"A rigorous and comprehensive exploration of the many manifestations of space in and of psychoanalysis ... Pushes the boundaries of psychoanalytic geographies by ushering in exciting new voices and perspectives from Argentina, France, Germany, Italy, and Poland."

Paul Kingsbury, *Professor of Geography and Associate Dean, Faculty of Environment, Simon Fraser University, Canada*

Space in Psychoanalysis, Psychoanalysis in Space

Space in Psychoanalysis, Psychoanalysis in Space explores the immense potential of psychoanalytic thought to questions of spatiality.

The international contributors combine the symbolic, the corporeal, the libidinal and the affective aspects of human experience, using psychoanalysis to reveal numerous facets and aspects of spatiality which remain invisible or blurred from other points of view. The focus moves from readings of the very physical space of the analyst's consulting room and spatiality of the analytic situation through philosophical analyses of spatiality of the body, subjectivity, love and materiality, to specific applications of psychoanalytic insights in a wide variety of fields from architecture to economics.

Space in Psychoanalysis, Psychoanalysis in Space will be of interest to psychoanalysts in practice and in training as well as scholars of psychoanalytic theory, cultural theory, literary theory, psychology, urban studies, space studies and philosophy.

Agata Bielińska is a PhD student at the Graduate School of Social Research affiliated with the Institute of Philosophy and Sociology of the Polish Academy of Sciences, Poland. Her research interests include contemporary philosophy of the subject and the philosophical implications of psychoanalytic theory. She is co-editor of the journal *wunderBlock: Psychoanaliza i Filozofia* (*wunderBlock: Psychoanalysis and Philosophy*) and contributor to the Center for Psychoanalytic Thought.

Adam Lipszyc is the head of the Center for Psychoanalytic Thought in the Institute of Philosophy and Sociology of the Polish Academy of Science, Poland. He teaches at the Graduate School for Social Research and at the Franz Kafka University of Muri.

Space in Psychoanalysis, Psychoanalysis in Space

Edited by
Agata Bielińska and Adam Lipszyc

Routledge
Taylor & Francis Group
LONDON AND NEW YORK

Designed cover image: gremlin © Getty Images

First published 2024
by Routledge
4 Park Square, Milton Park, Abingdon, Oxon OX14 4RN

and by Routledge
605 Third Avenue, New York, NY 10158

Routledge is an imprint of the Taylor & Francis Group, an informa business

British Library Cataloguing in Publication Data
A catalogue record for this book is available from the British Library

ISBN: 978-1-032-56578-1 (hbk)
ISBN: 978-1-032-56577-4 (pbk)
ISBN: 978-1-003-43618-8 (ebk)

DOI: 10.4324/9781003436188

Typeset in Times New Roman
by Taylor & Francis Books

Contents

Figures

Contributors

Agata Bielińska is a PhD student of Philosophy at the Graduate School of Social Research affiliated with the Institute of Philosophy and Sociology of the Polish Academy of Sciences, Poland, where she is preparing a dissertation on the (post)psychoanalytic philosophy of love. She is co-editor of the academic journal *wunderBlock: Psychoanaliza i Filozofia* (*wunderBlock: Psychoanalysis and Philosophy*) and contributor to the Center for Psychoanalytic Thought.

Thomas Dojan is a PhD student of Philosophy at the Graduate School of Social Research in Warsaw, Poland, and the University of Cologne, Germany (his thesis is on the intersection of phenomenology of embodiment and psychoanalytic theory of sexuality). He is a certified psycho-oncologist and is currently training as a psychoanalyst. He is working as a research assistant at the Center for Palliative Medicine at the University Hospital Cologne.

Tomasz Drzazgowski is a psychologist, psychotherapist and group analyst. He is a member of the Institute of Group Analysis "Rasztów" in Warsaw. Among his interests is the mutual influence of psyche and space. He has conducted workshops on the mindfulness of the city and its understanding, and he also runs a blog (available at psychologyandspace.net).

Steven Jaron is a clinical psychologist and psychoanalyst working in Paris, France. Before studying Psychology at the University of Paris-7 and Psychoanalysis at the Psychoanalytic Society for Research and Training (SPRF), he obtained a PhD in French and Comparative Literature from Columbia University, USA. He has published books such as *Edmond Jabès: The Hazard of Exile* (Legenda, 2003) and *Christopher Bollas: A Contemporary Introduction* (Routledge, 2022).

Andrzej Leder is Professor at the Institute of Philosophy and Sociology of the Polish Academy of Sciences. He focuses on political philosophy and philosophy of culture, applying phenomenological and psychoanalytical tools.

He has published books in Polish, English (*The Changing Guise of Myths*, 2013), and German (*Polen im Wachtraum: Die Revolution 1939–1956 und ihre Folgen*, 2019).

Adam Lipszyc is Professor at the Institute of Philosophy and Sociology of the Polish Academy of Sciences and head of the Center for Psychoanalytic Thought. He teaches in the Graduate School for Social Research and at the Franz Kafka University of Muri. In his work, he focuses on the philosophical implications of psychoanalysis, philosophy of literature, as well as on 20th-century Jewish thought. Most recently, he published (in Polish) a book on Freudian thought and a book on Herman Melville. He is the editor in chief of the academic journal *wunderBlock: Psychoanalysis and Philosophy.*

Marta Olesik is Assistant Professor at the Institute of Political Studies of the Polish Academy of Sciences. She is the author of two books (in Polish): one on Kierkegaard, absolute and bourgeois subject (*Mieszczanin na górze Moria*, 2014) and one on Descartes, Georges de La Tour and the conceptual vicissitudes of matter (*Kwadrat przebity włócznią*, 2020).

Cosimo Schinaia is a psychiatrist who worked as the Director of the Mental Health Department of Central Genoa, Italy, for many years. He is a training and supervising psychoanalyst of SPI (Italian Psychoanalytical Society) and a full member of IPA (International Psychoanalytical Association). He is the author of many books, including *Psychoanalysis and Architecture: The Inside and the Outside* (2016) and *Psychoanalysis and Ecology: The Unconscious and the Environment* (2022).

Anna J. Secor is Professor of Human Geography at Durham University, UK. She is a political and cultural geographer with interests in material and psychic space. She is co-editor of *The Wiley Blackwell Companion to Political Geography* (2015) and *A Place More Void* (2021) and, from 2016 to 2023, an editor of the academic journal *cultural geographies* (SAGE).

Santiago Sourigues is a CONICET (Scientific National Research Council) doctoral research fellow and teaching assistant at the Chair for Phenomenological and Existential Psychology at the University of Buenos Aires, Argentina. He is a psychoanalyst and a licensed psychologist. He is a former guest doctoral researcher at the Husserl-Archives, University of Cologne with a DAAD (German Academic Exchange Service) bi-nationally supervised doctoral degree research grant.

Gabriela Świtek is Professor of Art History at the University of Warsaw. She is a graduate of the University of Cambridge, UK. Her research interests include the history and philosophy of architecture, methodologies of art history, and art and architecture exhibition histories. She is the author of

Writing on Fragments: Philosophy, Architecture, and the Horizons of Modernity (2009). She has also published several books in Polish.

Antoni Zając is a PhD student at the Doctoral School of Humanities at the University of Warsaw. In his work, he focuses on twentieth- and twenty-first-century Polish literature, philosophy of literature, as well as psycho-analytic literary criticism. He recently co-edited a volume entitled *Languages of Contemporary Literature* (2022). He is an editor of the online literary journal *Wizje*.

Acknowledgements

We would like to thank Claudia Guderian, the owner of the copyrights for the images presented in Chapter 1 of this publication, for her kind permission to use them.

We would like to thank Penguin Random House for their permission to use the poem "The Age of Anxiety" in Chapter 2 in the print editions in North America and the Philippines, and Curtis Brown, Ltd for granting permission for the print editions in the rest of the world and for the e-book.

"The Age of Anxiety," Copyright © 1947 by W.H. Auden. Reprinted by permission of Curtis Brown, Ltd.

"The Age of Anxiety," Copyright 1947 by W.H. Auden and © renewed 1975 by the Estate of W. H. Auden; from COLLECTED POEMS by W.H. Auden, edited by Edward Mendelson. Used by permission of Random House, an imprint and division of Penguin Random House LLC. All rights reserved.

Chapter 8 is reprinted from A.J. Secor (2023) Spacetimeunconscious. *Dialogues in Human Geography*, DOI: 10.1177/20438206231191763.

Every effort has been made to contact the owners of the copyrights for Figure 10.4 used in Chapter 10. The editors of the present volume will be glad to respond to any legitimate demands regarding this matter.

Finally, we would like to thank Barbara Klicka for permission to use the translation of her poem "Allel" in Chapter 11 of this publication.

Introduction

Spacing Psychoanalysis

Agata Bielińska and Adam Lipszyc

I The Time of Time, the Time of Space

The first few decades of the twentieth-century European philosophy of the human being were, arguably, a time of time. In many cases, reflection on the temporal dimension of our lives substantiated a critical diagnosis of the contemporary state of European humanity and suggested ways of thinking about the human being in a renewed way. The spreading conviction that in the age of high capitalism the emancipatory promises of modernity were turning more and more into their opposite, with new forms of enslavement and alienation towering over the weakened individual, tended to find one of its most interesting expressions in the insight that late modernity robs us of our authentic temporality and replaces it with an alienated one.

New, fascinating models of time had appeared already in post-Hegelian philosophy, with Friedrich Nietzsche's thinking about history, memory and the eternal return (Nietzsche, 1873–1876/1997, 1883–1885/2003) or Søren Kierkegaard's innovative insights into the nature of repetition being some of the most interesting among them (Kierkegaard, 1843/1983). However, it was Henri Bergson who really blazed a trail for the renewed reflection on temporality, as he pointed to the subjective living experience of durée, which is ensnared and misrepresented by the positivistic, bourgeois, capitalist understanding of time (Bergson, 1889/2001). Hijacking Bergson's perspective, Georg Lukács would attempt to both historicize it and give it a dialectical twist by embedding Bergsonian inspiration firmly within the Marxist framework (Lukács, 1923/1972). The diagnosis that in late modernity human time freezes in a state of deadly alienation and mechanization was thus combined with a Marxist analysis of reification, while the utopia of liberation was shifted from Bergsonian subjectivism to the vision of a disalienating revolution that would rescue human temporality; or even discover it, *nomen omen*, for the first time.

Meanwhile, a robust perspective on human temporality as distinct from the reified time of late modernity was already developing within the phenomenological school. This perspective was given a breathtaking twist when,

DOI: 10.4324/9781003436188-1

drawing on Edmund Husserl's theory of retention and protention (Husserl, 1991), Martin Heidegger proposed his understanding of the ek-static temporality of the radically finite *Dasein*, a temporality conceived as clearly distinct from the distorted, flattened vision of time characteristic of the natural sciences and of what Heidegger called *das Man* (Heidegger, 1927/2001). Finally, the empty and homogeneous time of natural scientific and cheerfully progressive thinking found itself under attack in the writings of Walter Benjamin, who experimented with the radically discontinuous models of historical time and remembering, in which isolated moments of past and present meet in explosive constellations, forming what he called the Now-Time of dialectics (Benjamin, 1940/2003). Here, Benjamin endeavored to find a path of thinking about time which would avoid both the segmented, reified vision of temporality characteristic of positivism and the continuous, subjectivized understanding of time characteristic of *Lebensphilosophie* and phenomenology – both visions being perceived by him as explicitly or implicitly reactionary or, in his parlance, "mythical."

Now, in Bergson, and in Lukács after him, the name for the reified vision of time is … space. More accurately, the distorted understanding of temporality is modeled on homogeneous space, perceived as an empty container to be filled with objects. However, other thinkers of the temporal renaissance were often more careful in distinguishing various ways of looking at space, and would increasingly appreciate its significance in a fuller vision of the human. This is surely the case with phenomenology and, most importantly, with Heidegger's insistence on the fact that the lived space is not an empty vessel for things, but rather is a crucial aspect of being-in-the-world, of the situatedness of the radically finite *Dasein* in its condition of being-thrown (Heidegger, 1927/2001, pp. 122–148). Even more remarkably, in Benjamin's writings, space occupies as much space as time does. Following and radicalizing Georg Simmel's groundbreaking analyses of the lived spatiality of the big city dwellers (Simmel, 1903/1972), as well as entering into a most fruitful dialog with Siegfried Kracauer's novel insights into these very matters (Kracauer, 1995), Benjamin's work literally brims with fascinating ideas about borders, thresholds, interiors, streets, suburbs and, surely, those most paradoxical spaces that, just like dreams, lack an exterior, namely the famous arcades (Benjamin, 1999).

This interest in space can be seen as a dialectical continuation of that very same development which resulted in a renewed interest in time. Thus, if some thinkers, such as Husserl and Cassirer, were still trying to rescue old humanism and old humanity from the reifying forces of late modernity, figures such as Heidegger and Benjamin were, rather, reinventing the human. What they were defending was not the Cartesian or idealist subjectivity that ultimately was free from the material, but rather the subject in its radical finitude, a post-transcendentalist, non-autonomous agent, embedded not only in time, but also in language, body and affects. But if it is impossible to think of finitude seriously without thinking of the body, it is also impossible to think of the body seriously without thinking of space. Therefore, as one follows this line of exploration to its more radical conclusions, the spatial dimension of human existence grows in prominence. However, it was only in later decades of the twentieth century that space became central to philosophical reflection and to the humanities in general.

The shift from Heidegger's vision of *Dasein* to Maurice Merleau-Ponty's phenomenology of embodiment is a case in point (Merleau-Ponty, 1945/ 2002). For even though Heidegger stressed the finitude of *Dasein* as strongly as possible, and even though he did pay some attention to the spatial dimension of existence and a lot of attention to its affective aspect, it is debatable whether his thought really acknowledges our bodily condition. Rushing through the ek-static temporality, confronted with the drama of decision at every single moment of its life, *Dasein*, understood as "being towards death," is a spiritually athletic, even violent individual will, which effectively overcomes its own finitude by fully accepting its mortality, with its everyday embeddedness in body and space becoming irrelevant in the face of the sublime decision of choosing oneself and its ownmost possibility, i.e., death. For his part, Merleau-Ponty, while surely deeply indebted to Heidegger in terms of existential phenomenology, carefully and wisely avoided the decisionist collapse. Following but also radically transcending Husserl's late philosophy of embodiment, Merleau-Ponty managed to develop a non-Heideggerian rival phenomenology of existence, which is much more convincing in keeping the promise of offering a vision of the finite subject. And it is in the work of Merleau-Ponty that the link between human finitude, embodiment and spatiality is so consciously and skillfully drawn; it is in his work that space, body and movement are shown to be the very conditions of there being any intentional subjectivity in the first place, and so it is in his work that the focus of philosophical attention shifts so decisively from time to space – a space that, surely, never lacks its temporal dimension in itself.

Following this shift, in the second half of the twentieth century, thinking about and conceptualizations of space were steadily growing in significance within the philosophical attempts to develop post-Cartesian conceptions of subjectivity. However, it became equally crucial within the related attempts undertaken in various fields of the humanities, which sought to break with a euro/andro/heterocentric perspective of a homogeneous, hegemonic historical narrative and to replace it with a puzzle of co-existing, overlapping spaces linked by a complex network of relations: domination, recognition and subversion. As a result, with or without reference to Merleau-Ponty as the grand predecessor, some of the greatest minds of the second half of the twentieth century and the beginning of the twenty-first century developed a plethora of exciting theories of space.

Hence Hannah Arendt made us aware of the necessary connection between human plurality and what she called the space of appearance, the political space of mutual manifestation and recognition of subjectivities (Arendt, 1958, pp. 175–212). Guy Debord analyzed in detail the spatial dimension of the great spectacle of late capitalism and developed his psychogeographical tactics of its local-but-effective sneak subversions of the ways in which urban spaces are arranged (Debord, 1967/2014). Michel de Certeau insightfully described the semiotics of "walking in the city" and drew our attention to the existential and political significance of the spatial practices of our everyday life (de Certeau, 1984). Gilles Deleuze and Felix Guattari developed their thought around the spatial notions of deterritorialization, reterritorialization and nomadism, as well as around the key distinction between the striated and the smooth spaces (Deleuze & Guattari, 1987). Jacques Derrida managed to conceptualize his break away from structuralism by resorting to the pivotal idea of spacing the text (Derrida, 1978), and to his novel interpretation of the Platonic *khora* as the third destabilizing element of would-be dualistic metaphysics, which subverts and deconstructs all totalities and oppressive identities (Derrida, 1995, pp. 89–130). Michel Foucault continuously related his groundbreaking analyses of power-knowledge and subjectification to the ways in which the spaces we inhabit are designed and administered (Foucault, 2001). Edward Said showed the radical consequences of the Foucauldian perspective for thinking about colonial and post-colonial space (Said, 1979); Daphne Spain taught us to understand the gendered character of working spaces (Spain, 1992), while Giorgio Agamben discovered the spaces of exception spreading over our planet (Agamben, 2000). Frederic Jameson showed us how the logic of late capitalism requires accounting for the overwhelming character of global hyperspace, and suggested an aesthetics of cognitive mapping that would make human agency within that space at least partly possible (Jameson, 1991). Jean-Luc Nancy offered a powerful vision of the constitutionally plural embodied singularities, both sharing and dividing between each other the space of touch and communication (Nancy, 2000). Adriana Cavarero developed a whole new theory of embodied, affective, relational subjectivity and a feminist ethics of inclinations by focusing on the significance of bodily postures in the lived space (Cavarero, 2016). Karen Barad used paradoxes of *timespacematter* deduced from her interpretation of quantum mechanics in order to queer our all-too stable and oppressive visions of being and living (Barad, 2007). Homi Bhabha developed the idea of subversive hybridization within what he called the "Third Space" in-between the colonized and colonizing cultural domains (Bhabha, 1994).

This "thirdness" of the space, which returns both in abstract philosophical speculations and most specific and concrete analyses, requires some attention. One of the greatest twentieth-century philosophers of space, Henri Lefebvre, who taught us to perceive the lived space as socially produced and who proposed the revolutionary idea of the right to the city (Lefebvre, 1996), later developed powerfully by David Harvey (Harvey, 2012), suggested that every reflection on space as such has to avoid two complementary illusions (Lefebvre, 1991, pp. 27–30). First, it needs to beware of the "realistic illusion," the misconception that space is an objectively existing container that only later is filled by people, things, plants and animals. Second, it needs to beware of the "illusion of transparency," the misconception that space, being a socially produced human affair, is a fully intelligible element, a coherent cloth of human meanings woven by a collective, transcendental subject, a dimension ultimately indistinguishable from a mental space.

These two illusions and the need to escape from the dilemma between them show how difficult it is to think on that seemingly simple thing called space. Following Lefebvre, Edward Soja suggested the term "Thirdspace" for this strange status of the spatial element of our existence (Soja, 1996). Thirdspace – or, in fact, space proper – is not an objective container; however, it always manages to escape from our hermeneutic grasp. Indeed, it is both real and mental, it is both lived and estranged, it is both ours and not ours at the same time. Never homogenous, shot through by complex forces of power, exclusion and domination, charged with desire and anxiety, space is the unhomely home of our bodily existence, neither fully external nor fully internal, always evading our full comprehension, always – third. Consequently, we shall never map it. And yet, we shall always be in need of new instruments that will help us to navigate through this familiar/unfamiliar element. The heterogeneous, lively tradition of thought and practice, which was inaugurated by Sigmund Freud, may be of much use in this respect.

2 Psychoanalytic Extensions

The relationship of the multifaceted intellectual constellation known as psychoanalytic theory to the category of space is by no means a simple one. Owing to its unique perspective, which combines the symbolic, corporeal, libidinal and affective aspects of human experience, psychoanalysis reveals numerous aspects of spatiality that remain invisible or blurred from other points of view. At the same time, however, in its approach to space, psychoanalytic thought gets caught up in various conceptual tensions, which may be both fruitful and problematic.

Undoubtedly, spatial metaphors are omnipresent in psychoanalytic writings. Freud makes repeated efforts to outline the topography of the human mind, starting from the complex quasi-biological system of neuronal pathways and barriers introduced in the *Project for a Scientific Psychology* (Freud, 1950[1895]/1966) up to the famous model of the so-called second topography from *The Ego and the Id* (Freud, 1923/1961a) and beyond. His thinking about the psyche (which, according to his famous if enigmatic statement, "is extended and knows nothing about it" [Freud, 1941/1964, p. 300]) is torn between the purely metaphorical uses of spatial illustrations and the genuine belief that the unconscious can be explained through cerebral localization. As noted by Virginia Blum and Anna Secor (2011), Freud struggled with the Euclidean model of space that was insufficient to capture the psychic phenomena that psychoanalysis had unearthed. Recognizing the non-Euclidean character of the unconscious, Jacques Lacan in his reinterpretations of Freud's work uses not topographies but topologies: dynamic, three-dimensional, paradoxical structures such as the Möbius strip, which problematize the relationship between the interior and the exterior, surface and depth. He introduces the spatial concept of extimacy (Kingsbury, 2007), stressing the crucial psychoanalytic fact that what is most intimate and internal to the subject has its source outside, in the very exteriority and alienness of the other. Such a de-centered notion of subjectivity challenges the post-Cartesian, self-transparent "I," but also counters the phenomenological revisions following Merleau-Ponty that try to establish a new center in the form of the body-in-space, rather unproblematically inhabited by consciousness.

While Freud and Lacan use spatial models to illustrate the structure of the subject, Melanie Klein and her followers focus more on the relationships between the ego and its objects. The Kleinian logic of projection and introjection portrays the subject's interaction with the object as a continuous spatial exchange that alternates between outward expulsion and inward absorption. Klein also develops the notion of the inner world produced by successive introjections, mapping the psyche as a dense, multi-layered landscape populated by a multitude of very tangible objects that enter into various spatial relations with one another. This cartographic aspect comes to the fore particularly in her famous analysis of little Richard, a boy who gave shape to his phantasmatic "family romance" by drawing maps of a divided empire – his own family, the European continent torn by the ongoing war and his mother's body (Klein, 1961/1998). The spatial metaphor of maternal agency was also employed and elaborated upon by Wilfred Bion, who coined the pairing "container" and "contained" (Bion, 1962/1984). For Bion, the mother acts as a container when she is able to bear the stream of raw, primitive mental elements ("the contained") projected into her by the infant and convert them into actual feelings. By framing mental development as the deepening of one's capacity to contain foreign, anxiety-provoking objects, Bion implicitly places the category of space at the heart of his theory.

All these concepts provide invaluable tools for thinking about the spatiality of our being. However, because of their never-really-literal-and-always-somehow-figurative character, their connection to the actual experience of the space that surrounds us – rooms, buildings, cities – is never fully clear. The tension between the figurative and the literal use of spatial concepts is perhaps particularly evident in Donald Winnicott's theory of potential or transitional space (Winnicott, 1971/2005). Neither purely external nor internal, this third space serves as a model for multiple subjective experiences, such as those connected to culture and art; yet above all, it is an actual space between the child and the mother shaped by her non-intrusive presence. Focusing on the infant's holding environment and turning attention to the transitional aspects of "the place where we live," Winnicott inaugurates a psychoanalytic tradition of thinking about the lived space that will be continued by Christopher Bollas. Far from treating spatiality merely as a metaphor, Bollas develops the concept of the individual's spatial idiom, a distinctive, desire-driven way of inhabiting and moving through physical space (Bollas, 2009). As a counterpart to the idiomatically spatial subject, he posits equally idiomatic "evocative" objects that populate our surroundings, preventing the space around us from becoming merely a screen for our projections. Evocative objects and places not only contain us but also process us according to their specific qualities, shaping and reshaping our self-experience (Bollas, 2003). It was also Bollas who suggested the explicit application of the Winnicottian idea of the holding environment to the idea of architecture, and by extension to the ways in which actual buildings and cities manage to hold us.

The tension between space as a lived experience and space as a metaphor must be coupled with another tension within psychoanalysis, one that runs parallel to the discussions known from twentieth-century philosophy: the tension between space and time. Psychoanalytic approaches to temporality – intricate, original and invigorating – continue to have a profound impact on the humanities, for good reasons. The introduction of the concept of *Nachträglichkeit*, afterwardness or deferred action, revolutionizes thinking about memory and sexuality, allowing one to frame the properly human time as a non-linear one. According to the logic of retroactive attribution, events of a prematurely sexual and therefore traumatic nature are only experienced as such after the fact, thereby creating a peculiar time loop that constitutes the core of the psyche's perpetually belated temporality. Another psychoanalytic model of temporal entanglement initiated by linearity-shattering trauma is repetition compulsion, the unconscious tendency to re-enact the traumatic experience *ad infinitum*, linked by Freud to the circular death drive. Here, the overbearing excess bends time into a spiral, which is sometimes referred to as destiny. Psychoanalysis problematizes the relationship between the conscious and the unconscious as well as the present and the past in the notion of the return of the repressed, the uncanny haunting of present situations by displaced unconscious elements. Seemingly domesticated time, therefore, has its eerie double in the paradoxical, shattered, fragmented yet indestructible time of the unconscious. Precisely this strange temporality governs the dreamwork that weaves different timelines into an enigmatic knot – the navel of the dream.

In comparison to the conceptually impressive reflections on the complexities of time, the spatial aspects of Freud's thought seem much less pronounced. However, upon closer inspection, it can be noticed that psychoanalytic temporal concepts are rarely unrelated to space. Moreover, it is only by taking spatiality into account that their full philosophical potential can be discovered. This is indicated, for example, by the fate of one of the leading metaphors in Freud's oeuvre, namely the archaeological metaphor. Freud often evokes the work of an archaeologist who excavates the past from the rubble as an analogy for the role of the analyst. Human psyche resembles the ruins of a city that conceal deeply buried past material waiting to be extracted (Freud & Breuer, 1895/1955, p. 139). Although the metaphor of archaeology seems to refer mainly to time – the collective and individual past that can be traced back from the present state – it nevertheless relates at least as much to space. The excavation site is, after all, a *place* with its own specific topography. Traces from other times can only be retrieved archaeologically as elements of this particular space, detached from their original spatial context. In the case of the ruins of the city, the past also impinges on the present in the persistent form of space. Precisely because of this stubborn spatiality of the archaeological metaphor, Freud ultimately abandons it. In *Civilization and its Discontents* (1930/1961b) he compares the psyche to the city of Rome only to find this comparison untenable, since we would have to imagine such an "Eternal City" in which all the previous stages of development coexist with the most recent ones. The unconscious knows no destruction or oblivion – if it were a city, its oldest buildings would still stand in the same site as the newest constructions, ruined and preserved at the same time. Freud is incapable of imagining such a paradoxical density in any real place, so he discards his otherwise tempting metaphor. However, what he fails to see is that his comparison tells us something new and ultimately true about space, both the mental space and the space we inhabit. Not only is our time haunted by other ghostly times, but also our everyday space is always pervaded by another space. This superposition of places, near and distant, familiar and foreign, cosy and threatening, and inner and outer, accounts for the eerie spatiality of dreams, no less strange than their temporality. Psychoanalysis shows that spaces that matter to us – our psyches and our cities – are impossible to map fully, just as it is impossible to untangle the temporal knots at the root of our sexuality.

The true task is not to replace time with space but rather to see how the two are always interconnected: to spatialize time and to temporalize space. Such a manoeuvre opens up new possibilities in speculative psychoanalytical thinking and brings into focus insufficiently explored aspects of well-known conceptions. The non-linearity of time can and should be examined in conjunction with the inconsistency of space, while the circularity of repetition compulsion must also be understood as a certain topological model of a spiral or loop. Conversely, reflections on corporeality ought to take into account that the surface of the body is punctuated with inscriptions of desire from different times (Quindeau, 2013) and that it constitutes a libidinal space of remembrance. What applies to our bodies and individual remembering is also true of external sites and collective memory: a place can be saturated with, and haunted by, history as well as marked by the attempts to obscure it. Innovative geographers have already known for some time that psychoanalysis can be most helpful in our attempts to grasp these phenomena (Pile, 2005; Kingsbury & Pile, 2014).

The psychoanalytic spatial turn allows for the introduction of new threads into the study of key topics in the discipline. By reflecting on the category of space in different contexts, it is possible to create conceptual constellations in which metaphorical and literal aspects converge, and the spatiality of the psyche merges with the spatiality of the inhabited world. Spatial characteristics significantly contribute to the rethinking of different structures and perturbations of subjectivity. They are essential for analysing the complex topology of subject positions, as well as for explaining the subject's relationship to particular places that reflect their genesis or confront them with their own alienness. Categories useful in these kinds of psychoanalytical and philosophical investigations include liminal spaces and non-places, but also fullness and emptiness, darkness and undifferentiation, openness and enclosure. Spatiality sheds new light on the psychoanalytic concept of trauma: one of the ways to interpret the controversial trauma of birth is precisely to see it as a spatial trauma (Rank, 1924/2010), an overbearing excess of outer space or the loss of the original environment of the womb – the exit of the primordial sea (Ferenczi, 1924/1968). The notions of disorientation, displacement and replacement prove to be productive in conceptualizing the trauma of separation or the accompanying sibling trauma (Mitchell, 2003), the shocking loss of the position previously occupied by the child due to the arrival of a new baby.

Without spatial categories it is also impossible to think about pleasure and sexuality. The dialectic of closeness and distance that constitutes human intimacy unfolds in space, turning the erogenous spheres into privileged, particularly susceptible areas of the body. Space, as opposed to time, has become especially important in feminist psychoanalytic interventions. Female sexuality, almost entirely omitted by Freud in his account of human psychosexual development, has been linked by subsequent theorists to the experience of space (Erikson, 1968; Bassin, 1982; Benjamin, 1988). Spatial aspects play a vital role in feminist investigations of the maternal realm as distinct from the paternal symbolic sphere, most notably in Julia Kristeva's conception of the feminine, semiotic *khora*, the spacious origin of linguistic communication (Kristeva, 1980). Finally, the psychoanalytic space also represents the space of relations – the space that extends between the subject and the Other, as well as the space in which multiple subjects negotiate their interdependencies. Different spatial configurations enable different types of relationships by introducing boundaries into the intersubjective world. Both the space of the analytic pair and the "triangular space" of the Oedipus complex (Britton, 1989) can and should be examined also from this perspective.

All in all, the relationship between psychoanalysis and spatiality requires a dialectical attitude if it is to bear fruit. On the one hand, spatial concepts and metaphors are omnipresent within the field of psychoanalytic theory, but their status is often unclear and their presence is sometimes only implicit. Bringing spatial dimension to the fore can rearrange psychoanalytic theory, show new aspects of psychoanalytic ideas and help them to realize their full cognitive potential. In such an endeavor, much can be achieved by looking at psychoanalysis though the lens of philosophical theories of space developed in recent decades. On the other hand, once we draw out the presence of spatial problematic in psychoanalytic theory, we can fully benefit from the psychoanalytic insights into the spatial dimension of our existence, insights which are largely missing from philosophical reflection on the topic. If, as Freud claimed, psyche is extended and knows nothing about it, then psychoanalysis itself is, sometimes unknowingly, about *res extensa*. Once extended by bringing its spatial potential to the fore, it can, in turn, extend – nay, revolutionize – our thinking about space.[1]

3 Mapping the Book

On 24 February 2022, the Russian army initiated a full-scale invasion of the territory of Ukraine. Among the multiple reasons for this disastrous event was a wound that the Russian nation had suffered with the collapse of the Soviet Union and the tragically misguided notion, fueled by Kremlin propaganda and the narcissistic anxiety of an aging despot, that the wound could be healed by the restoration of an imperial space. Three weeks later, a conference on "Space and Psychoanalysis," organized by the Center for Psychoanalytic Thought based in the Institute of Philosophy and Sociology of the Polish Academy of Sciences, took place in a virtual space officially anchored in Warsaw, Poland, with the ongoing war adding peculiar urgency to the issues under consideration. For two days, psychoanalysts, philosophers, geographers, art historians and literary scholars from Argentina, England, France, Germany, Italy, Poland and the US discussed the potential of psychoanalytic theory for understanding space. With minor shifts and additions, the present book follows the program of the conference.

We begin with a chapter by one of the most eminent scholars of the day, who reflects upon psychoanalysis and space, especially in relation to architectural and ecological problems. In his chapter, Cosimo Schinaia focuses on the most concrete space of the consulting room and shows its significance for the therapeutic process. He traces the move from the "too full" packed spaces of the early consulting rooms through the ascetic, the too empty spaces of later analysts, up to the most recent trend of a balanced, sober manifestation of the analyst in the analytic relationship through a personalized design of consulting room – a trend he advocates. By evoking the most telling examples, he shows the importance of furniture and the spaces adjacent to the consulting room, not to mention its entrances and thresholds. Finally, foregrounding two clinical vignettes, he illustrates how the sound, the light, the size of the room and its windows, as well as the possible bodily postures of the analyst can affect the process of interpretation.

Steven Jaron, the author of Chapter 2, also focuses on the clinical space, but moves beyond its literal, material understanding. In an argument which can be seen as complementary to that of Schinaia, Jaron discusses not so much architecture, design and furniture as the spatial anatomy of the therapeutic experience. Beginning with intriguing references to W.H. Auden's *Age of Anxiety* and Gaston Bachelard's idea of topoanalysis, Jaron proceeds to define the threshold nature of psychoanalytic experience with the help of the idea of liminality borrowed from Arnold van Gennep and Victor Turner. The analytic field, understood by Jaron after Madeleine and Willy Barangers, with its curious, ambiguous status of the realm in which things are and are not, is a liminal space par excellence. It is in this space that we can be exposed to the experience of our self, as described by Winnicott and Bollas. Finally, Jaron searches for the most accurate characterizations of this space in Freud's idea of *Zwischenreich* of transference and Bion's notion of caesura which Jaron uses in order to present this liminal space as the site of passage and break, as the caesural inter-zone of encounter with the unexpected and other within our own selves.

With Thomas Dojan's chapter we move beyond the therapeutic dimension of psychoanalysis and into the realm of the psychoanalytical understanding of the human body and its surface. Dojan draws the reader's attention to the standard notion of erogenous zones and shows its immense richness and intellectual potential. Dojan reaches his conclusions by means of a careful analysis of two short but dense fragments from Freud's letters to Wilhelm Fliess and some of his other early writings on sexuality, as well as by reference to Adam Phillips' brilliant insights into the nature of tickling. Dojan argues that in the original Freudian rendering, the erogenous zones are not defined by biological function. Rather, potentially appearing all over our body, they are spots of irritability marked by mnemic traces of past encounters, relational aiming at other persons and expectation of coming pleasures. Entangled in the loops of *Nachträglichkeit* and memory, the libidinal space of the body lives in several temporal moments at the same time. Ultimately, it is psyche that explains soma, not otherwise, and the surface of our sexualized body turns out to be intersubjectively defined, talkative and inventive.

In Santiago Sourigues' chapter, the body is asleep. His starting point is Maurice Merleau-Ponty's phenomenological take on embodied subjectivity in general, and his groundbreaking analyses of dream, sleep and being awake. Sourigues extracts the main results of these analyses and then proceeds to his own original phenomenology of the dark space surrounding the passive sleeping body. He distinguishes between two modes of experience, the syncretic and the discretic, which are characteristic, respectively, of the sleeping and waking life. The syncretic mode of experience, the mode of the sleeping body in the dark space in which spatiality and temporality are marked by odd superpositions, is presented here as the more primary layer present under or behind the discretism of being awake. Sourigues identifies these two modes with Freudian distinction between consciousness and the unconscious, thus arriving at the elegant conclusion that the unconscious is founded on the passive operation of the structures of the body. Moreover, Sourigues shows how the main features of primary processes identified by Freud (condensation, displacement, absence of contradiction and timelessness) sit most naturally with the structure of the syncretic mode of spatiotemporal experience he describes in his chapter.

The link between the body and the unconscious is crucial also for Adam Lipszyc's chapter. Lipszyc begins with a discussion of Freud's famous note on the extended character of the psyche. In order to show the full potential of Freud's idea, he resorts to the interpretation suggested by Jean-Luc Nancy according to which the soul is identical to the body, while its constitutive unawareness of this identity is identical with the unconscious. While praising Nancy's take and his vision of exposed plural bodies interacting in space, Lipszyc suggests a psychoanalytic revision of this theory. He stresses the psychoanalytic idea of the decentered character of the subject and the way in which the embodied subject *and* his or her lived space are constituted together by the act of decentering. This take makes it possible to identify the main features of the lived space – our originary alienation in the spatial element and our irrevocable misplacement – as well as the reasons for the unease and uncanniness that we feel in the open space. This abstract model is then put to the test in a close reading of Elfriede Jelinek's *The Piano Teacher*, a brilliant novel about bodies, spaces, stifling closures and desperate openings.

Lipszyc's chapter ends with a reference to love as a more hopeful relation between exposed bodies in the open space. And it is the spatial dimension of love that is the main topic of Agata Bielińska's chapter. While acknowledging the omnipresence of spatial metaphors in Freud's vision of psyche and his understanding of object-relation, Bielińska points to the deficiency of Freud's original take on love, with the Freudian subject barely moving beyond its narcissism into the outer space. Thus, she moves on to develop a psychoanalytically inspired conception of love which would make up for this deficiency and show how even if the external space is a space of insecurity it is also the only space of actual love. Bielińska weaves her conception from a variety of threads: Donald Winnicott's theory of objects and his idea of the capacity to be alone, André Green's notion of the trauma-object, Christopher Bollas's thinking about the spatial idiom of the subject and Jessica Benjamin's idea of intersubjectivity. She concludes with the idea of love as sharing space, a vision of a being together in which what is shared by the lovers is, paradoxically enough, the very break within their spatial realities produced by the painful, surprising and joyful presence of the real other.

With Andrzej Leder's chapter we move deeper into the psychoanalytically inspired philosophical reflections on the very nature of human subjectivity in its relation to the spatial. Taking as his starting point the tension between two dictionary definitions of the subject – grammatical and philosophical – Leder resorts to Lacanian theory of the relation between the subject, the signifier and representation in order to move beyond the dilemma and arrive at the idea of the "subject's position" conceived on the model of "the lyrical subject." The sum of all the subject's positions forms what Leder calls "the subject's space," a space with a shape, limits and overall topology, which determines the ease with which one can move from one subjective position to another. The differences between the topologies of particular subject spaces are determined by different forms of early symbolizations of what Lacan perceived as the crucial, always traumatic encounter with the Real, re-encountered or missed at the moment of awakening. Most importantly, beyond the supposed unity of the punctual subject, this psychoanalytico-topological perspective allows us to see a fundamental "split" and a multiplicity of conflicted "fields," both at the intrapsychical and the interpersonal and collective level.

Anna Secor also draws on the Lacanian sources and the idea of the traumatic awakening. Her aim, however, is to explore the role of the unconscious knowledge beyond subjectivity in the becoming of the spatiotemporal materiality. She addresses Karen Barad's notion of spacetimematter which accounts for the paradoxical, non-linear foldings and unfoldings of materiality in accordance with Barad's queer-and-quantum metaphysics. Secor suggests a crucial supplement of Barad's vision, derived from psychoanalysis and captured by the idea of the spacetimeunconscious. Drawing on a variety of examples such as the physics of freezing and lightning, a poem by Primo Levi, Marcel Proust's novel and a video by Ali Ali, as well as on Lacan's idea of the unconscious-in-the-real, the theory of montage and Steve Pile's notion of the "distributed unconscious," Secor develops a theory of the functioning of unconscious knowledge in the ongoing articulation of the world. Analyzing the play between dream, traumatic awakenings and being awake, she is able to show the superposition of spaces as one with Freud's *Nachträglichkeit* and with a complex "psycho-topology" of spatiotemporal materiality entangled with unconscious knowledge.

Gabriela Świtek presents the uses of psychoanalysis for thinking not so much about the spatiality of matter as such, but about man-made architecture. She defines her perspective by discussing Maurice Merleau-Ponty's philosophy of space and his insightful reading of psychoanalysis, as well as Rudolf Arnheim's understanding of architectural forms. Thus, she weaves together Gestalt thinking on perception, a phenomenological approach to architecture and a psychoanalytic take on space. Then she proceeds to discuss the mythical and historical significance of the idea of labyrinth and its meaning as a symbol of the unconscious in Jungian psychoanalysis, as exemplified by certain striking clinical cases. Instead of sliding into the well-worn discussion of archetypes, she stresses the state of spatial and existential disorientations confronted with the labyrinth of their own unconscious. This allows Świtek to move on to her detailed analysis of Thomas De Quincey's meditations on Piranesi's *Carceri*. Drawing on Anthony Vidler's analyses of the architectural uncanny, she is able to present these meditations as a particularly striking description of spatial disorientation and a projection of De Quincey's dreams into the space of Piranesi's etchings.

Staying within the architectural realm, but going out into the public space, Tomasz Drzazgowski analyzes one particular building, namely the so-called Gdańsk Shakespeare Theatre located in the city of Gdańsk in northern Poland. Drzazgowski constructs his theoretical framework by first referring to Aristotle's definition of place as preceding the thing, and from there he turns to Heidegger and his analyses of a thing having ontological precedence over place. He points to the seeming incompatibility of the two perspectives, but is determined to find a "bridge" between them both. Thus, with the help of the Kleinian idea of the play of projection and introjection, the psychological notion of "affordance," Winnicott's idea of potential space and Bollas's thinking on the city space, he builds an ontology of space composed of places that are "outside" the subject, but are also saturated with "internal" meanings; and so, ultimately, they transcend the dichotomy. Armed with these ideas, Drzazgowski proceeds to his analysis of the Gdańsk Shakespeare Theatre and the plethora of conscious and unconscious meanings that surround the project. He ends on a powerful note, revealing a piece of context that makes it inevitable to turn to the reflections on proper forms of mourning in the public space.

Winnicott's theory plays an important role also in the chapter authored by Antoni Zając, which is devoted to literature rather than to architecture. Zając develops the notion of psychotopography, borrowed from Victoria Nelson. The idea here is to study literary works as the space within which the interplay between the self and the outside world is played out. In order to develop this notion, Zając refers to Mikhail Bakhtin's idea of the chronotope and, most importantly, Winnicott's theory of potential space, transitional objects and cultural experience – a theory which, however, he re-reads along more melancholic lines than it was originally conceived, stressing the importance of the mourning processes enacted within the potential space. For Zając, literature can be seen as a potential metaspace within which authors play out versions of themselves, scattered among characters, architectural constructions and landscapes. The constant play between real and fictional, between inner and outer, between actual and potential is to be captured by the concept of metalepsis which Zając borrows from Gérard Genette. Finally, this complex methodological perspective is put to the test in a close reading of a poem by Barbara Klicka, which can be seen as a metacommentary to the psychotopographical project as such.

In the final chapter, authored by Marta Olesik, we move into the spaces of world economy. In this bold and passionate argument, Olesik weaves together Daniel Schreber's schizophrenic theory of divine rays (freed from Freud's Oediplizing disciplinary machine of interpretation), Nicolas Malebranche's post-Cartesian occasionalist theology, and the paradoxes of the financial market of late capitalism. She discovers surprising analogies between the three realms, with the spatial perspective opening the very possibility of the comparison. In all three, the regular processes of symbolization, coupled with signs referring to things, are replaced by strange, abstract envelopes, freed from any referential link to reality, but touching and oppressing the individual mind, or indeed global society as such. Thus, having identified the schizophrenic, tactile semiosis of capitalism, Olesik may be perceived as ending on a very bleak note: "The logic of the efficient market is that of 'perverted touch.' It is a body of conjectures, a structure of debilitating knowledge dripping down on the social body. ... An anal, solar wealth is generated in the indissoluble connection between finance and the network of social codes – an economy of an approaching end of the world."

Whether the world is going to end, we shall most certainly see. Meanwhile, having moved from the space of the actual consulting room and the space of the analytic encounter, through the surface of the skin and the dark space that surrounds the sleeping body, through the body's closures and openings, through the space in which we love, the speculatively conceived space of the subject and the spacetimeunconscious of materiality, and onwards as far as the architectural, urban, literary and economic spaces, it is at this juncture that our book ends. The journey has led us through a complexity of landscapes with a variety of different climate zones; however, it surely has not mapped the immense territory which extends before us once we begin to think and see psychoanalysis and space as conjoined. Rather, by cutting through the land, the trajectory of our book may be read as a sequence of possible points of departures for other travelers. We hope that, swerving away from our trail at the spots of their choosing, these same travelers will forge their own journey spaces and return to tell us their stories – before the world ends.

Note

1 A number of collected volumes discuss the encounter between space and psychoanalysis, including Colomina (1992), dealing with the topic of space mostly from the perspective of gender studies; Savio et al. (2007), focusing mainly on the problems of migration and dislocation; Kingsbury & Pile (2014), with contributions from experts in human geography, Friedman & Tomšic (2017), stressing mostly the Lacanian approach, as do Burnham & Kingsbury (2021) who focus on the environmental issues.

References

Agamben, G. (2000). *Homo Sacer* (D. Heller-Roazen, Trans.). Stanford University Press.
Arendt, H. (1958). *The Human Condition*. University of Chicago Press.

Barad, K. (2007). *Meeting the Universe Halfway*. Duke University Press.

Bassin, D. (1982). Woman's Images of Inner Space: Data Towards Expanded Interpretive Categories. *International Review of Psycho-analysis*, 9, 191–203.

Benjamin, J. (1988). *The Bonds of Love. Psychoanalysis, Feminism and the Problem of Domination*. Pantheon Books.

Benjamin, W. (2003). On the Concept of History. In H. Eiland & M.W. Jennings (Eds.), *Selected Writings*. The Belknap Press of Harvard University Press, Vol. 4, pp. 389–400. (Original work published 1940.)

Benjamin, W. (1999). *The Arcades Project* (H. Eiland & K. McLaughlin, Trans.). The Belknap Press of Harvard University Press.

Bergson, H. (2001). *Time and Free Will* (F.L. Pogson, Trans.). Dover Publications. (Original work published 1889.)

Bhabha, H. (1994). *The Location of Culture*. Routledge.

Bion, W. (1984). *Learning from Experience*. Routledge. (Original work published 1962.)

Blum, V., & Secor, A. (2011). Psychotopologies: Closing the Circuit Between Psychic and Material Space. *Environment and Planning D: Society and Space*, 29(6), 1030–1047.

Bollas, C. (2003). *Being a Character. Psychoanalysis and Self Experience*. Routledge.

Bollas, C. (2009). *The Evocative Object World*. Routledge.

Britton, R. (1989). The Missing Link: Parental Sexuality in the Oedipus Complex. In R. Britton, M. Feldman, E. O'Shaughnessy, & J. Steiner (Eds.), *The Oedipus Complex Today: Clinical Implications*. Karnac.

Burnham, C., & Kingsbury, P. (Eds.). (2021). *Lacan and the Environment*. Palgrave Macmillan.

Cavarero, A. (2016). *Inclinations* (A. Minervi & A. Sitze, Trans.). Stanford University Press.

Colomina, B. (Ed.). (1992). *Sexuality & Space*. Princeton Architectural Press.

Debord, G. (2014). *The Society of the Spectacle* (K. Knabb, Trans.). Bureau of Public Secrets. (Original work published 1967.)

de Certeau, M. (1984). *The Practice of Everyday Life* (S. Rendall, Trans.). University of California Press.

Deleuze, G., & Guattari, F. (1987). *Thousand Plateaus* (B. Massumi, Trans.). University of Minnesota Press.

Derrida, J. (1995). *On the Name* (T. Dutoit, Ed.). Stanford University Press.

Derrida, J. (1978). *Writing and Difference* (A. Bass, Trans.). University of Chicago Press.

Erikson, E.H. (1968). Womanhood and the Inner Space. In *Identity, Youth and Crisis*. W.W. Norton & Company.

Ferenczi, S. (1968). *Thalassa: A Theory of Genitality* (H.A. Bunker, Trans.). W.W. Norton & Company. (Original work published 1924.)

Foucault, M. (2001). *Power* (J.D. Faubon, Ed.). The New Press.

Freud, S. (1961a). The Ego and the Id. In *The Standard Edition of the Complete Psychological Works of Sigmund Freud*, Vol. 19 (J. Strachey, Ed. & Trans.). The Hogarth Press. (Original work published 1923.)

Freud, S. (1961b). Civilization and its Discontents. In *The Standard Edition of the Complete Psychological Works of Sigmund Freud*, Vol. 21 (J. Strachey, Ed. & Trans.). The Hogarth Press. (Original work published 1930.)

Freud, S. (1964). Findings, Ideas, Problems. In *The Standard Edition of the Complete Psychological Works of Sigmund Freud*, Vol. 23 (J. Strachey, Ed. & Trans.). The Hogarth Press. (Original work published 1941.)

Freud, S. (1966). Project for a Scientific Psychology. In *The Standard Edition of the Complete Psychological Works of Sigmund Freud*, Vol. 1 (J. Strachey, Ed. & Trans.). The Hogarth Press. (Original work published 1950[1895].)

Freud, S., & Breuer, J. (1955). Studies on Hysteria. In *The Standard Edition of the Complete Psychological Works of Sigmund Freud*, Vol. 2 (J. Strachey, Ed. & Trans.). The Hogarth Press. (Original work published 1895.)

Friedman, M., & Tomšic, S. (Eds.). (2017). *Psychoanalysis: Topological Perspectives: New Conceptions of Geometry and Space in Freud and Lacan*. Transcript Verlag.

Harvey, D. (2012). *Rebel Cities*. Verso.

Heidegger, M. (2001) *Being and Time* (J. Macquarrie & E. Robinson, Trans.). Blackwell. (Work originally published 1927.)

Husserl, E. (1991). *On the Phenomenology of the Consciousness of Internal Time (1893–1917)* (J.B. Brough, Trans.). Kluwer Academic Publishers.

Jameson, F. (1991). *Postmodernism, or the Cultural Logic of Late Capitalism*. Duke University Press.

Kierkegaard, S. (1983). *Fear and Trembling/Repetition* (H. Hong & E. Hong, Trans.). Princeton University Press. (Original work published 1843.)

Kingsbury, P., & Pile, S. (Eds.) (2014). *Psychoanalytic Geographies*. Ashgate.

Kingsbury, P. (2007). The Extimacy of Space. *Social & Cultural Geography*, 8(2), 235–258.

Klein, M. (1998). *Narrative of a Child Analysis*. Vintage. (Original work published 1961.)

Kracauer, S. (1995). *The Mass Ornament* (T.Y. Levin, Trans.). Harvard University Press.

Kristeva, J. (1980). *Desire in Language: A Semiotic Approach to Literature and Art* (T. Gora, A. Jardine & L.S. Roudiez, Trans.). Columbia University Press.

Lefebvre, H. (1991) *The Production of Space* (D. Nicholson-Smith, Trans.). Blackwell.

Lefebvre, H. (1996). *Writings on Cities* (E. Kofman & E. Lebas, Trans.). Blackwell.

Lukács, G. (1972). *History and Class Consciousness* (R. Livingstone, Trans.). MIT Press. (Original work published 1923.)

Merleau-Ponty, M. (2002). *Phenomenology of Perception* (C. Smith, Trans.). Routledge. (Original work published 1945.)

Mitchell, J. (2003). *Siblings: Sex and Violence*. Polity Press.

Nancy, J.-L. (2000). *Being Singular Plural* (R.D. Richardson & A.E. O'Byrne, Trans.). Stanford University Press.

Nietzsche, F. (2003). *Thus Spake Zarathustra* (T. Wayne, Trans.). Algora Publishing. (Original work published 1883–1885.)

Nietzsche, F. (1997). *Untimely Meditations* (R.J. Hollingdale, Trans.). Cambridge University Press. (Original work published 1873–1876.)

Pile, S. (2005). *Real Cities: Modernity, Space and the Phantasmagorias of City Life*. SAGE.

Quindeau, I. (2013). *Seduction and Desire: The Psychoanalytic Theory of Sexuality Since Freud* (J. Bendix, Trans.). Karnac.

Rank, O. (2010). *The Trauma of Birth*. Martino Fine Books. (Original work published 1924.)

Said, E. (1979). *Orientalism*. Vintage Books.

Savio Hooke, M.T., & Akhtar, S. (Eds.). (2007). *The Geography of Meanings: Psychoanalytic Perspectives on Place, Space, Land, and Dislocation*. Routledge.

Simmel, G. (1972). *On Individuality and Social Forms* (D.E. Levine, Ed.). University of Chicago Press. (Original work published 1903.)

Soja, E. (1996). *Thirdspace*. Blackwell.

Spain, D. (1992). *Gendered Spaces*. University of Carolina Press.

Winnicott, D.W. (2005). *Playing and Reality*. Routledge. (Original work published 1971.)

Chapter 1

The Space of the Consulting Room

Cosimo Schinaia

The quality of the analytic relationship and the space in which such a relationship occurs is not only constituted by the cognitive and emotional context but also by the immediate and pervasive physical context.

> The analytic room should have the capacity to evoke different kinds of associations and be able to accommodate richly variegated desires of the occupants. The effect of the architecture on the analytic relationship, and hence the analysis, in direct and indirect awareness, is profound.
>
> (Danze, 2005, p. 123)

When defining the analytical field, Giuseppe Civitarese and Antonino Ferro (2015) say that it contains not only psychological processes inside the minds of the analyst and patient, linked like two dynamic systems that interact in real time, but also everything that furnishes the place in which the two persons find themselves, largely because it is a possible source of productive stimuli.

The organization and distribution of the external space (i.e., of the consulting room itself) is strongly influenced by the analyst's way of functioning: their personality, technical assumptions, feelings and opinions about the relational space, the degree of involvement in the analytic relationship (or, *mutatis mutandis*, how much they intend to be neutral), and how much their internal objects can be in contact with the analysand's internal objects in transference/countertransference dynamics. In the same way, the architectural, aesthetic, and functional organization of the physical space containing the psychoanalytic sessions' setting (i.e., the consulting room) cannot be immutable and repetitive. Rather, it must deal with the need for continuously contextualizing tastes, communications, or habits and modifying building materials, furniture, forms, and uses of light – all things that continuously change. In spite of a fundamental need to consider all these sociocultural and technological modifications, I believe that we cannot ignore the foundations of psychoanalytic theory and practice, or the relevance of the demands of a deep level of communication that, after Freud, focus on the

DOI: 10.4324/9781003436188-2

pre-oedipal phases of the mind and the care of psychotic states. I think that we must consider the necessities of the analytic couple not according to already defined modalities, but according to creative ones.

1 From Freud's Analysis Room to Contemporary Ones

If we were able to go back in time and observe Freud's consulting room, we would see a narrow space, interconnected with domestic spaces, and thus with its smells and noises. It was neither a neutral nor an institutional space, but rather a common place evoking everyday life. It was full of furniture, carpets, decorative objects, and relics able to give clear indications of the tastes and cultural interests of the analyst. Because all these objects were familiar in the analyst's everyday life, we can say that they functioned so as to reduce his solitude (we can say that this solitude was often emphasized by a continuous contact with the uncanny). Further, because these furnishings highlighted some aspects of the analyst's privacy, they were able to "organize this place of intimacy" (Eiguer, 2007, p. 6) and certainly to become part of the contents of the analysand's fantasies. Thus, by exhibiting his collections, Freud was literally able to reveal certain things about himself. In other words, he

Sigmund Freud, London

Figure 1.1 Sigmund Freud's consulting room in London, UK
Source: The photographs in this chapter are printed with the permission of Claudia Guderian.

Figure 1.2 Sigmund Freud's consulting room in London, UK
Source: The photographs in this chapter are printed with the permission of Claudia Guderian.

was able to operate a *self-disclosure* which allowed him to put together the past of the single person and that of civilization.

For some years now, we have seen an increasing number of published photographs of consulting rooms. This is curious because it contrasts with the well-known discretion of psychoanalysts about their personal lives and therapy places. From 2000 to 2004, the magazine *International Psycho-analysis* published pictures of the consulting rooms of the members of the International Psychoanalytic Association. The German photographer Clau-dia Guderian's 2004 book *Magie der Couch* (*The Magic of the Couch*) can be considered the first exploration of the contemporary consulting room with a camera. The pictures draw attention to the modifications of space and

Figure 1.3 Anna Freud's consulting room in London, UK
Source: The photographs in this chapter are printed with the permission of Claudia Guderian.

furniture over time not only by virtue of scientific and ideological assumptions, but also of sociocultural changes in the environment.

Freud's and the first Freudian analysts' rooms can be described as *too full spaces* (Figure 1.1, Figure 1.2, Figure 1.3, Figure 1.4).

Traces of some of this can also be found in the rooms of some contemporary analysts from Vienna and London (Figure 1.5, Figure 1.6).

Thereafter we witness the idea of reduction, simplification, and deprivation (this idea is based on the German architect Ludwig Mies van der Rohe's maxim *less is more* and his *skin and bone* architecture) in the *too empty spaces* of the subsequent analysts' rooms (Figure 1.7, Figure 1.8, Figure 1.9).

These rooms are generally furnished in a Franciscan style; that is to say, they are simple, frugal, essential, cold, almost anonymous. On the one hand, these studies are affected by the American Puritanism of the 1940s with its tendency toward uniformity and stability so that, for many decades, nothing could be changed in the analyst's study or wardrobe (Guderian, 2004); on the other hand, we may discern the minimalist claims of modern architecture. There is only an armchair, a couch, sometimes a writing desk and closet. No

Sadie Gillespie, London

Figure 1.4 Sadie Gillespie's consulting room in London, UK
Source: The photographs in this chapter are printed with the permission of Claudia Guderian.

books, no paintings on the walls, and no decorative objects are allowed: they could give indications of the analyst's personality and interfere with the analysand's phantasmatic and associative freedom. The basic idea is to reduce as much as possible the analysand's projections to objects that belong to the analyst and, in a certain sense, to foster the analysand's expression of dreams, fantasies, and experiences without any supporting material provided by the analyst.

Thus, the neutrality of the room allows for a mediation between the physical and psychical, and the fostering of a safe separation; that is to say, a safe passage from the center of the world (represented in the analytic relationship) to the external world for both the analyst and the analysand.

In general, the most recent generations of analysts have had to deal with the issue of the emergence of the presence of the analyst as something fundamental for the analytic relationship (Figure 1.10, Figure 1.11, Figure 1.12, Figure 1.13, Figure 1.14, Figure 1.15, Figure 1.16).

Figure 1.5 George Brownstone's consulting room in Vienna, Austria
Source: The photographs in this chapter are printed with the permission of Claudia Guderian.

It is clear that there are different degrees through which the analysts can reveal themselves as persons. The definition of the setting is between two polarities, one in which the analyst has the function of a "blank screen" or "hanger" and one in which he or she makes an excessive use of inter-subjectivity. This use can lead one to excessively define the setting on the basis of the analyst's personal tastes and his or her self-disclosure. What I mean by this is the analyst's act of conscious and deliberate revealing of personal information to the analysand. It is something completely different from the accidental and "unconscious" revealing of personal information. It can strongly interfere with the analysand's tastes and experiences, and with their freedom to express them.

I think that today the presence of a plain interior design, a place that is capable of communicating the analyst's aesthetic-cultural interests, is no longer something to be avoided. I think that it is necessary that analysts maintain, as Stefano Bolognini contends, "their good sense and good taste in limiting themselves to a perceptible but usually sober personalization of the environment, avoiding a narcissistic invasion of the working field with the exhibition of their private iconography" (Bolognini, 2011, p. 8).

Figure 1.6 Helmut Figdor's consulting room in Vienna, Austria
Source: The photographs in this chapter are printed with the permission of Claudia Guderian.

2 The Inside and Outside in the Analytic Room: Two Clinical Vignettes

Other commentaries on various photographs of analysts' studies have discussed the spatial dimensions of the rooms, the height of their ceilings, and the size of their doors and windows that, together with the spatial subdivision and the position of the pieces of furniture and decorative objects, define the horizontal and vertical position between two bodies by measuring and defining their architectural scale.

In general, the spaces of the European analysts' consulting rooms are smaller than those we find in the United States. This means that the distances between the analyst's armchair and the analysand's couch and between the analysand's perspective and the room's various pieces of furniture are

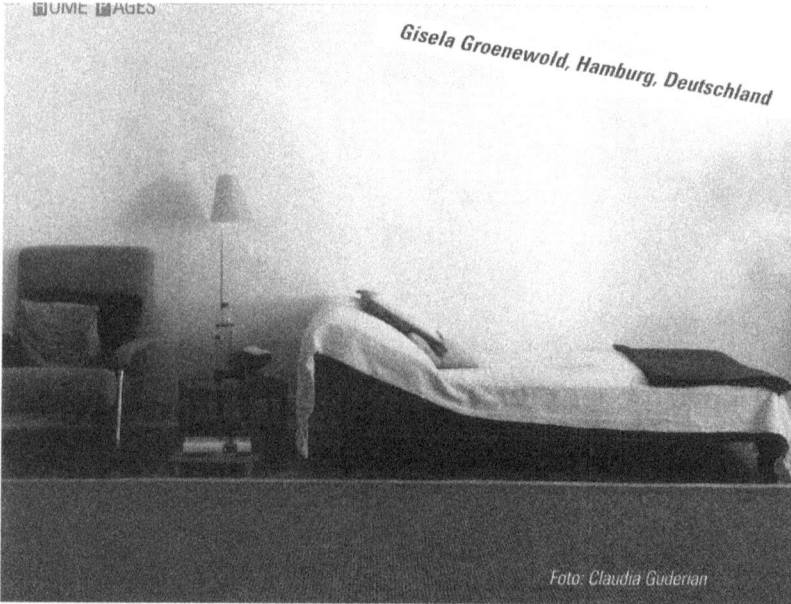

Figure 1.7 Gisela Groenewold's consulting room in Hamburg, Germany
Source: The photographs in this chapter are printed with the permission of Claudia Guderian.

Figure 1.8 Alex Tarnopolsky's consulting room in Toronto, Canada
Source: The photographs in this chapter are printed with the permission of Claudia Guderian.

Figure 1.9 Ulrich Stuhr's consulting room in Hamburg, Germany
Source: The photographs in this chapter are printed with the permission of Claudia Guderian.

smaller, too. In this sense, the room seems to hearken back to a primitive refuge. This implies a change at the perceptual level; that is to say, a different mutual way of listening, of visual observation, and of proprioception in relation to proximity and separation, but also to materials, acoustics, lights, and all the physical elements we must consider. "Rooms of different forms and material reverberate in a different way" (Rasmussen, 1962, p. 224).

I received positive comments from patients when I substituted my consulting room's chaise longue, designed by Le Corbusier, for a wider and softer couch. This is probably because the shape of the former imposed an objective spatial constraint and created difficulties for the patients in terms of their movement, whereas the shape of the latter fostered relaxation in their bodily movements and thus helped them with the remembering of their dreams and fantasies.

I remember the experience of temporariness and promiscuity of a patient who, before asking to start analysis with me, had been in treatment with an

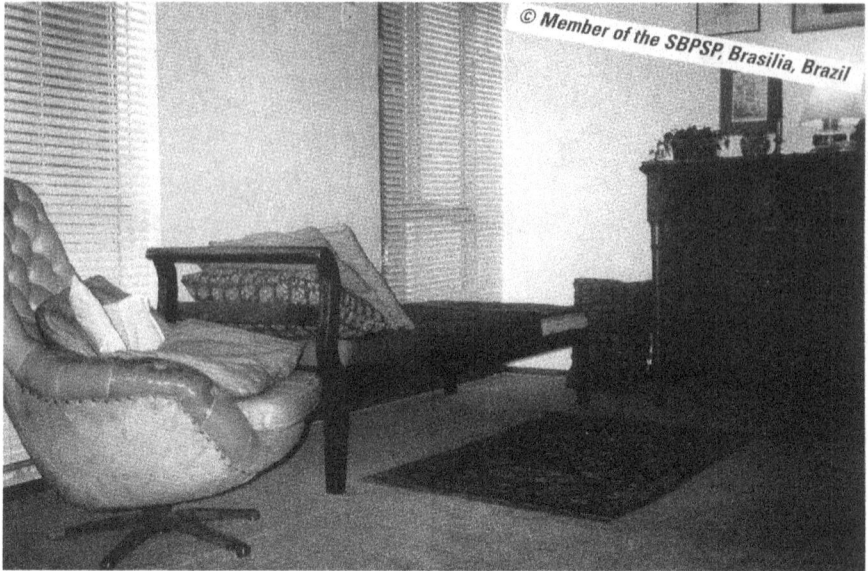

Figure 1.10 Consulting rooms of an unknown member of the SBPSP in Brasília, Brazil, and Hélène Goutal-Valière in Paris, France

Source: The photographs in this chapter are printed with the permission of Claudia Guderian.

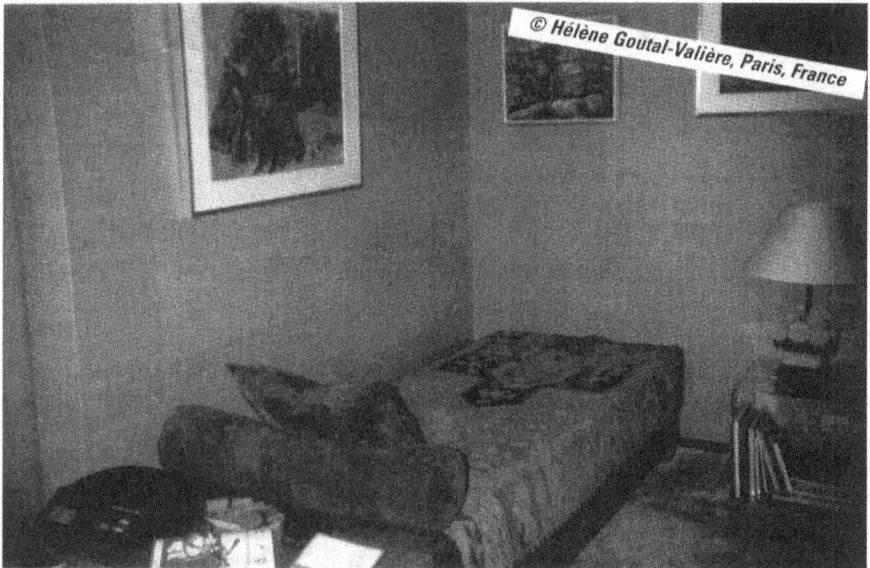

Figure 1.11 Consulting rooms of an unknown member of the SBPSP in Brasília, Brazil, and Hélène Goutal-Valière in Paris, France

Source: The photographs in this chapter are printed with the permission of Claudia Guderian.

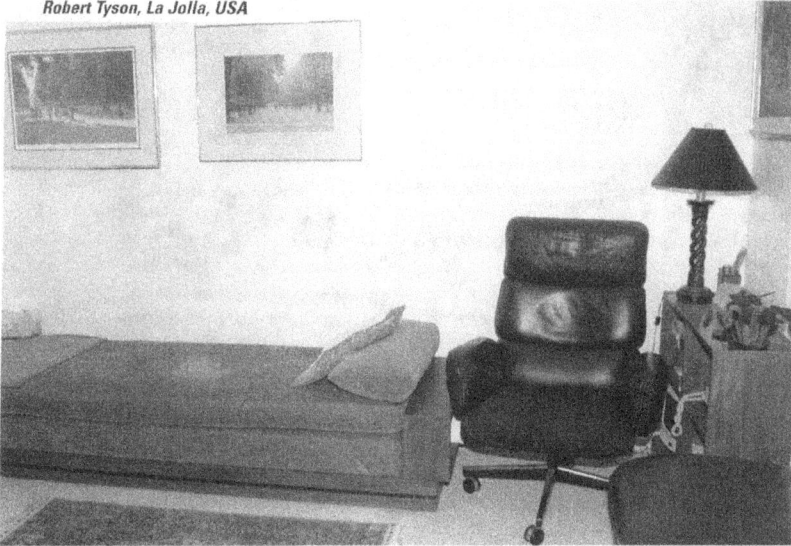

Figure 1.12 Robert Tyson's consulting room in La Jolla, USA
Source: The photographs in this chapter are printed with the permission of Claudia Guderian.

Figure 1.13 Hans Geigenmüller's consulting room in Busswil, Switzerland
Source: The photographs in this chapter are printed with the permission of Claudia Guderian.

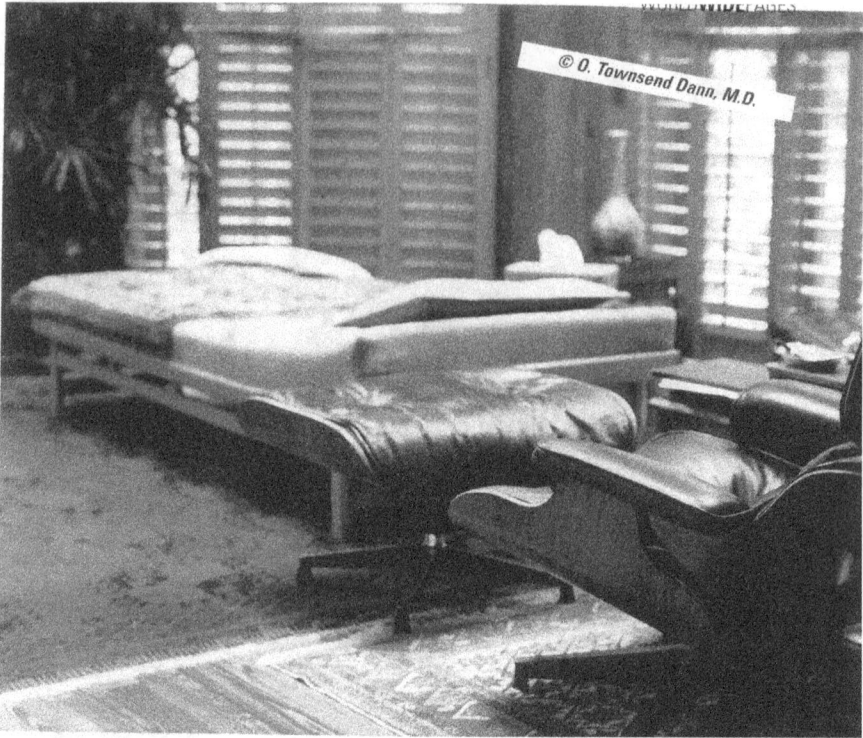

Figure 1.14 O. Townsend Dann's consulting room
Source: The photographs in this chapter are printed with the permission of Claudia Guderian.

analyst who had made him lie down on a common living room sofa. The patient fantasized that on this sofa his analyst used to drink coffee with his guests. In this sense, he fantasized that no place, that sofa included, could be a non-promiscuous place for him. He thought that he could not have an intimate place only for himself and with a well-specified function.

I believe that we cannot speak of the consulting room without considering the adjacent spaces. The sequence of arrival contains many thresholds and subtle and powerful elements in establishing territory and the dialectic between inside and outside (Malnar & Vodvarka, 2004). The reception desk of a building, its hall, its stairs, its elevator, its anteroom, its waiting room, and also its toilets are examples of the spatial sequence we must cross from a public space to a private home. "As one enters the building's precinct and proceeds towards the analytic room, layers of space are penetrated slowly, at a walking pace, preparing for the inner sanctum, while insulating the analysand and the analyst from the outside world" (Danze 2005, pp. 120–121). Esther Sperber writes that

Figure 1.15 Manuel Isaías López Gómez's consulting room in Mexico City, Mexico
Source: The photographs in this chapter are printed with the permission of Claudia Guderian.

> [a]rchitecture could be viewed as a series of suggestions and experiments on the nature of internal and external relations, a machine programmed to manipulate and regulate these links. Therefore, one can see architecture as a sublimation in which we bind our experiences of being connected to nature and society while maintaining sophisticated levels of differentiations from those same ever-present larger unities.
>
> (Sperber, 2014, p. 514)

Architecture is a reflection on entering and exiting, a reflection capable of defining the frames containing our lives (Sperber, 2015).

Entering, greeting and exiting are fundamental parts of the analytical experience. The borders are certainly physical and concrete, but can occur in many different ways. Some are clearly visible, others are invisible, and still others are only implicitly suggested but nonetheless are strongly felt at the physical and emotional level. The real or imaginary borders of the room refer to the real or imaginary borders of the analytic relationship also at the spatial level.

The role of connective architectural space, as well as that of interstitial space, is to connect the inside with the outside and to mediate conjunction

Figure 1.16 Ruth F. Lax's consulting room in New York, USA
Source: The photographs in this chapter are printed with the permission of Claudia Guderian.

and separation. Before entering the analytical space, you must pass through many doors that represent parts of the space indicating (at least to a certain degree), intermediate or transitive situations. These situations do not necessarily indicate exclusions but can be experienced as crossings, passages, or filters that can prepare you to meet the other, or that can be inaccessible barriers. In his *Arcades Project* (1972/2002), written between 1927 and 1940, Walter Benjamin shows how inadequate thresholds are. He also calls them transitions and relates them to the rites of passage that in turn have evident consequences on the articulation and the organisation of space.

By proposing two little clinical vignettes, I look to stress the differences in transference and countertransference relationships, which refer to different qualities of the consulting rooms.

2.1 The Sound

The sound can be hard or soft, reflected or absorbed, depending on the different features of forms and material. In this sense, these features can define in many different ways the issues of proximity, security, and fear, that the presence or absence of sounds near the consulting room can provoke (I am referring to those sounds or voices coming from the street or the waiting room). Further, it would be beneficial that there be between analyst and analysand a sensible listening and a continuous dialogue, similar to what happens in an execution of a work for a piano four hands. ... This execution requires piano players to have continuous critical attention, good taste and a common capacity of letting emotions go.

(Petrella, 2010, pp. 33–34)

Every time Franca spoke of her repressed and coerced sexuality, she did so with a subtle and feeble voice, a sort of whisper. This forced me to get close to her by moving my neck and my head in order to improve my hearing through an improbable enlargement of my ears. So, she forced me to get close to her and thus make a further effort to comprehend words that could not be completely said. Her fear that I could not listen to her was projected onto me. I was not able to listen adequately. Her childhood need to be listened to accompanied her narcissistic demand to have me close to her, as if she were asking whether I would really listen to her words.

The change of my posture in the armchair due to Franca's whispers helped me to feel how much she desired to be understood by me and, like a mother, identify her needs without her making the effort to make me "feel" them. I felt like a mother who is able to individuate her child's needs without attempting to feel them. Perhaps in a larger place and with a bigger distance between the couch and the armchair I would have not felt at the counter-transference level that she needed to maintain her privacy and I would have received and understood only a faint message from her. Perhaps, in a bigger room, I would have felt the urgency of an interpretation about her narcissism, I would not have been able to listen to her, and I would have not understood her need to be listened to. Thus, my later interpretation about her need to be understood has been favored by this possibility of acoustic intimacy (Schinaia, 2019).

2.2 The Light

The experience of intimacy is reinforced by the presence of a window that marks the distinction between the unmeasurability of the outside and the intimacy of the inside. If this experience can be called into question by distractions caused by big windows, a view of the horizon or of distant places, then we may have a concrete idea of the infinite. On the other hand, the sense of closure of the interiors reminds us of something finite and tangible. Each polarity needs the other for its fulfilment (Danze, 2005).

The quantity and the quality of natural light for a consulting room is very important because, in architecture, all the things that the eyes see and the other senses perceive are determined by light and shadow (Holl, 1994). The rooms of American analysts seem to have much more light than those of European analysts not only because of the size of the windows, the color of the walls, or the use of material, but because of the combination of these three elements. All these factors influence the perception of natural light, which can be excessive for an intimate and private place such as a consulting room.

On beautiful and sunny days, before starting the session, Giovanna could put on a pair of sunglasses to protect herself from what she felt as an excess of brightness in the room. This brightness could blind her and prevent her from looking at herself. This is because she had the sensation that brightness did not leave space for the need for privacy and intimacy, unlike semi-darkness. The use of sunglasses was a clear indication of her degree of tolerance for my interpretations. When she was wearing them, it was as if she said to me that she would have experienced my interpretation as if I were turning on a very intense light in a dark place. This is more or less like the actions of an inspector who questions someone under investigation for a crime. When she did not wear her sunglasses, it was as if she took my interpretations as flashes in the dark, as fireflies in the countryside at night (Schinaia, 2019).

Also in such a case, the presence of wide and luminous windows should have invalidated my possibility of perceiving certain indications. Perhaps Giovanna would have had more difficulties in representing her degree of tolerance of my interpretations without her sunglasses.

3 Conclusion

Of course, I have no intention of proposing an architectural model for a consulting room. I am aware of the risk of having excessive simplifications and reductions making us pay less attention to the unique and original features of every consulting room, as well as to the integration between the spatial and perceptual spaces, the patient's internal world, and the peculiarities of analysand-analyst relationship. In spite of this, I believe it is useful to stress certain historical (for example, it is a matter of fact that, unlike American analysts, European analysts tend to have their consulting rooms inside their homes), geographical (external spaces are wider in America than in Europe; this means that the population density is smaller and the extension of living spaces is bigger), architectural (it is a historical fact that American analysts have more interior illumination than their European counterparts; the interiors of European studies are less illuminated than the American ones probably due to the old age of the buildings and to the historical necessity of having reduced spaces and little communication with the external world in order to maintain heat), sociological (this point deals with, for example, the increase of professionalization of the psychoanalytic work and the consequent display of certificates as trophies), and technical aspects (in this case, I think of the various theoretical models in psychoanalysis). All these facets can have a non-neutral role in the constitution of the analytic setting and also in the experience and interpretation of transference and countertransference. I think that knowing and scrutinizing the effects of the architectural aspects and furniture of consulting rooms on the analytic relationship's dynamics can promote an assessment of the different components of the rooms. The same applies to the assessment of the consulting room as such.

The architect Peter Zumthor writes: "In my buildings I try to enhance what seems to be valuable, to correct what is disturbing, and to create anew what we feel is missing" (Zumthor, 1999, p. 24). I believe that this can be a source of inspiration for architects, psychoanalysts, and all creative talents.

References

Benjamin, W. (2002). *The Arcade Project* (R. Tiedemann, Ed., H. Eiland & K. McLaughlin, Trans.). The Belknap Press of Harvard University Press. (Original work published 1972.)

Bolognini, S. (2011). *Secret Passages: The Theory and Technique of Interpsychic Relationships* (G. Atkinson, Trans.). Routledge.

Civitarese, G., & Ferro, A. (2015). *The Analytic Field and Its Transformations.* Routledge.

Danze, E. A. (2005). An Architect's View of Introspective Space: The Analytic Vessel. *Annals of Psychoanalysis*, 33, 109–124.

Eiguer, A. (2007). *L'Inconscio della Casa* (A. Benocci Lenzi, Trans.). Borla.

Guderian, C. (2004). *Magie der Couch: Bilder und Gespräche über Raum und Setting in der Psychoanalyse.* Kohlhammer.

Holl, S. (1994). Questions of Perception: Phenomenology of Architecture. In S. Holl, J. Pallasmaa, & A. Perez-Gomez (Eds.), *Questions of Perception: Phenomenology of Architecture.* William Stout.

Malnar, J.M., & Vodvarka, F. (2004). *Sensory Design.* University of Minnesota Press.

Petrella, F. (2010). Interpretazione psicoanalitica e interpretazione musicale. In G. Gabbriellini (Ed.), *Psicoanalisi e Musica.* Felici.

Rasmussen, S. (1962). *Experiencing Architecture.* MIT Press.

Schinaia, C. (2019). *Psychoanalysis and Architecture: The Inside and the Outside.* Routledge.

Sperber, E. (2014). Sublimation: Building or Dwelling? Loewald, Freud, and Architecture. *Psychoanalytic Psychology*, 31(4), 507–524.

Sperber, E. (2015, June 9). The Architecture of Psychotherapy. *New York Times.*

Zumthor, P. (1999). *Thinking Architecture.* Birkhäuser.

Chapter 2

Liminal Experiencing in the Psychoanalytic Field

Steven Jaron

1 "Language Spaces" and Psychic Life[1]

I'll begin with a short quotation about space and the imagination and the inner world: "[A]n unprejudiced space in which nothing in particular ever happens, and a choice of physiological aids to the imagination whereby each may appropriate it for his or her private world of repentant felicitous forms, heavy expensive objects or avenging flames and floods."

I should state right away that this is *not* a definition of the psychoanalyst's consulting room, despite the terms used to convey its neutral, non-judgmental quality ("an unprejudiced space") and the apparent lack of activity within it ("in which nothing in particular ever happens") other than the subjective appropriation of the space, that is, how the patient makes it his or her own through bringing the specificity of their psychic history and problematic to it. No, notwithstanding a certain resemblance to the space of psychoanalysis, psychoanalytic treatment is not played out there. It is not a definition of its setting but rather W.H. Auden's description of where the better part of his dramatic poem, *The Age of Anxiety* (1948), begun in the midst of war and published shortly after its resolution, takes place: nothing more than a bar located on Third Avenue in Manhattan and, after closing, in one of the character's apartments on the West Side. And yet while it is not a matter of psychoanalysis, *The Age of Anxiety* derives part of its content from psychoanalytic thinking, specifically Jung's. Four characters represent his conception of the four faculties of the psyche: Thought (Malin), Feeling (Rosetta), Intuition (Quant), and Sensation (Emble) (Fuller, 1998, pp. 369–387). They may be conceived as constituting differing qualities of a single psyche. The poem is subtitled *A Baroque Eclogue*, and while there are elements of pastoral landscapes within it, it may perhaps be better understood as an allegorical drama treating the fate of the soul – its failings and foibles, its perplexities about the past, and aspirations for the future – at a deeply troubling time as the action takes place during the wartime conflict on an All Souls Night, a purgatorial, anxiety-charged liminal moment during which, as Hamlet on his nocturnal ghost watch might have uttered, within "this distracted globe" the "time is out of joint" (Shakespeare, 1601/1954, pp. 29 and 33).

DOI: 10.4324/9781003436188-3

Gaston Bachelard, in *La poétique de l'espace* (*The Poetics of Space*), would see in the figurative scenography of *The Age of Anxiety* "espaces de langage" ("language spaces") forming the object of study of a topoanalysis which, drawing on Jean-Bertrand Pontalis, he described as "cet espace fibré parcouru par la simple impulsion des mots vécus" ("this fibered space crossed through by the simple impulse of lived, experienced words"). Quoting Pontalis, he writes: "Le sujet parlant est tout le sujet" ("The speaking subject constitutes the entire subject") (Bachelard, 1958, p. 11), since the poetics of space is the space in which speech embodies the subject. In giving primacy to the speaking subject, Pontalis was perhaps alluding to Lacan's Rome report (1953) on how speech and language function in psychoanalysis, later developed in his concept of *parlêtre* which combines *speaking* and *being* and for Lacan replaces – audaciously, need it be said – the Freudian unconscious, "la parole bien entendu se définissant être le *seul lieu* où l'être ait un sens" ("speech of course defined as being the *sole place* in which being has meaning") (Lacan, 1975, p. 566; emphasis added). Bachelard for his part saw topoanalysis as an auxiliary, a sub-branch of psychoanalysis (Bachelard, 1958, p. 27), and he was perhaps thinking of how Freud wrote at the near end of his life, "[s]pace may be the projection of the extension of the psychical apparatus. No other derivation is probable" (Freud, 1941, p. 300). In topoanalysis, the sense of the past is not dispensed with but is more a matter of spatial ontology, a poetics of being in space within which time is experienced. In this key passage, Bachelard writes:

Dans le théâtre du passé qu'est notre mémoire, le décor maintient les personnages dans leur rôle dominant. On croit parfois se connaître dans le temps, alors qu'on ne connaît qu'une suite de fixations dans des espaces de la stabilité de l'être, d'un être qui ne veut pas s'écouler, qui, dans le passé même quand il s'en va à la recherché du temps perdu, veut "suspendre" le vol du temps. Dans ses mille alvéoles, l'espace tient du temps comprimé. L'espace sert à ça.

(In the theater of the past which is our memory, the stage setting maintains the characters in their predominant roles. We sometimes believe that we know ourselves in time, whereas all we are familiar with is a succession of fixations in the spaces of the stability of being, a being which does not wish to pass and which, even in the past as it sets off in search of lost time, aspires "to suspend" the flight of time. Through its great many alveoli [cells, compartments, or cavities], space recalls time compressed. This is how space is used).

(Bachelard 1958, p. 27)

In my understanding, Bachelard's topoanalysis allows for a rememorial sense of the past to infuse present consciousness. However, it places greater weight on the subjective, inner experience of spatial ontology and how space resonates throughout the ever-shifting qualities of psychic life.

Despite its allusions to Jung's thought, Auden's poem is not a figuration of psychoanalytic space. The "choice of physiological aids to the imagination" are not the objects typically found in the consulting room (minimally, two armchairs and a couch and, along with them, the psychoanalyst), but rather the bar, barstools, tables, and beverages served by a bartender – a bartender who, like the analyst in classical psychoanalysis, in the poem is largely out of sight and silent, the only external voice heard being that of a radio news-caster penetrating the barroom ambiance as he reads one nerve-racking headline after another, an endless flow of external reality reflecting the great inner upheaval in that deeply agitated age characterized as anxious:

> Now the news. Night raids on
> Five cities. Fires started.
> Pressure applied by pincer movement
> In threatening thrust. Third Division
> Enlarges beachhead. Lucky charm
> Saves sniper. Sabotage hinted
> In steel-mill stoppage. Strong point held
> By fanatical Nazis. Canal crossed
> By heroic marines. Rochester barber
> Fools foe. Finns ignore
> Peace feeler. Pope condemns
> Axis excesses. Underground
> Blows up bridge. Tibetan prayer-wheels
> Revolve for victory. Vital crossroads
> Taken by tanks. Trend to the left
> Forecast by Congressman. Cruiser sunk
> In Valdivian Deep. Doomed sailors
> Play poker. Reporter killed.
> (Auden 1948, pp. 17–18)

But what of "nothing in particular ever happens" when in fact, despite occasional appearances to the contrary, something in particular always happens? The physical characteristics of the psychoanalytic setting offer a space in which the patient speaks and associates freely while the analyst listens without prejudice. Auden's "unprejudiced space" thus seems especially apt to me as "unprejudiced" is also used by Freud, or rather Freud's translator, to describe how, in the days when he still believed in his seduction theory, he kept his "critical faculty in abeyance so as to preserve an unprejudiced and receptive attitude" (Freud, 1925/1959, p. 34), with the German reading "unparteiisch," which literally means "impartial" (Freud, 1925a, p. 59). Analytic listening is conducted intuitively, and in a mental state of reverie, a term used by W.R. Bion for whom maternal reverie or the alpha-function contains and then transforms the infant's raw, unmentalized, and unrepresentable beta-elements into tolerable, meaningful, and perceptible alpha-elements (see, for example, Bion, 1962/2014, p. 303) and as such bears a certain likeness to how the analyst listens to the analysand during the session.

2 Liminal Experiencing in the Psychoanalytic Field

Liminal experiencing in the psychoanalytic field belongs to both parties, the analysand and the analyst. An individual who comes for psychoanalysis and gives him- or herself over to the psychoanalytic process – in essence, undergoing a change of mental status in becoming an analysand – experiences the field liminally. Recounting dreams or fragments of them, associating without censoring oneself, living the transference at the juncture of the illusory and the real, and creating thereby something wholly specific to the juncture, are all instances of liminal experiencing, just as each partner's psychosexuality is conveyed by the drives. But this way of experiencing belongs to the analyst as well, though not in the same way; rather, the analyst's liminal experiencing is a function of the material the analysand brings to the field. As Thomas Ogden puts it, the analyst's reverie is "simultaneously a personal/private event and an intersubjective one," adding:

> As is the case with other highly personal emotional experiences of the analyst, he does not often speak with the analysand directly about his experiences, but attempts to speak to the analysand *from* what he is thinking and feeling. That is, he attempts to inform what he says by his awareness of and groundedness in his emotional experience with the patient.
>
> (Ogden, 1997, pp. 158–159; emphasis in the original)

Here's how I understand the two expressions in the title of this chapter. By *liminal experiencing*, I mean an experience of the self – self experience, a notion to which I will return – undergone across, or rather, within a threshold (*liminal* having its roots in the Latin *limen*, "threshold"), which the anthropologist Victor Turner characterized as "betwixt and between" (Turner, 1967). The liminal state is not a neither/nor dimension of experiencing; it is rather *one-and-the-other*. It is not exclusive but inclusive, functioning to collapse the separateness of the binary. Turner used the term "liminal" in relation to initiation rites to describe a transitional state found between an immature state towards a mature state. It was a matter of transformational growth across a somato-psychic continuum. In doing so, he was drawing on his predecessor, Arnold van Gennep, whose work on rites of passage dating from the early twentieth century provides the basic outline of liminality: an individual is *separated* from a group to which he or she belongs; there then occurs the *transition* to another state affected by the rite of passage; and afterwards the individual is *incorporated* into the group anew, having changed through the course of the transitional period (Turner, 1974, pp. 56–58). The transitional state is referred to as liminal and is nestled between the pre-liminal and post-liminal states.

In referring to liminal experiencing within the *psychoanalytic field*, I am not thinking entirely in the anthropological sense but more in terms of intrapsychic and intersubjective dynamics as they play out within the analytic setting. How might this field be conceived? There exist a great many ways of describing it but I will focus on a single one chosen because highly suggestive later conceptualizations, in particular post-Bionian ones (Levine, 2012, p. 26; Civitarese, 2012/2016; Ferro & Civitarese, 2015; Levine, 2022), in part draw on it.

In the early 1960s Madeleine and Willy Baranger wrote of the "analytic situation as a dynamic field" (Baranger & Baranger, 2008), that combines on the one hand a "spatial structure" in which "[t]wo individuals meet in the same room, and are generally located in constant and complementary positions within it" (p. 796) and on the other a "temporal dimension" whose "field is constituted by the prior agreement concerning the duration and frequency of the sessions, as well as the interruptions (vacations, etc.) that may break up the uniformity of the field" (p. 797). Furthermore, the "analytic field is ... structured according to a basic functional configuration contained in the initial commitment and agreement" which "explicitly distributes the roles between the two participants in the situation," that is, the analysand who communicates so far as possible "his or her thoughts" and "co-operate[s] with the other's work and pay[s] for this work" and the analyst, who tries "to understand the former, to provide help in resolving conflicts through interpretation and promises confidentiality and abstention from any intervention in the other's 'real' life" (p. 797). The analytic field is bi-directional, a term that accounts for the transferential-countertransferential dynamic which, as Ogden (1977) explains, is also asymmetrical by definition. The Barangers further describe the "essential ambiguity of the analytic situation" since it is "experienced in the 'as if' category," that is, "that each thing or event in the field be at the same time something else" (Baranger & Baranger, 2008, p. 799). The potentiality of what is uncertain or movable is opened up by means of the patient's transference onto the analyst of unconscious or inadequately represented affect states such as fear or resentment or dissatisfaction or hope or desire. Crucially, this experience *is felt* as real by the patient but is nevertheless "as if," a hypothetical way of being that places at the fore an essential ambiguity.

Ambiguity, and its related notion, illusion, are thus constitutive of the psychoanalytic field. Something at once is and is not, someone at once is and is not. Mechanisms such as unconscious fantasy and projective identification make this possible. Coming to terms with what comes to be understood as ambiguity and illusion in the course of psychoanalysis takes up a great deal of psychic work for both partners. Since the analyst is trained in how their appearance may be expressed within the psychoanalytic field, he or she will bring this functioning to the attention of the analysand at meaningful points in the cure. The analysand then becomes increasingly conscious of them and will reflect on how the roles that are assumed within it might somehow be meaningful in everyday life outside the analytic relationship. A patient who feels persecuted by the analyst, for example, will in time come to relate the feeling of persecution to his or her relationship with a spouse or superior in the workplace, and having a precedent in earlier object relations. While to my knowledge the Barangers do not refer to the analytic situation as liminal, its inherent ambiguity and illusory quality leads me to suggest that self experiencing within it is liminal.

3 Two Conceptions of Self Experience

I would like to turn to the question of self experience because I believe that it deepens our understanding of liminal experiencing in the psychoanalytic field. Artists of all sorts investigate the intricacies of self experience by means of their creative work. Experience of the self, how it is encountered or made known or discovered, endured or tolerated or dismissed, is likewise the object of analytic reflection and here I turn to those of Donald Winnicott and Christopher Bollas.

Winnicott developed a number of fundamental concepts that fall under one form or another of intermediary experiencing which he called "transitional phenomena." Among them is the "transitional object," an infant's "first possession" "related backwards in time to auto-erotic phenomena and fist- and thumb-sucking, and also forwards to the first soft animal or doll or hard toys" (Winnicott, 1971, p. 14). Transitional objects and phenomena, Winnicott argues, "belong to the realm of illusion which is at the basis of the initiation of experience" (p. 14) and he further specifies that the experiences lived within this realm are part of both inner and outer reality (the former being subjective while the latter is shared) and form the basis for sublimated self experiences belonging to imagination, art, religion, or science. For Winnicott, cultural experience is *located* (pp. 95–103). We live in a *place* (pp. 104–110) characterized as an "intermediate zone" (p. 105), a "neutral" third area in which culture is experienced and which accounts for

> the highly sophisticated adult's enjoyment of living or of beauty or of abstract human contrivance, and at the same time ... the creative gesture of a baby who reaches out for the mother's mouth and feels her teeth, and at the same time looks into her eyes, seeing her creatively.
>
> (p. 106)

The space *between* mother and baby is termed a "potential space":

> [A] hypothetical area that exists (but cannot exist) between the baby and the object (mother or part of mother) during the phase of the repudiation of the object as not-me, that is, at the end of being merged in with the object.
>
> (p. 107)

Within the potential space, "it is in play and only in playing that the individual child or adult is able to be creative and to use the whole personality, and it is only in being creative that the individual discovers the self" (Winnicott, 1971, p. 54). Here Winnicott was developing a theory of the exploration and meeting of the self through play. He stood in awe at how an infant arrives at an integrated sense of self out of an unintegrated state in part due to internal factors but also to the quality of his or her environment.

Relaxation and trust are essential at different moments, Winnicott further held, to the search for one's self in a psychoanalysis. The free-associating patient (either a child playing with toys or drawing or an adult lying on the couch and speaking with no consciously directed purpose) "must be allowed to communicate a succession of ideas, thoughts, impulses, sensations that are not linked except in some way that is neurological or physiological and perhaps beyond detection" (Winnicott, 1971, p. 55). The analysand thereby comes across, in the liminal sense, differing aspects of his or her self experience.

A second equally compelling account of self experience is found in Christopher Bollas's *Being a Character: Psychoanalysis and Self Experience* (1992). Self experience, Bollas suggests, is "an inner psychic constellation laden with images, feelings, and bodily acuities" (Bollas, 1992, p. 3). Left unhyphenated, this particular use of the expression does not imply a reflexive or "auto" experience but rather one which is untethered and, as such, the motor of a broadening and deepening of the self with a distinct somato-psychic ontology. It cannot be distilled to the memory of an event in one's life, even if recollecting such and such a moment evokes a certain sense of self. Self experience is constituted out of what the individual chooses and receives, consciously or unconsciously, as material originating in inner experience but further out of what is encountered throughout the outer, spatial world. The two dimensions "oscillate" within one's psyche and body and thereby contribute to creating "psychic textures that bring us into differing areas of potential being" (p. 4), a transformational process at the basis of psychic growth (see, further, Jaron, 2022, p. xi).

Christopher Bollas lays emphasis on the fundamentally vast portion of unconscious self experiencing and this dimension is inherent to the psychoanalytic encounter in which "two people, occupying this most interesting space, select narrative and mental objects to bring about inner states in one another" (Bollas, 1992, p. 5). This encounter is compared to Winnicott's intermediate zone (pp. 17–19; Jaron, 2022, p. 77). In "What Is This Thing

Called Self?," which expands on his observations in *Being a Character*, Bollas states that the self is "an object of an internal dialogue – one talks to oneself, for example, which suggests another. But we also define shifting states of self, particularly of emotional experiences" (Bollas, 1995, p. 146). While knowledge of self experience – either the analysand's or the analyst's – can only be partial – "a matrix beyond representation" (p. 147) – it is nevertheless potentially in part knowable through what occurs between the two individuals in the space of psychoanalysis, the analytic situation. In other words, while self experience cannot entirely be known because it is in large part unconscious (constituting elements of which Bollas terms the "unthought known"), it may nonetheless be glimpsed or even grasped through the exchanges made in the course of psychoanalysis in which, while relating to the analyst and by means of the analyst's interpretations, the analysand comes to perceive and describe his or her own distinctive "way of being" (p. 179). I understand this conception of self experience as a form of liminal experiencing in the psychoanalytic field.

4 Freudian Foundations of Liminal Experiencing

While later analysts contribute to our understanding of the clinical foundations of liminal experiencing in the psychoanalytic field, its seeds are in fact found in Freud's thinking. Freud sought to come to terms with the workings of the patient's repetition compulsion (or constraint) in which, due to uncontrollable drive necessity, the not-so past past repeats itself in the "nowness" of the analytic process as enacted in the transference and handled by the analyst such that the unconscious underpinnings of an idiosyncratic way of being might emerge into an enlarged conscious memory or piece of knowledge. The transference dynamic arouses a transference neurosis, an "artificially constructed transference illness" (Freud, 1916–1917/1963, p. 454), through which the patient's symptomatology may then be analyzed. It is a paradox of the psychoanalytic process, and certainly one that may arouse misunderstanding, that, as a precondition to treating the patient's character disorder, it needs to be expressed in the form of an *artificial reality* or *real artifice* in relation to the analyst. This is in contradistinction to other forms of treatment which either minimize or even eliminate the role of the practitioner as, to use Christopher Bollas's expression, "transformational object" (Bollas, 1987, pp. 13–29).

The language Freud uses, the very terms devised to describe what he observed in the setting, cannot be overlooked, so significant as they are. Here are two instances of how he described this process. In the first, found in *Remembering, Repeating and Working-Through*, he writes of the space in which transference occurs as a "specific region" ("bestimmten Gebiete"; Freud, 1914/1946, p. 134) likened to a "playground" ("Tummelplatz"), a word which, I would like to think, caught Winnicott's attention as he was formulating his own ideas on the conditions that facilitate or inhibit psychic growth. In terms that would have prompted Winnicott to even greater thought, Freud writes: "The transference thus creates an *intermediate region* between illness and life through which the transition from the former to the latter is made" (Freud, 1914/1958, p. 154; translation modified and emphasis added) ("Die Übertragung schafft so ein *Zwischenreich* zwischen der Krankheit und dem Leben, durch welches sich der Übergang von der ersteren zum lezteren vollzieht" (Freud, 1914/1946, p. 135; emphasis added). In the second instance, intrigued by the patient's transferential illness, Freud observed that it "is not something which has been rounded off and become rigid but ... [is] *still growing and developing like a living organism*" (Freud, 1916–1917/1963, p. 444; emphasis added), and thus continuously evolving even during, and in particular due to, the ongoing treatment. He next suggests an image by which this growth may be understood by comparing it to the "cambium layer in a tree *between* the wood and the bark, from which the new formation of tissue and the increase in the girth of the trunk derive" (Freud, 1916–1917/ 1963, p. 444; emphasis added), a highly suggestive ecological analogy. In both cases, it is a matter of living growth that takes place in a space-between.

Translating *Zwischenreich*, a Freudian neologism, into English is a harrowing affair even if it is a compound of two common words. If I were to do so, I would have to consider a prerequisite question, specifically, what does Freud mean by this expression? Meaning and language use go hand in hand and Strachey gives (as above) "intermediate region." *Zwischen* – in fact used twice by Freud: *ein Zwischenreich zwischen*, as if to stress the psychoanalytic process's foundational quality of *betweenness* – means simply enough "between" or "in-between" and *Reich*, "empire," "kingdom," or "realm" (see also Civitarese, 2012/2016, p. 174). The latter is found in the translation of Freud's letter of April 16, 1896 to Fliess in which *Zwischenreich* is first used: "I can record only a very few ideas arising from my daily work about the *in-between realm*" (Freud, 1985, p. 181; emphasis added). Pontalis, summarizing the birth of Freudian thinking in a single sentence and in reference to this very letter, writes: "Notre royaume est celui de l'entre-deux" (Pontalis, 1977, p. 9; see also Jaron 2002, p. 209 and note 6 on that page). The French term, *entre-deux*, can only be approximately translated into English, perhaps because it is, as Pontalis writes in his reflection on the range of psychosexuality and sexual difference, "insaisissable" ("elusory," "impossible to grasp") (Pontalis, 1977, pp. 101–115). Notwithstanding, making a stab at translating it is instructive: "Our realm is that of the gap, the divide, interface, the in-between state, the space-between." The novelist William Burrough's expression, *interzone*, also seems to fit. But this is used in a very different way as Burroughs had in mind the "international zone" in post-World War Two Tangiers, the interzone subsequently worked into his drug-induced, hallucinatory *The Naked Lunch* (1959). Perhaps "inter-realm" is a more suitable candidate. What is certain is that for Freud, within this space there occurs a "crossing," a "transition" (*Übergang*) in which the patient's transference is induced. Any translation of *Zwischenreich* can only approximate the German because the concept itself only approximates self experience, which, we have seen, can never be fully known due to its immeasurable unconscious depth. Within this space, however, transference occurs and working with it constitutes an essential part of the cure.

Regression is central to liminal experiencing in the psychoanalytic field and, like resistance, is stirred up by the setting as the movements of the life and death drives churn within the analysand's and the analyst's psyches. Topographical, temporal, and formal regression are the forms of regression Freud described in a paragraph added in 1914 to *The Interpretation of Dreams*. Pontalis wrote of topographical regression in the dream as a "subjective experience of the dreamer dreaming, an intersubjective experience in the treatment in which the dream is brought to the analyst, at once offered and guarded, speaking and keeping quiet" (Pontalis, 1977, p. 19). And yet the dream recounted, in which lie traces of the patient's infantile sexuality, is but one aspect of regression, perhaps the most apparent one, which refers to "a revival of the dreamer's childhood, of the drive movements which dominated it and the methods of expression which were then available" (Freud, 1900/ 1953, p. 548; translation modified). Temporal regression concerns a return to seemingly outmoded archaic psychic developmental stages (Klein's term, "position," is perhaps more accurate; here too appears repressed infantile sexuality) while formal regression designates primitive behavioral modalities of expression, of ways of relating and being, which take the place of habitual, present-day ones. The combined dimensions of regression may be, when broken down into constituent parts, hypothetically associated individually with space (the topographical), time (the temporal), and shape (the formal). Michael Balint summarized these three dimensions of regression as follows:

> [T]he "backward" movement of mental processes, "transforming thoughts into images" [here quoting from Freud], does not take place only in space, that is, between the various instances of the mental apparatus, but also in time, from the present towards earlier experiences. And lastly, *perhaps the most important characteristic in the clinical observation*, that during regression the mental experiences apparently disintegrate into their past components, and *simpler forms of experience* re-emerge into the mental apparatus.
>
> (Balint, 1968, pp. 120–121; emphasis added)

It seems significant to point out that this reappearance or resurfacing of "simpler forms of experience" occurs *within* the analytic situation since, as bounded space is made infinite and delimited time is returned to timelessness, they are rendered disjointed into a regressed way of being and relating born out of the analytic relationship. Self experience (the analysand's) forms itself in relation to the other's self experience (the analyst's) and as such transference takes on an intermediary shape or form that is specific to moment during which this relationship occurs. The form of regression within the transferential-countertransferential dynamic occurs precisely within the *Zwischenreich*.

There thus exists two *Zwischenreiche*, the first belonging to intrapsychic workings and the second to the clinical setting, the space of psychoanalysis. The first is an individual psychic arena. It consists in both the dream-work but also the whole of psychic life. The second is a topoanalytical arena and, in addition to comprising the intrapsychic, consists in the intersubjective dynamic in the clinical encounter through which the distinct qualities of the transference appear and are analyzed, the analyst using his or her countertransference as a source of insight into what is occurring in this relationship.

5 The Liminal Caesural Space

At around the time the Barangers were working out their conceptualization of the analytic field, Wilfred Bion published *Learning from Experience* in which he refers to the *synapse* which, he reminds us, Freud spoke of as a "contact-barrier" (Bion, 1962/2014, p. 285). Bion was not using this term in a neurophysiological sense but as a metaphor to describe "the point of contact and separation *between* conscious and unconscious elements" (p. 285; emphasis added). In other words, in what Bachelard would consider a topoanalysis, Bion is applying a biochemical process found in neurology to psychoanalytic understanding. That entity is the space where one neuron meets another and communicates with it, for example through neurotransmitters. The cleft between the two neurons is called the synapse. A topoanalytical way of understanding Bion here consists in apprehending the signification of the link *between* two objects or, on the contrary, where, to use his language, it is *attacked*. In a later paper, he called this space a *caesura* and he implored his reader to "[i]nvestigate the caesura; not the analyst; not the analysand; not the unconscious; not the conscious; not sanity; not insanity. But the caesura, the link, the synapse, the counter-transference, the transitive-intransitive mood" (Bion, 1975/2014, p. 49). Avner Bergstein, drawing on Bion, formulates this liminal psychic arena in his own terms: "That is where emotional aliveness lies, but that is also where the threat of drowning lurks" (Bergstein, 2019, p. 31) or again,

> The caesura is … a model for the gap, that raging river between two banks. It is the place where catastrophic change occurs but where lies the danger of catastrophe as well. This is the impossible place Bion asks us to be in – the emotional turbulence – without gripping onto any of the banks in a way that halts movement.
>
> (p. 32)

Christopher Bollas refers to narratology to describe how unconscious perception and meaning might arise within the caesura:

> Unconscious thinking is not held in any single mental idea, but takes place as a logical process. It is revealed not in one narrative unit … but in the *links between* narrative units. In the caesura one finds the logical possibilities. It is exactly *in and through these gaps* that the logic of thought occurs.
>
> (Bollas, 2007, p. 91; emphasis added)

I hold that the caesura may be understood as an interstitial, liminal space. As in the neurophysiological model, there is a pre-synaptic neuron and a post-synaptic neuron. The space between – the synapse – is liminal. Further, as with the analytic field I highlight the caesura's essentially ambiguous, illusory qualities. James Grotstein describes it as a "third entity," as "extraterritorial" (Grotstein, 2007, p. 57), while Nilofer Kaul specifically relates the caesura to the concept of liminality (Kaul, 2022, pp. xxii–xxiii). The liminal caesura may be described as an abyss or a void, a gully or pit, a cleft or a breach. It is a space-between, not a rite of passage but a *site of passage*, a passage that is wholly other and in which unfamiliar, perplexing thoughts and feelings are perhaps experienced and made representable. This brings to mind Pierre Fédida's expression, "le site de l'étranger" ("the site of the stranger"), in which foreignness or strangeness, alterity, in a word, is at the fore (Fédida, 1995, pp. 53–69). Psychoanalytically, within the liminal caesural space there occurs potential linking and unlinking but further a pause and resumption, a rent and reparation. The liminal caesural space *is* axiomatically psychoanalytic.

The concurrent and relational experiences of undergoing and carrying out psychoanalysis is complex, a source of puzzlement and wonder that attracts and repels insofar as it raises a basic question, namely what is happening within and between the partners? For each, there may be moments of the regressed release or discharging of painful affects, or of becoming aware of something which till then had been obscure, or "soul-eclipsed," in relation to one's self. Appreciating the liminal quality of the psychoanalytic field deepens our understanding of something specific to these experiences.

Note

1 I wish to thank Evelyne Sechaud for stimulating my thoughts on the specificity of psychoanalysis. Unless otherwise indicated, all translations are my own.

References

Auden, W.H. (1948). *The Age of Anxiety: A Baroque Eclogue*. Faber & Faber.
Bachelard, Gaston (1958). *La poétique de l'espace*. 2nd ed. Presses universitaires de France.

Balint, M. (1968). *The Basic Fault: Therapeutic Aspects of Regression*. Tavistock.

Baranger, M., & Baranger, W. (2008). The Analytic Situation as a Dynamic Field. *International Journal of Psychoanalysis*, 89, 795–826.

Bergstein, A. (2019). *Bion and Meltzer's Expeditions into Unmapped Mental Life: Beyond the Spectrum in Psychoanalysis*. Routledge.

Bion, W.R. (2014). Learning from Experience. In C. Mawson (Ed.), *The Complete Works of W.R. Bion* (Vol. 4). Karnac. (Original work published 1962.)

Bion, W. R. (2014). Caesura. In C. Mawson (Ed.), *The Complete Works of W.R. Bion* (Vol. 10). Karnac. (Original work published 1975.)

Bollas, C. (1987). *The Shadow of the Object: Psychoanalysis of the Unthought Known*. Free Association.

Bollas, C. (1992). *Being a Character: Psychoanalysis and Self Experience*. Routledge.

Bollas, C. (1995). *Cracking Up: The Work of Unconscious Experience*. Hill and Wang.

Bollas, C. (2007). *The Freudian Moment*. Karnac.

Civitarese, G. (2016). Intermediary as an Epistemological Paradigm in Psycho-analysis. In *Truth and the Unconscious in Psychoanalysis*. Routledge. (Original work published 2012.)

Fédida, P. (1995). *Le site de l'étranger: La situation analytique*. Presses universitaires de France.

Ferro, A., & Civitarese, G. (2015). *The Analytic Field and its Transformations*. Routledge.

Freud, S. (1946). Erinnern, Wiederholen und Durcharbeiten. In *Gesammelte Werke*, Vol. 10. Imago Publishing. (Original work published 1914.)

Freud, S. (1948). Selbstdarstellung. In *Gesammelte Werke*, Vol. 14. Imago Publishing. (Original work published 1925.)

Freud, S. (1953). The Interpretation of Dreams. In *The Standard Edition of the Complete Psychological Works of Sigmund Freud*, Vol. 5 (J. Strachey, Ed. & Trans.). The Hogarth Press. (Original work published 1900.)

Freud, S. (1958). Remembering, Repeating and Working-Through. In *The Standard Edition of the Complete Psychological Works of Sigmund Freud*, Vol. 12 (J. Strachey, Ed. & Trans.). The Hogarth Press. (Original work published 1914.)

Freud, S. (1959). An Autobiographical Study. In *The Standard Edition of the Complete Psychological Works of Sigmund Freud*, Vol. 20 (J. Strachey, Ed. & Trans.). The Hogarth Press. (Original work published 1925.)

Freud, S. (1963). Introductory Lectures on Psycho-Analysis. In *The Standard Edition of the Complete Psychological Works of Sigmund Freud*, Vol. 16 (J. Strachey, Ed. & Trans.). The Hogarth Press. (Original work published 1916–1917.)

Freud, S. (1964). Findings, Ideas, Problems. In *The Standard Edition of the Complete Psychological Works of Sigmund Freud*, Vol. 23 (J. Strachey, Ed. & Trans.). The Hogarth Press. (Original work published 1941.)

Freud, S. (1985). Letter of April 16th, 1896. In *The Complete Letters of Sigmund Freud to Wilhelm Fliess, 1887–1904* (J.M. Masson, Ed. & Trans.). The Belknap Press of Harvard University Press.

Fuller, J. (1998). *W.H. Auden: A Commentary*. Faber & Faber.

Grotstein, J. S. (2007). *A Beam of Intense Darkness: Wilfred Bion's Legacy to Psychoanalysis*. Karnac.

Jaron, S. (2002). Autobiography and the Holocaust: An Examination of the Liminal Generation in France. *French Studies*, 56(2), 207–219.

Jaron, S. (2022). *Christopher Bollas: A Contemporary Introduction*. Routledge.

Kaul, N. (2022). *Plato's Ghost: Minus Links and Liminality in Psychoanalytic Practice*. Phoenix.

Lacan, J. (1975). Joyce le Symptôme. In *Autres écrits*. Le Seuil.

Levine, H.B. (2012). The Analyst's Theory in the Analyst's Mind. *Psychoanalytic Inquiry*, 32, 18–32.

Levine, H.B. (Ed.). (2022) *The Post-Bionian Field Theory of Antonino Ferro: Theoretical Analysis and Clinical Application*. Routledge.

Ogden, Thomas H. (1997). Reverie and Interpretation. In *Reverie and Interpretation: Sensing Something Human*. London.

Pontalis, J.-B. (1977). *Entre le rêve et la douleur*. Gallimard.

Shakespeare, W. (1954). *Hamlet* (J.D. Wilson, Ed.). 2nd ed. Cambridge University Press. (Original work published 1601.)

Turner, V. (1967). Betwixt and Between: The Liminal Period in *Rites de Passage*. In *The Forest of Symbols: Aspects of Ndembu Ritual*. Cornell University Press.

Turner, V. (1974). Liminal to Liminoid in Play, Flow, and Ritual: An Essay in Comparative Symbology. *Rice Institute Pamphlet—Rice University Studies*, 60(3), 53–92.

Winnicott, D.W. (1971). *Playing and Reality*. Tavistock.

Chapter 3

Libidinal Spacing

Three Freudian Theses on Erogenous Zones[1]

Thomas Dojan

In the corresponding entry of Laplanche and Pontalis's *The Language of Psycho-Analysis*, "erogenous zones" are defined first generally as "[a]ny region of the skin or mucous membrane capable of being the seat of an excitation of a sexual nature" and then "[m]ore specifically, [as] one of those areas which are by function the seat of such excitation: the oral, anal, genital and mamillary zones" (Laplanche & Pontalis, 1988, p. 154). The more specific definition of erogenous zones, i.e., the one that takes recourse to regions of the body whose "function" is to be "the seat of sexual excitation," is at the same time the more familiar one. What first and foremost comes to mind when thinking about erogenous zones are regions such as the mouth, the anus, the penis, glans and scrotum, the vagina and clitoris, as well as the breasts. Of these bodily regions, Freud states that they are "predisposed" to function as seats of sexual excitation.

In the third of his *Three Essays on the Theory of Sexuality* – the one that is concerned with the "transformations of puberty" – Freud writes regarding the male body that sexual excitation "is a function of the accumulation of semen in the vesicles containing the sexual products." In line with "the fairly wide-spread hypothesis that the accumulation of the sexual substances creates and maintains sexual tension," he states that "[i]f the excitation of the erotogenic zones increases sexual tension, this could only come about on the supposition that the zones in question *are in an anatomical connection that has already been laid down* with these centres" (Freud, 1905/1953b, p. 213; emphasis added). These thoughts can be found in a passage that was added by Freud in the fourth edition of the *Three Essays* in 1920, under the influence of new research on the formation of the sex hormones in the gonads. According to this view, sexual excitation arises quite mechanically, as the result of a chemical process that begins to operate in the body once it has reached a certain state of anatomical maturity during puberty. And thus, the most oppressive of the Freudian oracles comes to mind: "Anatomy is Destiny" (Freud, 1924, p. 178) – everything will play out according to how it has "already been laid down."

Straightforward as this might seem, and in line with the depiction of Freud as the so-called "biologist of the mind" (Sulloway, 1992), the preface to the

DOI: 10.4324/9781003436188-4

earlier, third edition of the *Three Essays* already calls on us to take bio-chemical accounts of sexuality such as this with a grain of salt, as it were. Freud writes – perhaps surprisingly, considering the quote above – that his work is "*completely* based upon psychoanalytic research" and "*deliberately independent* of the findings of biology." Furthermore, Freud's aim "has rather been to discover how far psychological investigation can throw light upon the biology of the sexual life of man (*menschliches Sexualleben*)." As such, "the psycho-analytic method led in a number of important respects to opinions and findings which differed largely from those based on biological considerations" (Freud, 1905/1953b, p. 131; emphasis added). Thus, Freud reverses the direction of the epistemic relation between soma and psyche that the biologist would assume: *psyche explains soma, not otherwise.*

Some light, I believe, can be shed on this peculiar state of affairs if we turn our attention to Laplanche and Pontalis's more general definition of erogen-ous zones, which states that they are "[a]*ny* region of the skin or mucous membrane capable of being the seat of an excitation of a sexual nature" (Laplanche & Pontalis, 1988, p. 154; emphasis added). Based, of course, on Freud's own work, this definition can be traced to the first mentioning of erogenous zones in Freud's writings, in a letter to Wilhelm Fliess from 6 December 1896. In the context of a discussion on the pathogenesis of hysteria, Freud writes:

> Furthermore, behind this lies the idea of *abandoned erotogenic zones.* That is to say, *during childhood sexual release would seem to be obtainable from a great many parts of the body*, which at a later time are able to release only … anxiety … A hysterical attack is *not a discharge but an action*; and it retains the original characteristic of every action – of being a means to the reproduction of pleasure. … Attacks of dizziness and fits of weeping – *all these are aimed at another person* – but mostly at the prehistoric, unforgettable other person who is never equalled by anyone later.
>
> (Freud, 1985, pp. 212–213; emphasis added)

Is it not curious that the first written account of erogenous zones that can be traced in Freud's work is a negative one, commenting on "*abandoned* ero-genous zones" instead of explaining what they might positively be in the first place? It would seem that, just as Freud's interest in mental processes is pre-dominantly an interest in their latency – i.e., in the unconscious – his interest in sexual life is always tuned towards the repressed. What Freud has in mind here when he talks about "abandoned erogenous zones" might be such pleasurable parts of the body that lose their relevance when so-called phallic or genital primacy is established, and the sexual excitation of, say, the oral or anal zones – but really "a great many parts of the body" – releases anxiety rather than pleasure, potentially culminating in hysterical attacks. In such cases, Freud is far from evoking the vocabulary of machines that mechanically operate in blind, reactive response to adequate stimuli. Instead of passivity, activity – the "acting-out" of hysterical symptoms – is underscored along with their communicative function, their "being aimed at other persons." All this is grounded in the concept of erogenous zones, which thereby partake in such talkative activity. A second passage from a later letter, dated 14 November 1897, further explores this:

> We must assume that in infancy the release of sexuality is *not yet so much localized* as it is later, so that the zones which are later abandoned (and *perhaps the whole surface of the body* as well) also instigate something that is analogous to the later release of sexuality. ... A release of sexuality ... comes about, then, not only (1) *through a peripheral stimulus upon the sexual organs,* or (2) *through the internal excitations* arising from those organs, but also (3) from ideas – that is, *from memory traces* – therefore also by the path of deferred action.
>
> (Freud, 1985, p. 279; emphasis added)

With this, we are given a programme that distinguishes three options for the release of sexuality in erogenous zones: (1) through external stimulation; (2) through internal stimulation; and (3) through memory traces. Explicating these three theses as accounts of what can be called "libidinal spacing" is the aim of this contribution.

Starting with Freud's first two points – external and internal sexual stimulation – it may be instructive to recall that this motif lies at the heart of Freud's concept of "infantile sexuality." Infantile sexuality was introduced in the context of the so-called seduction theory that Freud developed in research following the *Studies on Hysteria* (Freud, 1896/1962b; 1896/1962c). Seduction theory holds that the class of childhood events that set up hysterical symptoms exclusively encompasses cases of sexual initiation – by adult strangers, by adult caregivers or by other children who had previously been "seduced" by adults (Freud, 1896/1962c, p. 208). The traumatic character of such experiences then explains the characteristic repression of the sexual factor observed in hysteria. Infantile sexuality is thus initially understood as a pathogenic phenomenon that is awakened by external stimulation. In this account, the sexual factor is not by itself an efficacious moment in the infantile psyche, and under ordinary conditions (i.e., without external stimulation) gains psychic relevance only later, over the course of physical maturation processes during puberty. How then are external and internal sexual stimulation to be understood?

In an earlier 1895 paper on anxiety neurosis, Freud took the concept of sexual excitation to capture the "irritability" and "sensitiveness" of the subject in response to sexual stimuli with "sexual need" – i.e., "libido" (Freud, 1895/1962a, pp. 92, 101, 102) – expressed in characteristic bodily and psychic reactions such as the preparation for and inclination to initiate sexual activity; reactions that are affectively experienced as tension (pp. 108–109, 112). The model case once again is given with recourse to the male body. In the neurological parlance of early Freud, we read that, somatically, sexual excitation "is manifested as a pressure on the walls of the seminal vesicles," releasing a "visceral excitation" which "will develop continuously" and "express itself as a psychical stimulus" once it has "overcome the resistance of the intervening path of conduction to the cerebral cortex," resulting in "the psychical state of libidinal tension which brings with it an urge to remove that tension" through "*specific* or *adequate* action" (p. 108; emphasis in original). Disentangling this jargonistic account, Freud is stating here that the organism responds to external sexual stimuli with sexual excitation, by giving rise to a kind of inner-somatic pressure that psychically translates into the experience of sexual need and the inclination to release this pressure through sexual activity. Thus, according to this view, sexuality is processed internally only under the condition that the organism reacts to external sexual stimuli.

This position was modified as the concept of infantile sexuality was advanced, once Freud renounced his early version of seduction theory in 1905 (Freud, 1905/1953b, pp. 190–191). Against the critics,[2] we should keep in mind, though, that Freud never *completely* withdrew from seduction theory, but only restricted its scope of application, no longer stating that it explained *all* cases of neurosis. Therefore, despite this change of view, he noted in a paper on aetiology in 1906: "there are two positions that I have never repudiated or abandoned – the importance of sexuality and of infantilism" (Freud, 1906/1953c, pp. 277–278). Instead of regarding infantile sexuality *exclusively* as a pathogenic phenomenon, Freud thus breaks through to a non-pathological account of infantile sexuality as ubiquitous autoaffection, already operative during earliest childhood. The "internal excitation" that Freud alludes to in the Fliess letters is, I think, of such a type. With this modified view, conscious and unconscious sexual fantasies about the self and others arise not only in response to external sexual stimuli but also from the internal sources of infantile sexuality. Such fantasies are operative in pathological and non-pathological experiences alike, because they do not originate from traumatic external sexual stimulation but from the autoaffection common to all humankind, i.e., from an internal sexual factor that is always already operative in the human psyche.

While this brings into view how external and internal excitation give rise to sexual release in a broad sense, passages from the *Three Essays* also shed light more specifically on the formation of erogenous zones in response to stimulation of privileged areas of the body. That this must not be thought of in the stimulus-response model that the biochemical hypothesis rests on is well portrayed in the example of the care work directed at the child during infancy. The "psychological examination" of the "child's intercourse with anyone responsible for his care" – especially with the mother who "strokes him, kisses him, rocks him" – reveals that such care work "affords him an unending source of sexual excitation and satisfaction from his erotogenic zones" (Freud, 1905/1953b, p. 223). From the psychological point of view, the most privileged erogenous zones – the oral, anal, genital and mammillary zones – are most responsive to external stimulation not simply by virtue of an inborn physiological mechanism that predisposes them to sexual functions, but have acquired their "irritability," "sensitiveness," *excitability* over the course of repeated experiences of intimate contact during childcare. This is more strikingly depicted in examples where erogenous zones arise in bodily regions that do not pertain to the oral, anal, genital and mammillary zones. Freud instructively alludes to the phenomenon of thumb-sucking, which also sheds light on how erogenous zones tap into memory traces. Quoting the entire respective passage from the *Three Essays* is worthwhile:

> Furthermore, it is clear that the behaviour of a child who indulges in thumb-sucking is determined by a search for some pleasure which has already been experienced and is now remembered. ... It was the child's first and most vital activity, his sucking at his mother's breast, or at substitutes for it, that must have familiarized him with this pleasure. *The child's lips, in our view, behave like an erotogenic zone ...* The child does not make use of an extraneous body for his sucking, but *prefers a part of his own skin* because it is more convenient, because it makes him independent of the external world, which he is not yet able to control, and because in that way *he provides himself, as it were, with a second erotogenic zone*, though one of an inferior kind.
> (Freud, 1905/1953b, pp. 181–182; emphasis added)

While the lips, of course, belong to the oral zone, in this example it is especially interesting how a part of the child's own skin, i.e., their thumb, can acquire the properties of an erogenous zone, "though one of an inferior kind." It does so as a substitute for the mother's breast, more specifically as a "mnemic symbol" that stands in its place. This resonates with Freud's concept of "somatic compliance," which he introduced in the case story of Dora (Freud, 1905/1953a, pp. 40–41), that designates the ability of the body and its organs to offer privileged mediums for the symbolic expression of unconscious desire. In the case of thumb-sucking, the libidinal cathexis of the breast is displaced onto the thumb, an area of the body which is not by physiological function designed to serve as an erogenous zone. Psychoanalytically conceived, the body is thus far from being the passive, dead matter of mechanical reactivity. It has its own peculiar kind of inventive activity that it responsively enacts vis-à-vis the other, both in their presence and absence. Instructively, further musing on thumb-sucking, Freud comments: "A rhythmic character must play a part among them [i.e., the conditions of its pleasure] and the analogy of tickling is forced upon our notice" (Freud 1905/1953b, p. 183), and although he does not elaborate on this digression, others have taken up the cue. The British psychoanalyst Adam Phillips wrote a commendable short essay, "On Tickling," which I quote from:

> Through tickling, the child will be initiated in a distinctive way into the helplessness and disarray of a certain primitive kind of pleasure, *dependent on the adult to hold and not to exploit the experience*. And this means to stop at the blurred point, so acutely felt in tickling, *at which pleasure becomes pain*, and the child experiences an intensely anguished confusion; because the tickling narrative, unlike the sexual narrative, has no climax.
>
> (Phillips, 1993, p. 2; emphasis added)

Tickling provides a good example of suitable intimacy between adults and children, and is, as such, much like childcare or consolation – an adult's proper response to the infantile sexuality of the child; it is at the same time obviously innocent and obviously sensuous. Offering a good example of how pleasure is so often at the tipping point of pain, tickling can also be made sense of as the whole body operating as an erogenous zone. Phillips' hint that the experience depends on being held (i.e., "contained" in a "holding environment") by the adult, though, alerts to the possibility of it being overwhelming. With regard to the latter, Freud speaks of the formation of so-called hysterogenic zones, a concept he took from Martin Charcot and advanced in his own psychoanalytic framework.

By means of example, consider the case of Elisabeth von R. from the *Studies on Hysteria* (Freud, 1895/1955, pp. 135–181), who came to Freud for treatment because she suffered from leg pain for which no somatic cause could be discerned. On differential diagnosis, Freud writes that "if one pressed or pinched the hyperalgesic skin and muscles of her legs, her face assumed a peculiar expression, which was one *of pleasure rather than pain*," and that Elisabeth cried out "as though she was having a voluptuous tickling sensation" – giving Freud reason to state "that the stimulation had touched upon a hysterogenic zone" (p. 137; emphasis added). Over the course of her treatment, Elisabeth confessed to Freud a secret love affair with a young man of which she had never spoken. She then established a connection to her suffering, and was able to name the origin of her hysterical symptoms, which now dawned on her: her suffering first manifested as she was nursing her dying, bedridden father, whom she dearly loved, and the leg pain spread from the very spot where her father's diseased leg had rested each morning as Elisabeth changed the bandages. Freud underscores the repetition operative in this morning ritual: "[t]his must have happened a good hundred times, yet she had not noticed the connection till now." Instead of being noticed, i.e., being consciously deliberated, it seems that in Elisabeth's case an experience of intimate touch was not properly contained, and thus, as it was inscribed into the body as a mnemic erogenous zone, took the form of a hysterical symptom with all the associated pain – and pleasure, as Freud is quick to add. "In this way," Freud comments, "she gave me the explanation that I needed of *the emergence of what was an atypical hysterogenic zone*" (p. 148; emphasis added).

One last loose thread needs to be tied up. When Freud writes in his letter to Fliess that sexual release may come about "from memory traces," he adds by means of explanation: "therefore also *by the path of deferred action*" (Freud, 1985, p. 279; emphasis in the original). Freud applied his concept of deferred action, *Nachträglichkeit*, to the case of Emma from the 1895 *Project for a Scientific Psychology*. Emma entered into treatment with Freud because she suffered from "a compulsion of not being able to go into shops *alone*" (Freud, 1950[1895]/1966, p. 353; emphasis in the original). In analysis, Emma recalled that her symptoms first manifested themselves at the age of twelve, i.e., shortly after puberty, according to Freud. On one occasion, she felt sexually attracted to one of two (male) shop assistants working at a store she frequented. The shop assistants laughed at Emma's dress as she entered the store, and in consequence Emma "ran away in some kind of *affect of fright*" (p. 353; emphasis in the original). Analysis uncovered that, at the age of eight (i.e., before puberty), Emma had been sexually assaulted by a grinning shopkeeper on the occasion of visiting his store alone, i.e., unaccompanied; "the shopkeeper had grabbed at her genitals through her clothes" (p. 354). After the incident reoccurred on another occasion, Emma "reproached herself for having gone there the second time, as though she had wanted in that way to provoke the assault" (p. 354). Emma was eventually able to identify an association between the two: "the laughing of the shop-assistants had reminded her of the grin with which the shopkeeper had accompanied his assault" (p. 354). The point is that now – after Emma had undergone puberty – this memory aroused "what it was certainly not able to at the time, a *sexual release*, which was transformed into anxiety" (p. 354; emphasis in the original).

Emma's case illustrates how past experience can be preserved in embodied memory and released once the conditions are in place that allow for this experience (however disturbing) to be processed *meaningfully*. There is no question that eight-year-old Emma's experience involved a transgression that must have been traumatic, and the anxiety she was unable to experience on the first occasion was released as an *adequate* response to the first experience in the second scene, where it seemingly no longer made sense. And this teaches us something about the tissue of the libidinal body: it does not exist exclusively in the here and now but is expanded through time, weaving and unweaving threads of unconscious fantasy that knot perception, memory and anticipation *meaningfully* together (Freud, 1908/1959, pp. 147–148). Libidinal space is thus not only the locus of the present experience of sexual release but also of the remembrance and anticipation of such release. On 3 January 1899, Freud wrote to Wilhelm Fliess: "To the question 'What happened in earliest childhood?' the answer is, 'Nothing, but the germ of a sexual impulse existed'" (Freud, 1985, p. 338).

*

Anatomy may or may not be destiny, but like every psychoanalyst after him, Freud always recognized that everybody struggles with their destiny. And even though the Freudian concept of "erogenous zones" may seem somewhat dated by the standards of today's discourse, I hope to have shown that it can well account for the talkative, relational and inventive life of the body. Freud's descriptions of the emergence of erogenous zones can be read as accounts of the "libidinal spacing" of the body. Through this "libidinal spacing", respective areas of the body become "irritable" and "sensitive" in response to external and internal stimulation with sexual need (i.e., "libido"). The polymorphously sexual tissue from which erogenous zones emerge is not limited to the privileged oral, anal, genital and mamillary zones but expands over the whole surface of the body. Erogenous zones then become localized when external or internal stimulations of the body have an impact that leads them to be inscribed with sexual meaning. Thus, erogenous zones may emerge in regions of the body that are physiologically predisposed to sexual functions, but they can also appear in parts of the body that are themselves non-sexual and yet "somatically compliant" towards the sexual. Erogenous zones operate in conjunction with a peculiar kind of bodily memory, in place of psychic functions, and can somatically substitute for psychic functions as hysterogenic zones. Erogenous zones are mnemic bodily tissue that quite literally remember experiences of past intimate touch and anticipate such experiences in future contact, striving to make sense of the riddle which sexuality is.

Notes

1 The author received funds from the National Science Centre (Poland), as part of the research project *Towards a "Depth Phenomenology" of Embodied Individuation*, grant agreement no. UMO-2019/35/O/HS1/042018.
2 See Masson (1984). Masson's view that Freud deliberately retreated from seduction theory because he refused to believe his analysands was reproached as polemic particularly by historians of psychoanalysis; see Gay (1985, p. 117, FN. 1 and 1988, p. 751). The standard account of Freud's views on seduction theory is given in Jones (1953, pp. 263–267).

References

Freud, S. (1953a). Fragment of an Analysis of a Case of Hysteria. In *The Standard Edition of the Complete Psychological Works of Sigmund Freud*, Vol. 7 (J. Strachey, Ed. & Trans.). The Hogarth Press. (Original work published 1905.)

Freud, S. (1953b). Three Essays on the Theory of Sexuality. In *The Standard Edition of the Complete Psychological Works of Sigmund Freud*, Vol. 7 (J. Strachey, Ed. & Trans.). The Hogarth Press. (Original work published 1905.)

Freud, S. (1953c). My Views on the Role Played by Sexuality in the Aetiology of the Neuroses. In *The Standard Edition of the Complete Psychological Works of Sigmund Freud*, Vol. 7 (J. Strachey, Ed. & Trans.). The Hogarth Press. (Original work published 1906.)

Freud, S. (1955). Studies on Hysteria. In *The Standard Edition of the Complete Psychological Works of Sigmund Freud*, Vol. 2 (J. Strachey, Ed. & Trans.). The Hogarth Press. (Original work published 1895.)

Freud, S. (1959). Creative Writers and Daydreaming. In *The Standard Edition of the Complete Psychological Works of Sigmund Freud*, Vol. 9 (J. Strachey, Ed. & Trans.). The Hogarth Press. (Original work published 1908.)

Freud, S. (1961). The Dissolution of the Oedipus Complex. In *The Standard Edition of the Complete Psychological Works of Sigmund Freud*, Vol. 19 (J. Strachey, Ed. & Trans.). The Hogarth Press. (Original work published 1924.)

Freud, S. (1962a). On the Grounds for Detaching a Particular Syndrome from Neurasthenia under the Description "Anxiety Neurosis." In *The Standard Edition of the Complete Psychological Works of Sigmund Freud*, Vol. 3 (J. Strachey, Ed. & Trans.). The Hogarth Press. (Original work published 1895.)

Freud, S. (1962b). Heredity and the Aetiology of the Neuroses. In *The Standard Edition of the Complete Psychological Works of Sigmund Freud*, Vol. 3 (J. Strachey, Ed. & Trans.). The Hogarth Press. (Original work published 1896.)

Freud, S. (1962c). Further Remarks on the Neuro-psychoses of Defence. In *The Standard Edition of the Complete Psychological Works of Sigmund Freud*, Vol. 3 (J. Strachey, Ed. & Trans.). The Hogarth Press. (Original work published 1896.)

Freud, S. (1966). Project for a Scientific Psychology. In *The Standard Edition of the Complete Psychological Works of Sigmund Freud*, Vol. 1 (J. Strachey, Ed. & Trans.). The Hogarth Press. (Original work published 1950 [1895].)

Freud, S. (1985). *The Complete Letters of Sigmund Freud to Wilhelm Fliess, 1887–1904* (J.M. Masson, Ed. & Trans.). The Belknap Press of Harvard University Press.

Gay, P. (1985). *Freud for Historians*. Oxford University Press.

Gay, P. (1988). *Freud: A Life for Our Time*. J.M. Dent & Sons Ltd.

Jones, E. (1953). *The Life and Work of Sigmund Freud* (vol. 1). Basic Books.

Laplanche, J., & Pontalis, J.-B. (1988). *The Language of Psycho-Analysis*. Karnac.

Masson, J.M. (1984). *The Assault on Truth: Freud's Suppression of the Seduction Theory*. Farrar, Straus and Giroux.

Phillips, A. (1993). On Tickling. In *On Kissing, Tickling and Being Bored*. Faber and Faber.

Sulloway, F. J. (1992). *Freud, Biologist of the Mind: Beyond the Psychoanalytic Legend*. Harvard University Press.

Chapter 4

The Dark Space of the Sleeping Body

The Syncretic Space of Dreams and the Unconscious

Santiago Sourigues

Space is neither a concept nor an issue of direct interest within psycho-analysis itself.[1] Nevertheless, this does not mean that we cannot make use of it as a means of analysis for studying the phenomena described by psycho-analysis to gain new insights into such descriptions. In this regard, we want to formulate the hypothesis that the primary spatial structure of subjectivity serves as a guiding thread for a deeper understanding of the relations between dream and unconscious, between the conscious and unconscious systems and between the unconscious and the body from a phenomen-ological perspective. Indeed, phenomenology provides interesting conceptual and methodological tools for approaching the question of spatiality from a subjective point of view, as well as for articulating such a matter with the study of dreams and the unconscious. Within phenomenological tradition, we find authors who have dealt with classical phenomena discussed by psy-choanalysis; as it is, for instance, in the case of Sartre's studies on dreams (Sartre, 1940) and Merleau-Ponty's elaborations in his course at the Collège de France (1954–1955) on passivity, memory, dream and the unconscious (Merleau-Ponty, 1954–1955/2017). Within the framework of this course, Merleau-Ponty sets the symbolism of dreams and the unconscious against the background of his developments on the body and the problem of passive dimensions of subjective experience, which are presupposed by active and waking consciousness. And it is Merleau-Ponty whom we draw on in the present chapter in order to discuss the question of the primary spatial struc-ture of subjectivity as a thread for analysing the inner relation between body, dream and the unconscious, and so to support the thesis that the structural relation between them is owed to their common spatial (de-differentiated and syncretic) organization.

I Merleau-Ponty's Account of the Dream Against the Background of the Sleeping and Wakeful Body

From the outset, it is important to emphasize that Merleau-Ponty's elabora-tions on his courses at the Collège de France presuppose the developments

DOI: 10.4324/9781003436188-5

made in his major work, *Phenomenology of Perception* (1945), and that they are in continuity with its conceptions of an embodied subjectivity which overcomes the mind-body dualism, intellectualism and a physiological and mechanistic reductionism of the body. According to this perspective, subjectivity is not a floating soul attached to a body; furthermore, the body is neither a mere sum of members nor a machine, but instead it is regarded as symbolic of the world and an expression of existence and its movement, being the "outward manifestation of a certain manner of being-of-the world" (Merleau-Ponty, 1945/2002, p. 64). Against this backdrop, the elaborations made in his courses at the Collège de France consist partly of a deepening and further development of such conceptions, with a special focus on the problem of passivity. The phenomena of dream and the unconscious show themselves in this context as privileged for the study of passive dimensions of subjectivity, which are at stake in them.

When analysing the dream from the perspective of his phenomenology of the body, Merleau-Ponty focuses on the phenomenon of sleeping, for the dreaming subject is primarily a sleeping body. An attempt to clarify the phenomenon of dreaming leads him thus to a phenomenology of the sleeping body, which includes the phenomenon of dreaming, and from there to dreamless sleeping. The focus of these analyses on the sleeping body as a preliminary condition for dreaming consciousness allows him to overcome some limitations which were imposed on Sartre's analysis due to the fact that his conceptual apparatus was centered on consciousness, i.e., on the dream as a phenomenon of imagining consciousness, which made it difficult, for instance, to account for dreamless sleeping. In this context, Merleau-Ponty, making recourse to his typical argumentative pathways, reviews some of the main theories of sleep of the time in order to show how both a physiological and a biological reduction of sleep are not sufficient to account for the same. Nevertheless, as it is also one of his classical manoeuvres, he points out some key points of such theories, which he then makes use of and interprets from a phenomenological and existential point of view.

First, Merleau-Ponty points out that from the physiological point of view in sleep we find an inversion of Babinski's elemental reflex,[2] as well as an inhibitory[3] reaction in Pavlov's sense and a de-differentiation[4] of chronaxies.[5] Second, from the biological point of view, he argues against the thesis that sleep is a mere biological phenomenon resulting from carbonic self-narcosis or intoxication, namely by referring to Piéron's experiments, which show that hypno-toxin does not act by producing direct intoxication, but rather by way of a defensive inhibitory response from the organism, which defends itself against exhaustion and intoxication through the inhibition of sensory and motor centers of the encephalo-medullary axis. In addition, Merleau-Ponty points out that old people and children show that there is no linear relation between the intoxication produced by states of exhaustion, tiredness and sleeping (1954–1955/2017, p. 41), for states of exhaustion do not necessarily go hand in hand with sleeping. These points allow Merleau-Ponty to state that sleep is not merely a natural phenomenon caused by external factors and externally received by consciousness, but a behavior, and that there is an intention of sleeping in a phenomenological sense. Therefore, we can add that it consists of an overall attitude, for whose account supposing a primary distinction between a physiological body and a disembodied soul or mind as a point of departure is misleading.

Thus, Merleau-Ponty is especially interested in the facts pertaining to the inversion of reflex, the inhibition of sensory and motor centers, and the de-differentiation of chronaxies, which he, from a non-dualistic epistemology, links to a statement by Freud which Lhermitte provides in his book on the dream; albeit without giving the exact reference:

> In the same way as when we undress each night, we bring our body back to its primitive state, when we fall asleep, we undress our psyche, we strip it of its acquisitions and we return, not only by the nakedness of our body, but also by the nakedness of our spirit, back to the state of a newborn[6] child.
>
> (Lhermitte, 1931, p. 64)

Freud's statement is convergent with the direction which Merleau-Ponty is interested in giving to his research: dream as an overall regressive phenomenon, i.e., of global regression which is both manifested on a physiological as well as on a psychical ground. The physiological regression is thus not the cause of the phenomenon of sleep, but a manifestation of a global style of experience, i.e., of an overall regressive attitude or intention, bodily manifested in the undressing, and psychically shown in the de-layering of the more recent organizations of subjective experience. As we shall see, this overall regressive attitude is also extended to the spatial dimension of experience.

In this context, Merleau-Ponty attempts to systematically distinguish sleeping from dreaming, by defining sleeping as distancing oneself from the world, whereas dreaming retains the same bond with the world. As nightmare shows, the dream is not a mere absence of the world and a deviation towards the pure power of desire and the overabundance of a consciousness freed to signify without limits. Instead, it is precisely the dream's remaining bond to the anxieties of waking life that brings the subject back again too close to the world and suppresses the distance from the world which is required by sleeping. And so, waking follows. Therefore, sleeping embodies distancing from the world instead of absence: "it is being at a distance" (Merleau-Ponty, 1954–1955/2017, p. 41). Regarding dream and its subject, the latter has major cascade consequences, and allows further distinctions: if dreaming is neither a simple absence from the world nor a simple phenomenon of the imagining consciousness freed to its own caprice of inventive and signifying power, what does the givenness of this distant world rely upon? Who is the subject of the dream? What agency can at the same time account for this passive givenness, which is neither wakeful presence nor inventive absence, but a sort of compromise between the two in the form of distant and passive presence?

> The body, then, as a perceptual attunement, in general, as a relation to situations of drama, is the subject of the dream, and not the "imaginative consciousness" [as Sartre would have it]. Sleeping is not the same as dreaming, but the return to the undifferentiated body. Symbolism, the compromise between the active body and the undifferentiated body, is not simply the collapse of the intention-*Erfüllung* structure, the absence of the real world.
>
> (pp. 41–42)

The body as perceptual attunement and scheme of praxic possibilities is the subject of the dream,[7] as a general capability and assemblage of experience. It is not only the collapse of the intention-*Erfüllung* structure that accounts for the dream. Nor is it explained by the distinction between the synthesis of coincidence (*Deckungssynthesis*) between intention and fulfillment in perceptive consciousness and its absence thereof in imagining consciousness. According to Merleau-Ponty, the imaginary still operates in the waking life and there is no such splitting, but the interweaving of the two. However, when we analyze the dream from the perspective of the body instead of consciousness (as Sartre did), and from the perspective of the experiential horizons instead of that which emphasizes the synthesis of coincidence, we arrive at more detailed results.

Following Merleau-Ponty, the clue to analysing the difference between dream and perception relies upon the structural differences between the openness of the experiential fields and the extendedness of horizons characteristic of the waking body and the waking life versus the closure of experiential fields and the unextendedness of horizons characteristic of the sleeping body and oneiric life, as well as their distant reference to the world. Thus, it is now interesting to further analyze the characters that this oneiric givenness assumes thanks to its relying on the structures of the sleeping body.

If the structure intention-fulfillment (*Erfüllung*), the extendedness of horizons and the proximity of the world, allow for greater differentiation of givenness, the distant horizon-lacking givenness is a de-differentiated one being correlative of the physiological de-differentiation e.g., manifested at a physiological level by the de-differentiation of chronaxies. In experiential terms, this de-differentiated givenness consists of a generalized givenness, namely a givenness that, due to its distance from the world, loosens its reliance upon what comes from the world, and thus only relies upon that which the body is already prone to perceive. It is a form of pre-givenness of that world-for-me, or quasi-world, in which the objects of the world are inserted and in which "I"[8] already "am" before the worldly supported givenness[9] is articulated, consisting of the typical pre-formulae of experience which are supported by "my" capabilities of experience, i.e., by the assemblages of body and its experiential fields, which pre-delineate the general sketches of experience and typical guidelines with which the worldly givenness is articulated, a certain basic bodily schematic pre-objective grammar for the text of world. Under these circumstances, it is no coincidence that what is left of experience is not an experience of discrete objects, but a pre-objective[10] and a de- or pre-differentiated experience in its most vague and general form, and as a general capability of typical situations or of typical matrix-events or schemata of experience, whereby the experience is given in its global outlines, i.e., as general styles of experience given in a sketched or typical form.

> We have to find the intentionality of the dream, not as intentionality of acts, which puts objects, but as the exhibition of concretions that "upholster" our life, not individual or conceptual content. The dream is made of events that form symbolic matrixes. The elements are thus not traversed by a ray of categorial thought.[11]
>
> (Merleau-Ponty, 1954–1955/2017, pp. 51–52)

According to this perspective, events given in dreams are not given in their particularity, but in a general form, as styles of experience or significant matrixes which configure the subjective landscape on which what is lived is inserted. Those significant knots which operate as familiar references in relation to which the experience assumes a subjective value. They become pre-categorial parameters according to which experience is appropriated and becomes the experience of one's own:

> To dream [is] to let all that affective field play, the familiarities, the allusions, the correspondences .... Dreaming is not "I think" (*ego cogito*) but thought according to significant knots which aren't present as objects.[12] ... We can let ourselves be carried away in an experience by styles, by safe relationships, without, however, possessing the meaning. And this is because the life of consciousness, finally, is not sense-giving (*Sinngebung*) in a constituent sense but the happening of something to someone (*sich ereignen*).
>
> (Merleau-Ponty, 1954–1955/2017, pp. 126–127)

At the same time, it is remarkable how by analysing the type of givenness, which is founded on the sleeping modality of the body, we arrived at the description of the symbolism of dream. Hence, the de-differentiation of the sleeping body founds the de-differentiated character of oneiric experience, and so the symbolism of dream and dream itself appear as founded on the structures of the body, i.e., as the compromise between the active body, dominant in waking life, and the passive and de-differentiated body, dominant in sleep. Hence, dream expresses at the same time a peculiar conjunction of the structural characters of both modalities of experience. Between the worldly experience of waking life and the quasi-zero givenness of sleep, we find the quasi-world of oneirism as the structural midpoint and synthesis. As a result of the latter, the structures of the symbolism of dream are founded on those of the body in its different modalities. Let us now analyze the further implications of this inner correlation between body and dream.

As in this form of givenness, there is distance from the world; conversely, it is all too close to "me,"[13] there is no distance between things and "myself" and between "myself" and "my" subjective life, and so a certain kind of passivity takes place in which there is an indistinction or a sort of fusion between things and subjective life[14] (Merleau-Ponty, 1954–1955/2017, p. 30). Without worldly barriers which make of the worldly givenness something more than the result of subjective life, this givenness is the result of the subject's fields of experience freed to its passive operation and turns so to speak into a private object, i.e., objects turn into projections[15] of subjective drama. In addition, without barriers which extend a field of tension between intention and fulfillment, between object and horizon, and structure a difference between them, the two become indistinct, and the intention is immediately fulfilled so that "the intention of seeing is immediately vision" (p. 38). In this context, it is interesting to analyze the attaining of the oneiric and unconscious processes to a pleasure principle (paying little regard to reality[16]) and to the characteristic of wish-fulfillment (which characterizes dream according to Freud's main thesis) as a result of this horizon-structure of the sleeping body. The contraction of the experiential fields and horizons in sleep and the de-differentiation between the object and its horizon of objectivation, its horizon-extendedness or its telos, result in the telos of givenness not being temporally extended; and thus, by losing its temporal length and depth, it is immediately fulfilled. Thus, the wish is allowed to immediately reach its telos and be fulfilled without temporal extension.

"The rule is here the indistinction and the exception, the differentiation" (Merleau-Ponty, 1954–1955/2017, p. 50). Analysing Merleau-Ponty's thesis more systematically, and trying to explore its further implications, we come to realize its usefulness for analysing different features of dream. This de-differentiation can be observed on multiple levels. In addition to the de-differentiation between embodied-consciousness and object (indistinction between things and self, i.e., ob-jects turning into pro-jects of subjective life) and to the de-differentiation between object and horizon or intention and fulfillment (previously interpreted as a precondition for dream's wish-fulfillment, which is conversely one of its clearest manifestations), we also find in dreams a *de-differentiation between spatial and temporal coordinates or positions*, i.e., a *de-differentiation of the spatial and temporal configuration of experience*, as well as a *de-differentiation between the experiential fields themselves.* As we shall further explore in the next section, these dimensions of the phenomenon of sleeping as a generalized phenomenon of regression and de-differentiation provide us with the structures which are found in the characteristics of the dream and the unconscious, such as timelessness, condensation, displacement, primary process and transference of intensities or mobility of cathexes and quotas of affect (*Affektbeträge*). Moreover, tracing back the experiential structures which precondition such types of givenness will also enable us to gain insights into *the structures of the sleeping body*, i.e., into the *passive operation of the structures of the body*, whose functioning is far from being limited to sleep and dream, even though they are privileged phenomena in which such structures are revealed in a relatively pure or isolated form.

2 The Dark Spatiality of the Sleeping Body: Syncretism and Discretism as the Two Basic Structures of Subjective Experience

Following Merleau-Ponty's thesis on sleep as behavior, which thus embodies an overall attitude, and at which a global phenomenon of de-differentiation takes place, by further examining the correlation between oneiric givenness and the sleeping body we may note that the phenomenon of sleep takes place not only accompanied by undressing[17] (as Lhermitte pointed out), but by a *dark space.* In the same way that undressing embodies a regressive global de-layering of more recent acquisitions, at which – as Freud points out, as cited by Lhermitte (Lhermitte, 1931, p. 64) – the regression of the bodily attitude of undressing is correlated with the psychical regression to more archaic organizations, we can observe that in the case of darkness a similar correlation takes place, namely a *correlation between the structural features of the dark space of the sleeping body and the spatial structure of the oneiric givenness.* Such a bodily regression is correlated to psychical regression in dreams, *the darkness of the bodily space is correlated to a dark organization of the oneiric space.* As a result, we can infer in advance that the phenomenon of darkness may also be considered a regressive one, especially when it comes to analysing its spatial structure.

What does this imply? Darkness is essentially a phenomenon of the non-differentiation and de-differentiation of objects, which become relatively indistinct and in-mixed, with diffuse edges and boundaries; their distinction and discreteness becoming state of con-fusion. Additionally, together with its effects on the objects, the perceptual horizon is also altered, indeed substantially reduced, made compact and un-extended. In fact, darkness is no object, but insofar as it affects the background out of which objects show themselves, it is eminently a horizon phenomenon. It is in principle a visual phenomenon which affects the configuration of visual space, i.e., the spatial horizon of the visual field, by contracting and enclosing it to the immediate surrounding proximity of the body, the given objects being increasingly limited to the objects which are in closer contact with "me," and tending to lose access to the givenness which is distant from "my body"; thus, it is more independent from its contact with "me." The phenomenon of darkness questions the independence of the givenness of the objects and reduces the horizon of givenness to objects dependent on their closer contact with the subject.[18] Thus, the distinction and discreteness between the objects and subjective life also become relative and fall into a relatively diffuse state of non-differentiation. Finally, darkness is thus also a regressive phenomenon, insofar as the deployment, enrichment, detail, inner discrimination and differentiation of the givenness regress to my more immediate horizon of visual and tactile proximity. Simultaneously, the primacy of vision in my experience regresses to the old primacy of the tactile; it is as if I came back to the times in which touch[19] was my dominant sense, without me being able yet to focus my sight[20] on things. In the darkness, it is as if I were for a moment again that child starting out in life, making the first exploratory attempts.

It is noteworthy to observe that these structural traits of non-differentiation, closure of horizons and of bodily and worldly regression to more archaic organizations of experience, which characterize the phenomenon of darkness, coincide with those of the sleeping body and those of (oneiric and unconscious) symbolism. We ask, then, how is this correlation to be understood? Does it have something to teach us, or is it just a curious coincidence?

Let us first examine these matters by asking: is this a correlation of isolated dimensions, which just run parallel to each other? If we answer in the affirmative, then we will be assuming that there is a primary distinction or original split between the experiential fields, which only secondarily enter into a correlation. But is that really the case? Does not experience show us that the opposite obtains; particularly once we get rid of the objectivistic prejudice, which observes and takes the outer-experience and third-person perspective as being the central rule and parameter for analysing experience? When we consider experience from the first-person perspective, the splitting between the senses and dimensions of experience is no longer so obvious or easy to assume as from the external perspective. If darkness were primarily just a visual phenomenon, and its transpositions on other dimensions of experience were marginal and of a derived and secondary nature, then only in pathological cases would small children be afraid of it, i.e., the contraction and narrowing of the dark space would only in exceptional circumstances represent an anxiety-giving value for them – the *eng/angosta* quality of the dark space would only hardly and exceptionally bear an affective state of *Angst/angustia*.[21] But experience shows us the contrary; in fact, it would even be more indicative of an exceptional or a pathological case if we saw a small child who had no fear of the dark. Indeed, the affective *transposition primary* and the *overall synaesthetic* contracting angst-value of darkness is the rule, and the *primary layer of experience* is such that it is an achievement in the child's development to overcome it by splitting the primary transposition and non-differentiation of the experiential fields; establishing barriers between the experiential dimensions which differentiate them: splitting darkness off as a mere visual phenomenon, confiscating it and reducing it to the visual field. That is, in fact, what parents say to their child in order to ease the child's fear of the dark: they tell the child that things are the same when the lights go out, just as with a simple change in the visual field. They aim to enhance the child's ability to establish discrete barriers between experiential dimensions, which is an achievement of a secondary nature, since it is an achievement for the child not to be threatened by monsters in the dark, or indeed by the monstrous character of darkness anymore.

Thus, the immediate primary transpositive and overall value of darkness shows us a primary layer of non-differentiated and transpositive unity of experience, which has as its precondition a primary layer of syncretic and non-differentiated intersensorial experience, prior to the discrete differentiation of the experience in separate experiential fields. *Our experiential fields are not primarily split from each other and there are not as many subjects as experiential fields*, which would only be secondarily synthesized and unified in a unitary subject with a unitary experience. Instead, we find *an* experience which has a primary syncretic unity or cohesion by non-differentiation and generalization, a subject which is a generalized embodied consciousness, a body which is a generalized subject, and an intention and behavior which are an overall existential attitude. As a result of this, what happens within a certain experiential field is not just limited to that field, but is generalized to the overall experience, and only secondary divergence within the boundaries of a certain field.

Before proceeding, let us make a digression. In the course of this chapter, and as can be particularly well observed in the phenomenon of darkness, we have systematized *two basic forms of structuration of sense and givenness, two basic modes of articulation of experience*. One of them is associated with the active body and the waking consciousness, i.e., with the structures dominant in waking life and in perception, where the basic structure trait of experience is its *discreteness as a result of horizon openness and extendedness*, i.e., the difference between the thus segregated components of the experience. This discreteness is extended to the experiential fields: conceived as separate to the objects; to the relation between the objects and subjective life; and to the temporal and spatial positions. As one of its emerging salient results, discreteness guarantees the identity, specification and particularization of such components with themselves and their difference from others.

On the other hand, we find another basic form of structuration of senses and articulation of experience, which results from the passive operation of the structures of the body and is best clarified by the sleeping body, the oneiric consciousness and the phenomenon of darkness. It is characterized by *non-differentiation, syncretism, horizon closure and generalization, con-*

fusion in indistinction, transposition, in-mixing or interweaving of identity of its elements, and therefore analogical symbolism by reciprocal expression. This structural feature can be observed in these phenomena when it comes to the relation between the fields of experience, between various objects, the objects and myself, and the configuration of space and time and their spatial and temporal positions, as we will show more fully later. Following our argument about darkness, if this second mode of articulation of experience can be regarded as nocturnal, the discrete experience corresponds with the structures of the daylight.

The phenomenon of fear of the dark in its diachronic development in small children enables us to see that these two basic forms of experience are not isolated from each other, but are articulated in a *genetic relation*, whereby the syncretic experience is primary to the discrete one, which has a derived and secondary nature and is relatively lately acquired throughout development, working as a step towards the subtraction of phantasy from the world, the objectivization of the world and gaining access to the shared objective world of the adults. Its primacy in the waking life of the adult is such that it can in fact be regarded as the main reason for our difficulties in observing and conceptualizing the syncretic experience and for our reiterated, always insistent, and hardly overcome tendency (also observed in the history of science) to consider experience as a sum of atomic disjunct elements, fields, objects, positions, etc., which are originally discrete and may only secondarily be reunited.[22] In accordance with the above, this primary character which is incorrectly assigned to the discrete experience is not the result of the primary configuration of experience itself, but is a result of the dominance that the discrete modality of articulation of experience has gained for the adult in the course of development – a dominance which is manifested and impregnates the adult's theories of experience themselves and makes it hard to unveil the primary syncretism. Thus, the objectivistic approach and its assumptions do not tell us that much about the structure of experience itself, but rather more about what structures are dominant in the experience and thought of the theorizing (adult). Maybe if the adult were to listen to the child's theories of their experience, it would not be so hard to arrive at syncretism. If the objectivism of the adults expresses the dominance of discretism in their experience, the animism of the infantile thought may be one of the phenomena in which the primary dominance of syncretism is manifest, just as the dream is the expression of the primary syncretism which, although more subtly and less directly observable than in the child, continues to operate in the subjective life of the adult. But the development of this second modality of discretism in the adult does not take place by way of an erasure of the primary structures. As the phenomena of sleep, dream and darkness show, experience has a dynamic character which lets it alternatively be articulated in a predominantly discrete or syncretic way and dynamically come back and forth, progressively and regressively, and the development of the structures of discreteness does not mean substitution or erasure of the primary syncretic structures, but rather a mantling or over-layering of newer and later structures on the bedrock of the more primary ones. The daylight finds the dark bedrock of subjectivity, but that does not mean that darkness is definitively overcome, for the sun sets each day and darkness shows that it remains there hidden and waiting, ready to present itself once more. It means, therefore, that the later structures of subjective experience become dominant in the later course of experience, thus becoming the surface structures with which the analysis first and more immediately comes upon the proverbial tip of the iceberg. The more primary structures of subjective experience, however, are still operative in the margins and at deeper, non-surface levels; as they are not dominant in the waking life, they only become indirectly accessible, namely in some phenomena which for structural reasons set aside the tip of the iceberg or suspend the dominance[23] of the structures of discretism of waking life and turn into privileged phenomena for the manifestation of the primary syncretic structures and a circumstantial regaining of the dominance it had in the childhood.[24] Hence, the peripheral and marginal character that syncretism achieves is correlated to the peripheral and marginal character of the phenomena in which it can be particularly well accessed, such as the phenomena of dream and darkness. Development is therefore not linear, but is stratified or layered, wherein the latter acquisitions do not substitute but are founded on the primary ones, which still keep operative in more subtle, indirect and non-surface ways. Indeed, although adults do not have the same predominance of syncretism in our waking lives that children have, the peripheral and underlying cooperating syncretism of the adult, shown in the oneirism of waking life, still provide us with a means for understanding dreams, without just being another person who dreams; and allowing us to understand the child and the infantile world without being separate species in simple discontinuity.

Finally, it is worth noting that these two modes of configuration of experience are congruent with Freud's distinction between the conscious/preconscious thought of waking life and the unconscious and their relations: provided that the first one coincides with what we elaborate under the title of the structures of discretism, i.e., of discrete experience, the structures of the unconscious are convergent with those of syncretism, which is the primary layer of syncretic experience. This is also convergent with Freud's thesis on the functioning of the psychism in accordance with two psychical processes, namely a primary process, characterized by sliding cathexes and quotas of affect between representations, and a secondary process, characterized by a fixed or stable bond between affect and representation. Additionally, Freud links the primary process to the unconscious, and the secondary process to the conscious and preconscious, which are thus also genetically ordered, being the unconscious primary in relation to the conscious-preconscious system (Freud, 1900/1953, p. 567).[25] Hence, our developments are finally also

convergent with Freud's genetic perspective, which presents dream as a phenomenon in which a regression to a primary and unconscious thought takes
place.[26] In this regard, given that oneiric regression comes back to *primary
structures* of unconscious thought, and that it regresses to an overall *primary
syncretic structured experience, the unconscious can be thus phenomenologically regarded as the primary layer of experience of syncretic structure*. If
this thesis is correct, we should find the main characteristics of syncretic
experience manifesting themselves most clearly in the phenomena which rely
upon the structures of the unconscious, a task which we shall attend to
presently.

3 The Syncretic Spatiality of Dreams and the Unconscious as the Primary Structure of Subjectivity

The correlation of the characteristics of de-layering, regression, non-
differentiation and horizon closure, shared between the phenomena of darkness, the sleeping body and the structure of oneiric givenness (i.e., the
dream's symbolism and wish fulfillment) is no coincidence. They show
instead that there is no secondarily established correlation between primary
differentiated dimensions, but a *primary overall structure of experience, a
unitary style of attunement, common and transversal to all fields of experience*,
which results from the regained regressive dominance of the primary layer of
experience and its syncretic, transpositive, generalized and non-differentiated
structure.[27] This structure gains primacy in sleep thanks to the de-layering of
the secondary and later structures of the waking life, which tend to discreteness, and differentiate the experience in fields separate from each other. From
this perspective, the darkness surrounding the sleeping body, the experiential
and physiological features of the sleeping body itself and the structure of the
oneiric givenness embody different aspects of a *unitary and overall experience
of horizon closure and regression to the primary pre-differentiated, generalized
and syncretic configuration of experience*.

Putting together what we have developed above, given that the structures
of syncretic experience do not appear ex nihilo but are founded on the passive operation of the structures of the body (and thus are particularly well
revealed by the sleeping body as one of its privileged manifestations), and
that the unconscious can be regarded as the primary layer of syncretic
experience, therefore the structures of the unconscious are also not ex nihilo,
neither are they the result of any caprice, nor are they contingent on any
inner or external influence: they are the structures which result from the
passive operation of the body. Hence, *the unconscious is founded on the passive operation of the structures of the body*. By means of this, it is much easier
not to understand the unconscious as a hidden double subject which is of
equal structure to the wakeful consciousness, or indeed as a sum of hidden
contents, but as the *living underlying primary syncretic layer of passive co-*

functioning of the structures of the body, which is not suppressed or overcome by the structures of waking life, but just kept living in the background in the marginal shades of subjectivity, remaining the dark reverse of the structures of the discrete experience predominant in the daylight and its horizon extendedness.

The affective value of seasons, the fact that it is easier not to be sleepy anymore when the sun rises, and that spring and summer dispose oneself to a state of activity, as well as it being easier to fall asleep when the room is dark and the grey and cloudy winter disposes oneself to a state of inactivity, can be traced back to this underlying co-functioning of the structures of syncretic experience. To fight the shadows of winter, it is important to try splitting the colors and the darkness off from their primary transpositive and generalized "sad," inertia-inducing "value." Those phenomena, in which the horizon configuration suggests an atmosphere-sensitivity and a certain summoning of the other dimensions of experience by the visual-spatial configuration of the surroundings, can be deemed the result of the integrated, pre-differentiated and multimodal-synaesthetic structure of experience in its primary syncretic layer, which allows the configuration of one dimension (as it is here the spatial one) immediately and irreflexively be transposed and generalized to the overall experience, gaining thus, for instance, an affective, bodily and behavioural value. Hence, the subjective effects of day and night, of light and dark, and summer and winter are by no means to be deemed mere blind and mechanical epiphenomenal results of phenomena that are "in truth" physiochemical. In other words, the transpositive generalizations of horizon extendedness and horizon closure. Instead, it would be interesting to regard physiological effects as the correlates of an overall experience of awakening to activity and falling asleep or turning to passivity, but not as the linear *causes* of them. The relation between landscape and subjectivity, more than a relation of cause and consequence, is to be better understood as a relation of inspiration and transpositive syncretic expression.

Following this, just as undressing embodies an overall attitude of regression that already bodily pre-announces the psychical regression and delayering of sleeping and dreaming; darkness, through its regress to a primary spatial configuration of horizon-closure, embodies an overall attitude of regression, which pre-announces on a bodily level the regressive horizon-structure of sleeping and dreaming, i.e., *darkness embodies an overall attitude of distance from the world, horizon-closure and non-differentiation*. It is in this regard that the space of the sleeping body and dreams shares a common dark or nocturnal character, namely a regressive syncretic and non-differentiated configuration.

Let us analyze the structure of this syncretic space of darkness, of the sleeping body and dreams. As noted earlier, the syncretism of the dark space and the regressive spatial and horizon-structure configuration of darkness are redoubled and generalized to an overall regressive experience of spatial syncretism and non-differentiation. Thus, what we find is that this regression to a syncretic configuration and horizon closure does not only concern the space of the sleeping body, but also time and the spatial-temporal structure of the oneiric givenness; and the different fields of experience and their reciprocal relations. In this generalized regression to a syncretic configuration of primary non-differentiation, we note that the systems of coordinates of experience – space, time and the experiential fields themselves – lose their particularity and specification (they lose their extendedness and discreteness) and assume a generalized and de-differentiated form. Thus, the experiential fields lose the spatial and temporal differentiation between their positions. According to this, if the discrete organization of time and space in waking life is that of systems of differentiated positions which found and guarantee the order and identity of objects and the spatial and temporal positions themselves in their discreteness and difference from each other, in dreams we have a de-differentiation and overlapping of spatial positions, of temporal positions and, thus, of the given objectivities which are ordered according to them. Hence, the de-differentiation of the spatial and temporal organization of the experiential fields established the oneiric de-differentiation of the identities of objects. Therefore, we have here the basic prerequisites and structures required for the foundation of the dream's symbolism.

If discreteness of space and time is regressively dismantled or suspended in the dark configuration of space of the sleeping body and the dark space of dreams, we arrive at a syncretic form of space and time, i.e., to a syncretic order of objectivities in which not only spatial and temporal positions, but also objectivities, are con-fusioned in non-differentiation, which allows the oneiric objectivities to work as emblems that analogically symbolize others, expressing them by mutual implication in this syncretic non-differentiated spatial-temporal configuration of experience.

If in the discrete configuration of space and time, i.e., the discrete configuration of the spatial-temporal structuration of experiential fields, we find extended and unfolded systems of differentiated positions, in the syncretic one it comes to a non-differentiated, non-divided and unextended organization, one that is more compact, curved or folded upon itself. The experiential fields have here a certain *primary* synthetic configuration; that is, a synthesis which is not the result of a first moment of difference between parts and a secondary moment of reunion or unification, but of an *original moment of primary unity in indistinction*. In this organization of space and time each position (and the objects within it) is not simply equal to itself nor neatly differentiated from the others. The objectivities given in them also overlap and lose their discreteness, equally turning non-differentiated, too.[28] In this syncretic organization of time and space, positions thus become con-fusioned and their distinctions become diffuse. Furthermore, given that space and time are two systems of order of presence, in such syncretic organization of time and space, objectivities may be present in two or more temporal or spatial positions at the same time, i.e., they are at least potentially simultaneous, ubiquitous, omnipresent or transversally present to the totality of overlapping positions of these syncretic and de-differentiated systems of presence. What does this mean? That the objectivities do not just occupy a discrete place in space and time, and therefore are in-mixed and con-fusioned with others, means that they turn into *equivalents, symbols or analoga* of one another, their general global outlines gaining prevalence over their particularity and specification.

> The renunciation of a direct, adequate expression, *Erfüllung*, is a consequence of sleeping, i.e. that one pushes away the discriminating element and goes towards indifferentiation, aphasia, apraxia (cf. Freud when he shows that one does not really speak in the dream, that there is no expression of logical relations in the dream). But this does not mean unlimited freedom of an arbitrary *Sinngebung* (sense-giving). It means the use of certain phenomena as analogues of certain others, according to pre-established connections, on the contrary, in their general outlines.
>
> (Merleau-Ponty 1954–1955/2017, p. 43)

If identities given in the objective, differentiated organization of space and time in waking life are discrete and cut off from others, i.e., one neatly ends when another begins, this basic structure is subverted by the dream: in the oneiric organization of time and space the generalized and syncretic organization of space and time allows for the identities of oneiric objectivities to overlap their positions or to blur their edges and lose their discrete boundaries, they are in-mixed or con-fusioned, one may extend itself, continue, be substituted, resignified or symbolized by another. As a result, *this de-differentiated, syncretic organization* of time, space, the experiential fields and the identities of objects founds *four fundamental characteristics of dream and the unconscious* pointed out by Freud: condensation, displacement, i.e., transference of intensities or mobility of cathexes according to primary psychical process, timelessness and absence of contradiction (Freud, 1915/1957, pp. 186–187).

First, condensation, i.e., the fact that the dream-content is *compressed* in comparison with the dream-thoughts (Freud, 1900/1953, p. 279). By means of the same, a single common element can be ambiguous and symbolize two or many others at the same time (p. 339). Hence, a single dream-thought may be represented by many dream contents (p. 653), i.e., multiple aspects of the subjective dynamics can be simultaneously distributed in many elements which express its different moments (e.g., two oneiric characters can represent different aspects of the father or two tendencies in conflict). This structural trait of oneiric givenness presupposes a spatial configuration, which is far from being discrete and is one where the identity of the elements and the spatial positions with themselves is not fixed; instead, it is a *compressed syncretic space* in which positions are non-differentiated, interwoven and confused. As a result, the dream-content is relatively compressed (p. 595) and short when compared with the dream-thoughts; only a few manifest elements rich in multiple senses are enough to express the latent thoughts, which are juxtaposed without the dream consisting of a faithful point-for-point translation of dream-thoughts (p. 281) but of common mediating elements which work as nodal points wherein many overdetermining associative chains converge. In this regard, the *overdetermination* of the elements of the manifest dream-content – that is, the fact that the elements of the dream-content are determined by the dream-thoughts many times over – also presupposes a space in which relations of determination are neither linear nor point-for-point, but instead are ambiguous, polyvalent and irradiating, simultaneously occupying a single manifest element in many non-differentiated positions; something which allows such an element to possess this inner nodal richness or sense-saturation.

Second, displacement consists more of a diverse centering of the dream than that of the dream-thoughts (p. 305), i.e., a de-centering of the focus of the material, whereby the affective intensity and focus are differently centered in the dream content in comparison with the dream-thoughts and that which plays an essential role in the latter may only be marginal in the former, whereas the peripheral components of the dream-thoughts become central in the manifest content of the dream. Thus, a psychical transvaluation takes place and the psychical emphasis and intensity of cathexes are displaced (p. 177), being differently placed and distributed between representations. Representations charged with a strong affect quantity transfer transvaluations to weak ones, which thus become strengthened and force their entry into consciousness (p. 177). In strong relation to it stands then the fact of *transference*,[29] by means of which an unconscious idea incapable of entering the preconscious "can only exercise any effect there by establishing a connection with an idea which already belongs to the preconscious, by transferring its intensity on to it [the preconscious idea] and by getting itself 'covered' by it" (p. 562). As a result, the preconscious idea acquires an undeserved degree of intensity (p. 563). In this regard, psychical value is not only transferred by content or a contiguity to neighboring elements closely associated in semantical terms, but also through many associative types depreciated in the waking life and relegated to jokes, such as verbal associations through similarity or homophony (p. 596). Both displacement and the transference of intensities presuppose that the field of psychical emphasis, intensity and affect has a spatial structure whose positions are not disjoined from each other, but rather are locked in an immediate reciprocal play of transposition, mutual expression and subduction, namely that the focus is distributed in a multi-centered, syncretic and non-differentiated way along the field of representations,[30] without having fixed spatial positions or locations.

This guideline also applies to the absence of contradiction of the unconscious. Indeed, thoughts and drives which are mutually contradictory persist in the unconscious side by side and arrive at compromises in which they are coordinated and exempt from contradiction, without being influenced by one another or doing away with each other (Freud, 1900/1953, p. 596, 1915/1957, p. 186). And so if the principle of contradiction is preconditioned by a spatial structure where there is only one position for either of the two mutual contradictory elements, and thus only one is imposed while the other is disregarded, then in a syncretic system of positions there is no such discrete differentiation of a single position for both of them to fight over. This means that there is no need for them to confront one another or for one of them to be disregarded, as there is space for both of them.

As regards temporality, the temporal order of the elements of experience in the waking life presupposes again a discrete structure where temporal positions are distinctly and unmistakably distinguishable from each other – a structure which Freud attributes to the work of the system *Cs-Pcs* (Freud, 1915/1957, p. 187). Conversely, the so-called timelessness of the unconscious, i.e., the fact that its processes are neither temporally ordered nor altered by the passage of time, without having reference to the characteristic of time[31] at all (p. 187.), presupposes a syncretic structure where temporal positions are non-differentiated, juxtaposed and interchangeably pre-sorted, and thus are in mutual transposition and reciprocal expression and substitution. This allows the elements to be simultaneously present in many points of this syncretic time. Thus, so-called timelessness, instead of being regarded as a mere absence of time (from an objective or realistic point of view), can hence be deemed a temporal ubiquity by a non-differentiation or pre-objective omni-temporality of the primary syncretic layer of experience as the experiential structure of the unconscious.

Conclusion and Final Remarks

Throughout this chapter, we have sought to analyze the spatial structure of the sleeping body and the unconscious. By doing so, we have found the limitations which are imposed on an analysis of dream and sleep that does not include a reference to either the body or the spatial features of the sleeping body and oneiric givenness. After coming to the importance of space for the analysis of these phenomena, we described the dark space of the sleeping body and the dark configuration of the oneiric space, thus finding common traits such as overall regression to a non-differentiated and syncretic mode of configuration of experience.

Following from this, we brought these analyses together with those of Freud. By observing that the oneiric regression comes back to the *primary structures* of unconscious thought, and that it regresses to an overall *primary syncretic structured experience*, we have posed the thesis that *the unconscious can be phenomenologically regarded as the primary layer of syncretic experience.* In these last analyses, we explored the syncretic spatial structure of experience which is presupposed by the main features of the dream and the unconscious, finding thus that the main structural traits of the unconscious and its manifestations (condensation, symbolism, displacement, transference of affect, absence of contradiction and timelessness) are founded on the syncretic and non-differentiated spatial-temporal structure of experience which is in turn founded on the passive operation of the structures of the body. Hence, the spatiality of the unconscious and its phenomena could be traced back to the spatiality of the body in its passive modality, thus revealing the pre-eminence of space and its key role as a guiding thread, allowing us to better understand the unconscious and its relations to the body from a phenomenological standpoint.

Notes

1 This work is funded by a DAAD (German Academic Exchange Service) scholarship programme for a bi-nationally supervised doctoral degree.
2 Van Gijn presents Babinski's (plantar) reflex and analyzes its significance in the following terms: "The plantar response is a reflex that involves not only the toes, but all muscles that shorten the leg. In the newborn, the synergy is brisk, involving all flexor muscles of the leg; these include the toe 'extensors', which also shorten the leg on contraction and therefore are flexors in a physiological sense. As the nervous system matures and the pyramidal tract gains more control over spinal motoneurons the flexion synergy becomes less brisk, and the toe 'extensors' are no longer part of it. The toes then often go down instead of up, as a result of a segmental reflex involving the small foot muscles and the overlying skin, comparable to the abdominal reflexes. With lesions of the pyramidal system, structural or functional, this segmental, downward response of the toes disappears, the flexion synergy may become disinhibited and the extensor hallucis longus muscle is again recruited into the flexion reflex of the leg: the sign of Babinski" (Van Gijn, 1995, pp. 645–648).
3 The concept of inhibition was used by Pavlov to account for the decrement in response to experimental extinction of conditioned responses. Cf. Wenger (1937).
4 These physiological facts are not to be regarded as physiological causes of sleep, but are mentioned here as physiological manifestations of sleep as an overall phenomenon of regression and de-differentiation.
5 According to the *Medical Dictionary* by Farlex, a chronaxie is defined as a measurement of excitability of nervous or muscular tissue; the shortest duration of an effective electrical stimulus having a strength equal to twice the minimum strength required for excitation. It is the minimum time at which an electric current must flow at a voltage twice the rheobase to cause a muscle to contract (Farlex, n.d.).
6 Cf. fn. 22.
7 Cf. fn. 10.
8 In some sentences, as is typical of Merleau-Ponty's style in his descriptions, we make use of the first-person singular, which we enclose between commas.
9 Cf. fn. 15.
10 In this direction, Merleau-Ponty states: "already in Freud himself: a return to the pre-objective organisation of the world, whose the subject is the body in the

general sense of assemblage for living, possession of *imagines*, body as a setting-up of the world" (Merleau-Ponty, 1954–1955/2017, p. 44).

11 Cf. fn. 15.

12 Cf. fn. 15.

13 Cf. fn. 8.

14 Better than fusion, we consider in this case *con-fusion*; for here we do not have a simple fusion or unification, but a relative loss of differences and blurring of the borders and edges between things and between things and subjective life; rather than a clear unification or simple fusion, a diffuse and non-discrete form of experience can be found here. "Con-fusion" is then used to mean "fusion" and "confusion" at the same time, which is related to the fact that the oneiric givenness is an undifferentiated one, in which the principle of identity is not operative, so that the identities of oneiric objects are mixed and confused.

15 I.e., *Ob-iectus* turns into *pro-iectus*, this is, givenness is not what is set against me as a result of what is thrown (*iactus*) in front of me (*ob-*) on the other – worldly – side, but is instead an outcome of my throwing (*iactus*) myself forth (*pro-*), towards the other side, consisting thus this givenness of a pro-jection of the pre-familiar and typical world for me in which I already am and in whose experiential (especially intersubjective and affective) fields and assemblages the worldly givenness is inserted, articulated and apprehended or set-up by familiarity. In addition, such apprehension by familiarity provides experience with a certain cohesion. *We do not dream with ob-jects but with pro-jects of subjective emblems and familiar analoga expressive of dimensions of subjective life.* That is, in fact, one of the structural reasons why the dream serves as such a good pathway to subjectivity.

16 "The Ucs. processes pay just as little regard to reality. They are subject to the pleasure principle; their fate depends only on how strong they are and on whether they fulfil the demands of the pleasure unpleasure regulation" (Freud, 1915, p. 187).

17 There is no normative claim in this statement. We are not using the term in an empirical sense. We are using it only as a metaphor that expresses the change of bodily attitude that occurs when the subject prepares for sleep (which is different from that which occurs during the day when preparing to face the vicissitudes of waking life), but which goes beyond a concrete undressing per se and is not necessarily expressed in that concrete empirical form, which depends on a variety of empirical (social, individual, etc.), factors.

18 In this sense, together with the regression of the givenness in the dark and in dreams to a private and proximal condition in contact with me, the other scene (*Schauplatz*, literally meaning show- or seeing-place) of dreams and the unconscious (Freud, 1900/1953, p. 48) can hence be regarded rather as a *Rührplatz* (our neological wordplay: touch-place), for what is seen in this place is eminently dependent on its contact with me.

19 Maitre et al. (2017) claim that touch is in neonates a cornerstone of interpersonal interaction and sensory-cognitive development, and that neonatal intensive care unit treatments used to improve neurodevelopmental outcomes rely heavily on touch. According to their research, supportive experiences (e.g., breastfeeding, skin-to-skin care) are associated with stronger brain responses, whereas painful experiences (e.g., skin punctures, tube insertions) are associated with reduced brain responses to the same touch stimuli.

20 Brémond-Gignac et al. (2011) state that visual development is incomplete at birth, particularly in premature infants. Thus, maturation of the visual system depends on many factors, including prenatal and postnatal nutrition and postnatal visual stimulation.

21 Here we are referring to the etymological community between the narrow (German: *eng*; Spanish: *angosto*) and the experience of being subjectively

narrowed and oppressed (German: *Angst*; Spanish: *angustia*, which is also suggested by homophony. Such a correlation between a spatial configuration and its redoubling, generalization and transposition into an overall attitude rich in affective and subjective value does not only take place in the phenomenon of darkness, but can be also be used for gaining insights into phenomena such as claustrophobia, wherein, as it is the case of darkness, there is a spatial configuration which works as a precursor and suggests a certain affective value, without however triggering it automatically in the sense of a causal relation nor independently of subjective conditions of proclivity to such a state of anxiety.

22 In the field of empirical science there is increasing evidence on the primary integrated character of sensory systems of perception. Baron-Cohen (1996) reviews findings regarding Maurer's neonatal synesthesia (NS) hypothesis (Maurer, 1993), which is still under discussion (Harvey, 2013), and evidence on cross-modal transfer (CMT). He states that "the NS hypothesis argues that early in infancy, probably up to about 4 months of age, all babies experience sensory input in an undifferentiated way. Sounds trigger both auditory and visual and tactile experiences. In contrast, the CMT hypothesis argues that objects can be recognized in more than one modality, as a result of infants being able to represent objects in an abstract form (Meltzoff & Borton, 1979). This implies, for example, that babies can recognize one object versus another from their appearance, even if they have previously only touched them without seeing them" (Baron-Cohen, 1996). He also shows that there is considerable evidence for the CMT hypothesis, and that it is widely accepted, refuting Piaget's conception that the senses are independent in the neonate and only after birth become gradually integrated (Piaget, 1952). In a convergent direction, Harvey (2013, p. 205) reviews evidence on cross-modal perception (CMP) and defines it as a perception involving the interaction of two or more sensory modalities. As an example, Harvey mentions Köhler's (1929) study on the "bouba/kiki" effect, which provides evidence of CMP through the association of the word "bouba" with curved shapes and the word "kiki" with angular shapes. A further example in favor of CMP is provided by the McGurk effect, which shows that hearing and vision interact in speech perception. This effect describes the phenomenon in which audition is altered by vision, such that seeing someone's mouth uttering the sound "Faa" while hearing the sound "Baa" elicits the hearing of the sound "Faa," even though it is not the sound that is actually displayed. He reviews evidence from fMRI and TMS disruption studies and considers that it is likely that with further research, CMP will be shown to have an increasing role in everyday sensory perception (p. 205). In the current chapter, however, we try to go a step further by interpreting CMT as the perceptual manifestation of a more generalized phenomenon of primary syncretic configuration of experience, which is not limited to manifesting itself at the level of sensory perception.

23 From the perspective of Husserlian's phenomenology, Brudzińska (2019) systematically develops the thesis of the bi-valence of two experiential orders of subjectivity between two structures of experiential consciousness, namely the apperceptive-impressional consciousness of the perceptive order and the imaginary-phantasmatic consciousness as the experiential structure of the unconscious, which co-function with alternative dominance alongside the different lived phenomena in a relation of tension between the pre-givenness of the impressional and the unbindingness of the phantasmatic, being the apperceptive impressional dominant in perception and the imaginary-phantasmatic dominant in dreams. According to our interpretation, there is a strong continuity between our

developments and those of Brudzińska. From the perspective of Merleau-Ponty's philosophy of the body, however, we additionally attempt to trace back the foundation of those experiential orders of subjectivity in the structures of the body, namely in the passive and active operation of the structures of the body. In addition, we consider that reconstructing this relation of foundation, at the same time, provides grounds, by means of the distinction between syncretism of the passive sleeping body and discretism of the active body of waking life, for a better understanding of how those two experiential structures are configurated and interwoven between each other.

24   "Dreams, which fulfil their wishes along the short path of regression, have merely preserved for us in that respect a sample of the psychical apparatus's primary method of working …. What once dominated waking life, while the mind was still young and incompetent, seems now to have been banished into the night – just as the primitive weapons, the bows and arrows, that have been abandoned by adult men, turn up once more in the nursery. *Dreaming is a piece of infantile mental life that has been superseded*" (Freud 1900/1953, p. 567; emphasis in the original). As we also deal with it throughout this chapter, such superseding is not absolute, and together with its pathological remnants (such as psychoses), there are many non-pathological remnants of the non-dominant underlying cooperation of the unconscious and the primary structures of non-differentiated syncretic experience in waking life, as it becomes clear by the analysis of the immediate and primary generalized transpositive character of the phenomenon of darkness.

25   Regarding the genetic relation between the primary process characteristic of the unconscious and the secondary process characteristic of the conscious-pre-conscious, Freud states: "The psychical process which we have found at work in dream-displacement, though it cannot be described as a pathological disturbance, nevertheless differs from the normal and is to be regarded as a process of a more *primary* nature (Freud, 1900/1953, p. 177); "When I described one of the psychical processes occurring in the mental apparatus as the 'primary' one, what I had in mind was not merely considerations of relative importance and efficiency; I intended also to choose a name which would give an indication of its chronological priority" (p. 603).

26   Cf. fns. 24 and 25.

27   On a perceptual level, this primary syncretism is expressed in the primary synaesthesic character of perception. In this direction, based on a series of experiments on perception presented by Werner (1930) and Stein (1928), Merleau-Ponty states that "synaesthetic perception is the rule, and we are unaware of it only because scientific knowledge shifts the centre of gravity of experience, so that we have unlearned how to see, hear, and generally speaking, feel, in order to deduce, from our bodily organization and the world as the physicist conceives it, what we are to see, hear and feel." (Merleau-Ponty, 1945/2002, p. 266). On the other hand, the thesis of a primary synaesthetic-syncretic configuration of the experiential fields and a "general function of unspoken transposition" (p. 195) in body schema does not mean they are not separable at all. In this regard, Dillon discusses Merleau-Ponty's theory of synaesthesia and claims that "the identity-within-difference of reversibility (developed in *The Visible and the Invisible* [Merleau-Ponty, 1964]) explains the synesthetic unification of the senses without obscuring their separability" (Dillon, 1997, p. 160).

28   This primary non-differentiation, which emerges from the primary layer of syncretic experience can be found in the different experiential fields. In the case of the social field of experience, for instance, Merleau-Ponty argues that the first phase of the child's relation to others is characterized by a "syncretic sociability"

(Merleau-Ponty, 1951/1964). In this direction, García approaches from a phenomenological point of view the problem of the different genetic levels of the experience of the other, and finds that "at this [primary] stage of 'pre-communication' there is not yet an individual facing another individual but only 'an anonymous collectivity' (Merleau-Ponty, 1951/1964, p. 312) or an undifferentiated multiple existence, as shown by the contagion of crying in a baby nursery, or mimetic behaviour such as that of the smile in the infant of a few months: there is here a "background of mimicry that is an irreducible function" (p. 322)" (García, 2015, p. 18). In accordance with this, Buffone studies the construction of the children's body schema from a merleaupontyan perspective and points out that "the recognition of the other and of oneself as an individuality dissociated from the environment" does not occur as a starting point. It is instead "a process that takes place during the first months of the baby's life" (Buffone, 2019, p. 297). "The baby structures its own body on the basis of a function that starts from itself, where the other as an isolated individuality different from its own will appear as a correlate of the baby's motor, spatial and perceptual organisation" (p. 317).

29 It is important to remark that in *The Interpretation of Dreams* (Freud, 1900/1953) Freud calls *transference* a structural trait of dream attaining the mobility of affect quantities of dream's representations and is thus different from the phenomenon within the relationship analysand-psychoanalyst with which Freud deals under the same name in his further works.

30 Displacement and transference of intensities show two constitutive moments: a first moment, characterized by mobility of cathexes and quotas of affect, and a second moment, characterized by a re-centering of the material which de-centers it with comparison to its centering in the waking life. We consider that these moments may not be regarded as having the same *status*. Whereas the first moment shows sliding, mobile and transposing quotas of affect, which is not in itself a factor convergent with censorship, the second one, by mistakenly or falsely centering the material, replacing the mobility with false connections, does play a functional role for the censorship. The first one may be well attributed and understood from the perspective of the primary syncretic spatial configuration of the affective field, which does not presuppose any fixed connection, but reciprocal expression via non-differentiation and regression of the givenness to its general outlines. It is not focal; it does not presuppose a space or relief of distinct positions between foreground and background, where something affects, and something does not. In this sense, rather than focal, it is transversal, global and floating. The second moment, however, is more convergent with the characteristics of discretism, for it does establish bonds between affect and representation, distinguishes a space of different reliefs, where some things affect in the foreground and some just remain on a minor plain, and substitutes the mobility and floating character of the first moment with bonds and focuses of misleading nature. Given that this second moment is more convergent with the characters of discretism and is functional to censorship, it may be attributed to a censoring side-operation of the conscious system, which is to be considered phenomenologically as a latent background cooperation of discretism in dreams.

31 Additionally, in his early *Draft M* (1897), Freud already observes that "chronological corrections seem precisely to depend on the activity of the system of consciousness. ... This and neglect of the characteristic of time are no doubt essential for the distinction between activity in the preconscious and unconscious" (Freud, 1897/1966, pp. 252–253).

References

Brudzińska, J. (2019). *Bi-Valenz der Erfahrung Assoziation, Imaginäres und Trieb in der Genesis der Subjektivität bei Husserl und Freud.* Springer.

Baron-Cohen, S. (1996). Is There a Normal Phase of Synaesthesia in Development? *Psyche*, 2(27), 2–27.

Brémond-Gignac, D.*et al.* (2011). Visual Development in Infants: Physiological and Pathological Mechanisms. *Current Opinion in Ophthalmology*, 22, 1–8.

Buffone, J. (2019). La construcción del esquema corporal infantil desde una perspectiva merleaupontyana. La propiocepción como fundamento del accouplement fenomenológico. *Revista de Filosofía*, 31(2), 297–320.

Dillon, M. (1997). *Merleau-Ponty's Ontology.* Northwestern University Press.

Farlex (n.d.). Chronaxie. In *Farlex Partner Medical Dictionary.* Retrieved 12 December 2022 from https://medical-dictionary.thefreedictionary.com/chronaxy.

Freud, S. (1953). The Interpretation of Dreams. In *The Standard Edition of the Complete Psychological Works of Sigmund Freud*, Vols. 4–5 (J. Strachey, Ed. & Trans.). The Hogarth Press. (Original work published 1900.)

Freud, S. (1957). The Unconscious. In *The Standard Edition of the Complete Psychological Works of Sigmund Freud*, Vol. 14 (J. Strachey, Ed. & Trans.). The Hogarth Press. (Original work published 1915.)

Freud, S. (1966). Draft M. In *The Standard Edition of the Complete Psychological Works of Sigmund Freud*, Vol. 1 (J. Strachey, Ed. & Trans.). The Hogarth Press. (Original work published 1897.)

García, E.A. (2015). Anonimato, conflicto y reconocimiento como figuras de la alteridad en la filosofía de M. Merleau-Ponty. *Tópicos. Revista de Filosofía de Santa Fe*, 29, 1–24.

Harvey, J.P. (2013). Sensory Perception: Lessons from Synesthesia: Using Synesthesia to Inform the Understanding of Sensory Perception. *Yale J Biol Med*, 86(2), 203–216.

Köhler, W. (1929). *Gestalt Psychology*, (1st ed). Liveright.

Lhermitte, J. (1931). *Le sommeil.* A. Colin.

Maitre, N.*et al.* (2017). The Dual Nature of Early-Life Experience on Somatosensory Processing in the Human Infant Brain. *Current Biology*, 27(7), 1048–1054.

Maurer, D. (1993). Neonatal Synesthesia: Implications for the Processing of Speech and Faces. In B. de Boysson-Bardies*et al.* (Eds.), *Developmental Neurocognition: Speech and Face Processing in the First Year of Life.* Kluwer Academic Publishers.

McGurk, H., & MacDonald, J. (1976). Hearing Lips and Seeing Voices. *Nature*, 264, 746–748.

Meltzoff, A., & Borton, R. (1979). Intermodal Matching by Human Neonates. *Nature*, 282, 403–404.

Merleau-Ponty, M. (1964). *Le visible et l'invisible* (C. Lefort, Ed.). Gallimard.

Merleau-Ponty, M. (1964). The Child's Relations with Others. In *The Primacy of Perception* (W. Cobb, Trans., J.M. Edie, Ed.). Northwestern University Press. (Original work published 1951.)

Merleau-Ponty, M. (2002). *Phenomenology of Perception* (C. Smith, Trans.). Routledge. (Original work published 1945.)

Merleau-Ponty, M. (2017). *La institución. La pasividad. Notas de cursos en el Collège de France (1954–1955). II – El problema de la pasividad: el sueño, el inconsciente, la memoria* (M. Larison, Trans.). Siglo XXI – Anthropos. (Original work published 1954–1955.)

Piaget, J. (1952). *The Origins of Intelligence in Children*. International University Press.

Sartre, J.-P. (1940). *L'imaginaire: Psychologie phénoménologique de l'imagination*. Gallimard.

Stein, J. (1928). Über die Veranderung der Sinnesleistungen und die Entstehung von Trugwahrnehmungen. In O. Bumke (Ed), *Handbuch der Geisteskrankheiten: Pathologie der Wahrnehmung* (Vol. 1, Part 1). Springer.

Van Gijn J. (1995). The Babinski Reflex. *Postgraduate Medical Journal*, 71, 645–648.

Werner, H. (1930). Untersuchungen uber Empfindung und Empfinden, I y II: Die Rolle der Sprachempfindung im Prozess der Gestaltung ausdrausdrucksmässig erlebter Worter. *Zeitschrift für Psychologie*, 121.

Wenger, M.A. (1937). A Criticism of Pavlov's Concept of Internal Inhibition. *Psychological Review*, 44(4), 297–312.

Chapter 5

Locked Bodies, Locked Selves

Freud, Nancy, Jelinek

Adam Lipszyc

I Das Unbehagen im Raum

Let me start with a text that is short but deservedly famous. On 22 August 1938 Sigmund Freud wrote: "Räumlichkeit mag die Projektion der Ausdehnung des psychischen Apparats sein. Keine anderes Ableitung wahrscheinlich. Anstatt Kants *a priori* Bedingungen unseres psychischen Apparats. Psyche ist ausgedehnt, weiss nichts davon" (Freud, 1941, p. 152). Or, in English translation: "Space may be the projection of the extension of the psychical apparatus. No other derivation is probable. Instead of Kant's *a priori* determinants of our psychical apparatus. Psyche is extended; knows nothing about it" (Freud, 1941/1964, p. 300).

This famous note is, of course, extremely exciting. Moreover, it seems to provide an unavoidable starting point for anyone wishing to reflect on the relationship between space and subjectivity within the Freudian tradition. It should be noted, however, that while this is a wonderful passage, it is also marked by a serious intellectual flaw. Here the weakness lies in the very term "projection." The danger is that if we become too attached to the term and to the very logic of the mechanism of projection, we may come to believe that (1) there is some well-defined inner sphere of the psyche, elegantly demarcated from an equally well-defined outer sphere; that (2) this inner sphere of the psyche is in some sense extended; and that (3) this extension of the inner sphere is projected onto the outer sphere, which gains its spatiality through this very projection.

Amicus Freud, but let's be honest: this is a very odd idea. First, it is difficult to say how one can speak of a well-defined external sphere preceding a projection that is supposed to establish its spatiality. Second, if we accept a model based on the idea of projection, it is difficult to say how we are to understand the very idea of the extension of the psyche. The idea sounds very interesting, but what does it actually mean? Are we to take it quite literally and consider, say, that our id is literally situated next to the ego within a certain extended internal forum? Seriously? This idea simply won't fly, unless we believe in the ancient Greek vision of the soul as an extended yet

DOI: 10.4324/9781003436188-6

subtle piece of matter; or, in a more contemporary mode, in the strict iso-morphism which would supposedly connect the Freudian model of the mind (or one of the post-Freudian models) with the map of the human brain. Or are we to think of the idea of the extension of the psyche in some metapho-rical way? Fair enough, but then, first of all, what is the cognitive value, the content of such a metaphor? What are we actually stating about the psyche when we metaphorically refer to it as extended? And, more importantly, if the idea is to be taken metaphorically, it seems that we first assume the existence of external spatial extension, and then we metaphorically relate it to the internal forum of the psyche itself, which in turn is supposed to be the source of the constitution of external extensibility, a constitution carried out by means of the mechanism of projection. It is quite clear that what we are dealing with here is not so much a dialectical reasoning, but rather a mere mess, or, at best, a vicious circle.

In order to show the intellectual potential of Freud's brief note and the powerful paradox it contains, we need to read it beyond the logic of projec-tion, insofar as this logic presupposes well-settled boundaries between the internal and the external, and beyond the binary distinction between literal and metaphorical understanding of the very idea of the extension of the psyche. How do we get there? An extremely helpful, even if still imperfect, guideline is offered by Jean-Luc Nancy. In his book *Corpus*, he writes most insightfully:

> Freud's most fascinating and perhaps (I say this without exaggerating) most decisive statement is in this posthumous note: *Psyche ist ausge-dehnt: weiss nichts davon.* "The psyche is extended: knows nothing about it." The "psyche," in other words, is body, and this is precisely what escapes it, and its escape (we may suppose), or its process of escape, constitutes it as "psyche," in a dimension of not (being able/wanting)-to-know-itself. ... It's not an accident that Freud was obsessed with the topical: the "unconscious" is the being-extended of Psyche.
>
> (Nancy, 1992/2008, p. 21)

I find Nancy's comment both brilliant and extremely revealing. Significantly, Nancy points out that the second part of Freud's aphorism – "knows noth-ing about it" – is not merely an epistemological addition to the ontological statement made in the first part – "the psyche is stretched" – but that this unknowing, *das Nichtwissen*, is linked to the very idea of the unconscious, *das Unbewusste*, and should therefore be read as an essential part of the ontological statement. Moreover, although Freud says nothing about the human body in his note (incidentally, I think that this is precisely why he gets himself into trouble), Nancy insists on linking the idea of extension appear-ing in this small text to the Cartesian vision of our bodies as slices of *res extensa*. It is this interpretive move that allows Nancy to step beyond the logic of projection and the overly stable dualism of interior and exterior associated with it – body properly conceived escapes this duality – and beyond the dichotomy between literal and metaphorical understandings of the psyche's extension in Freud's note. Paradoxically, the psyche can be defined simply as entity which is unable to grasp its identity with the extended body, an entity from which the knowledge about this identity constantly slips away. This very slipping means that the psyche never equals consciousness, and yet it is also this very slipping that makes it a psyche at all. It is not just that not the whole psyche is conscious (which is the fundamental inequality proposed by Freud). It is simply that a fully conscious – i.e., thus disembodied – psyche would not be a psyche at all!

Is, then, the psyche extended in a literal or metaphorical sense? It is neither, for it is not a separate, well-separated domain, which could then be regarded as extended in either of these two senses. Rather, it is extended-but-knows-nothing-about-it. It will be easier for us to come to terms with this literally vertiginous idea if we consider its opposite. If the psyche knew of its own extension, it would be capable of grasping itself, so that it could become a master in its own house, and thus sublate and neutralize its own extension – in which case it would become a punctual *res cogitans*. Incidentally, this peculiar character of the psyche also makes it possible to understand (at least to some extent) the bewildering, relentless proliferation of the psychoanalytic set of mechanisms, involving processes such as repression, foreclosure, denial, introjection, incorporation, etc., as well as the unrestrained metamorphoses and chronically precarious status of the psychoanalytic topographies of the mind itself. Wedged between the literal and the metaphorical, endlessly drawn and redrawn, these frenzied images – starting with that strange bulb with the cap worn awry that Freud presents in his treatise on the ego and the id – are expressions of both the necessity and the ultimate impossibility of mapping our psyche (Freud, 1923/1961, p. 24). A fully mapped unconscious would not be unconscious at all, but abandoning these mapping efforts could pave the way to the belief that the soul simply lacks extension, and thus, again, that there is no such thing as the unconscious.

Nancy himself is primarily fascinated by the ontological status of the human body. He continues the tradition initiated by Maurice Merleau-Ponty, who, following late Husserl, insisted on the embodied status of the psyche, on the primacy of motor intentionality over acts of "pure" consciousness, and on the fact that the body – neither internal nor external to the psyche – "is our anchorage in a world" (Merleau-Ponty, 1945/2002, p. 167). At the same time, however, Nancy seeks to avoid a certain fundamental flaw in this tradition, which – presumably with Merleau-Ponty's very theory in mind – was pointed out by Jacques Lacan in his highly malicious but extremely insightful remark: "After long centuries gave us a spiritualized body in the soul, contemporary phenomenology has made body a corporealized soul", a cosy Leib, a living body, which, without much friction and resistance, is permeated by soul and smoothly situated in the world (Lacan, 2004/2014, p. 219).

For Nancy, the body is a radically open, non-sovereign, exposed, vulnerable entity whose "soul" is not hidden in its "interior," but occurs on the surface, in its very openness and exposure, and is therefore never able to achieve fully reflective self-presence. The body is not an object among other objects, but neither is it primarily a seat of intentionality – motor or otherwise – situated in its own world like a hand in a glove. It is a surface entity, radically separate and yet defined by the otherness to which it remains exposed. The body is never identical with itself; it can never reclaim or master itself. It can only endlessly touch things around it and thus feel itself through that touch and touch itself through that touch, and yes, it can touch itself, but – as Karen Barad has brilliantly pointed out – touching oneself does not lead to the discovery of one's own identity within elegantly delineated boundaries: "self-touching is an encounter with the infinite alterity of the self" (Barad, 2018, p. 156). And, as Nancy himself elegantly put it: "The soul is the body's difference from itself, the relation to the outside that the body is for itself" (Nancy, 1992/2008, p. 126). This is why the soul, the body's extended-but-not-knowing, never-fully-established self, is constitutively unstable in terms of its boundaries, which it endlessly establishes and renegotiates – and is radically unstable when it comes to establishing what is within and what is without. This state of affairs causes an inescapable vertigo, a sense of the impossibility of self-determination, and thus gives rise to various more or less violent gestures of snapping, cutting off, fencing off and demarcating boundaries: existential, bodily and political.

And yet Nancy's position, however attractive, does need a fundamental revision. What is missing here? Nancy's body-soul is always a body among a plurality of bodies, a singularity-in-plurality. Nancy celebrates the vulnerability of body-souls which co-constitute a living space of mutual interaction; the bodies are always in motion and their configurations keep on being tentative. Fair enough. However, Nancy omits the conditions that make this very plurality and this very movement possible. These conditions, in turn, can be grasped by the psychoanalytic tradition, which Nancy reads with care and originality, while at the same time neutralizing it. However, by revealing these conditions of possibility, psychoanalysis also fundamentally modifies the very topology of the space occupied by the moving and interacting of plural bodies-subjects which can never master themselves or come to terms with their own extension.

From Sigmund Freud himself, through Melanie Klein and Jacques Lacan, to Jean Laplanche, André Green and Didier Anzieu – with all the fundamental differences between these masters of psychoanalytic thought – the key idea of the decentered subject remains the distinguishing feature of this tradition. This decenteredness is accomplished through the constitutive separation of the subject. We emerge through an act of separation from the maternal pre-object ("pre-" because it is only this separation that allows us to speak of objects at all). We constitute ourselves by leaving our center outside of ourselves. We are separate but non-sovereign, non-autonomous and non-central, sidelined, set aside. This is why we are necessarily plural bodies in Nancy's sense. We can be open, exposed, vulnerable bodies, never identical with ourselves, never sovereign, with souls extended-but-not-knowing-it, only as catastrophically separated, marked by constitutive loss, sidelined, with our center outside ourselves. This is why, moreover, we are bodies always unsettled by the dual entanglement of sexual desire (emphasized by Freud and Lacan) and the need for holding, caring and nurturing (emphasized by Winnicott and Anzieu). The magnificent, pathetic or haunted palaces of our sexuality, as well as the homes that keep us relatively safe, rest on the foundations of the groundlessness, the non-foundation of the abyss of catastrophic separation that makes them possible, necessary – but also, after all, ultimately impossible.

It seems almost obvious to say that, as a result of this very separation, space is also constituted as the medium of human life. This common source or transcendental condition for the constitution of both body and space gives their relation two essential features that are missing from Nancy's analysis and that only become apparent from the point of view of the psychoanalytic tradition. First, the relationship between body and space is marked by what might be called primordial alienation or primordial entrapment. The point is that the body-subject and the living space are constituted in the same movement, but their relationship is far from a cosy fit. Rather, it is that the exposed body remains inevitably trapped, overwhelmed and alienated in a space it is not itself by definition, a space it confronts, a space it cannot control. A body that has taken control of space is no longer a body. The space that has been mastered by the body is no longer space. The primordial or originary alienation of the body in space cannot therefore be eliminated without simultaneously eliminating both space and body.

Second, the relationship between body and space is defined by an originary derailment, by what Steve Pile has aptly called misplacement (Pile, 1996, pp. 121–144). This thought is as simple as it is most simply true. If space has been created as a result of the original separation, as a result of the loss of the center, then there simply is not and cannot be a place in space where our body feels in its proper place. Existing in space, we are always-already misplaced, always-already displaced, pushed aside, not by accident but constitutively so. This is where one should look for the source of all the displacements, movements, interactions that we sometimes call life, which would be neither necessary nor possible without this source derailment. But is not "home" where "we start from," as the title chosen by the editors for the posthumously published book by Donald Winnicott proclaims (Winnicott, 1986)? Indeed it is. But even before that starting point, there was something even more primordial, which is precisely what makes home necessary-though-not-originary: the primordial separation and originary derailment.

We need home, this fragile prosthesis of centrality, precisely because we are bodies misplaced and decentered in a lived space that itself arises with the loss of an absolute center, that comes to existence only when the center is always-already elsewhere. And if Freud suggested that we inevitably feel discomfort and unease in the social world, *das Unbehagen in der Kultur*, we can say with at least as much validity that the tradition Freud initiated makes us aware of our fundamental discomfort in space, *das Unbehagen im Raum*. It is due to this very unease that we so feverishly draw boundaries and find it so difficult to unlock our souls. Every time, however, that we draw the boundaries of home, of our *Heim*, we know (we feel it under our skin, we feel it in our bones) that – as constitutively exposed bodies entangled in space – sooner or later we will have to confront the tentative nature of these borders, with the impossibility of clearly demarcating the boundaries between inside and outside, which manifests itself as the essential uncanny-ness and non-domesticity – *die Unheimlichkeit* – of space itself.

2 Erika Goes Home

There are, of course, millions of ways in which we try to cope with our spatial condition, the condition of misplaced bodies-and-souls – both alienated in, and inextricably entangled with space – that are unable to grasp their own extension and must therefore constantly negotiate and renegotiate the relationship between the internal and the external. Let us now try to look at the paradoxes of a rather extreme strategy that can shed additional light on the whole dynamic and further complicate it. The person who follows this strategy is a literary character, but in many ways a very real one. The person I have in mind is Erika Kohut, the heroine of *The Piano Teacher*, Elfriede Jelinek's famous novel (Jelinek, 1983/2004).

The book is well known, but for the sake of clarity let us recall the outline of the plot. Jelinek's novel tells the story of a woman in her thirties who lives with her mother and works as a piano teacher at a conservatory in Vienna, Austria. Her sex life, after several early attempts at a relationship with one man or another, is now limited to regular visits to peep shows, where Erika watches naked women, and to the park on Prater, where she observes couples copulating in the bushes. The woman falls in love with one of her students, Walter Klemmer, who also seems interested in her. However, Klemmer is shocked by the sadomasochistic demands that Erika articulates in a letter addressed to him. After several twists and turns, the whole thing ends in a calamitous event: with Klemmer brutally raping Erika.

The book is designed with an incredible sensitivity to the relationship between embodied subjectivity and various spaces. In particular, Jelinek is simply an unrivalled expert and student of the torment to which the exposure of our bodies to the element of space condemns us, and of the profound need for closure, for the slamming, locking of the soul. A key role in the novel is played by a whole sequence of opening and closing spaces, from the peep show booth where Erika attempts to look inside a naked woman, to the booth in the school toilet from which Walter pulls Erika out prior to their first sexual encounter. However, the most important element of the sequence remains Erika's apartment. Significantly, the apartment is rented, and Erika's mother is slowly raising money for a flat that would already be fully owned by both women. Thus, she gets angry with her daughter every time the latter buys herself a new dress, for here Erika is wasting the very money that could have fed her savings. Either-or: either the final flat, where Erika will settle down with her mother for good, or a new dress, a second skin and an extra coat that would at least partially separate her from her mother.

Erika does leave home, of course, but in the end she always succumbs to an irresistible compulsion, and, driven out of town, returns again and again to the flat:

> Yet every day, the daughter punctually shows up where she belongs: at home. ... Mother has called her up, making her a laughingstock, and Erika is forced to admit: I have to go home now. Home. If ever you run into Erika on the street, she is usually on her way home.
>
> (Jelinek, 1983/2004, pp. 9–10)

And when it looks like some kind of relationship is beginning to emerge with the pupil, the teacher panics: "Erika wants to go home. Erika wants to go home. Erika wants to go home" (p. 123).

One may come to a rather too hasty conclusion that the apartment is the womb to which Erika, terrified of her separateness and dizziness in the open, of her anxiety in space and the terrible necessity of constantly redefining the inner and the outer, continually returns. One may even perceive it as the womb from which she never emerges for good. But it is not that simple. First, it is to be noted that the apartment is, crucially, endowed with internal architecture. In particular, it is possible to distinguish two essential zones within the apartment: the marital bed, in which Erika sleeps with her mother after the successful elimination of her father – that third, differentiating element – and Erika's separate room, which, however, has no bed and cannot be locked. Second, as we have already seen, the apartment remains temporary: the two women do not own it. Therefore, it is rather a prosthesis of the womb, something that is to substitute for it; it is an almost-womb, but this "almost" makes a fundamental difference, precisely because within this space of dwelling, difference is still possible and present. Moreover, Erika's aggressive attacks on her mother – the women argue and beat each other, but nevertheless they always end up sleeping in the same bed – and the dresses Erika buys for herself indicate that the daughter is, indeed, trying to break out of this daemonic cocoon. At the same time, however, when her non-relationship with Klemmer is already heading for disaster, the piano teacher launches an attack of a different kind on her mother, apparently trying to replace the prosthetic or metaphorical womb with a literal one:

> Erika is stronger. She winds around Mother like ivy around an old house, but this Mother is definitely not a cozy old house. Erika sucks and gnaws on this big body as if she wanted to crawl back in and hide inside it.
>
> (Jelinek, 1983/2004, p. 235)

New dresses and envelopes, which would at least relatively separate Erika from her mother, can be seen as a precondition for her leaving the apartment and opening up to someone else. However, this is certainly not a sufficient condition: for such an opening, Erika's body, a most peculiar entity situated at the very center of the carefully constructed architectonics of this novel, would have to be ready. The teacher sees it as something slammed shut: "Erika has closed everything about her that could be opened" (Jelinek, 1983/2004, p. 49). Or even more bluntly:

> Erika is a compact tool in human form. Nature seems to have left no apertures in her. Erika feels solid wood in the place where the carpenter made a hole in any genuine female. Erika's wood is spongy, decaying, lonesome wood in the timber forest, and the rot is spreading.
>
> (p. 55)

Therefore, at best, Erika's body can be filled with music, which, however, being icy cold, cannot become the rhythm of intercorporeal contact, the rhythm of the interaction of bodies: "Her body is one big refrigerator, where Art is well stored" (p. 25). No wonder, then, that when the student brings Erika out of the toilet cubicle and tries to have intercourse with her, Erika – while mechanically tinkering with his penis – keeps him at a distance, and no erotic resonance is generated between the two: "Erika holds him far away. A yawning abyss, made up of seven inches of dick, plus Erika's arm, and ten years difference in age, gapes open between their bodies" (p. 181). And so, finally, it is not surprising that Erika herself feels nothing during actual sexual intercourse.

This deaf and mute lockdown of the body does not, of course, mean that the novel's protagonist is free of the anxiety we all feel in space. Rather, it means that she remains fenced off from various ways of dealing with this anxiety. Therefore, Erika tries to put an end to this condition; and she does so by voyeuristically studying sexual acts and by incising her own body. Characteristically, the two instruments she employs in these activities – binoculars and a razor blade – belonged to her father. When watching an act of copulation, desire awakens in Erika, albeit in a peculiarly displaced, infantile form: the teacher feels an irresistible urge to urinate (she also feels it when she achieves a murderous triumph and manages to injure a schoolgirl, the object of her envy).

In comparison with these urethral, quasi-orgasmic openings, the compulsively undertaken acts of self-mutilation seem even more desperate: they are always unsuccessful, desperate attempts to unlock one's own body. The occasion for the first incision that Erika makes as a child becomes a confrontation with the penis of her narcissistic cousin. Even more significant is the moment when, with the help of a razor blade and a mirror, Erika makes a misguided attempt at defloration, apparently cutting her labia:

> SHE, however, cuts the wrong place, separating what the Good Lord and Mother Nature have brought together in unusual unity. Man must not sunder, and revenge is quick. She feels nothing. For an instant, the two flesh halves, sliced apart, stare at each other, taken aback at this sudden gap, which wasn't there before. They've shared joy and sorrow for many years, and now they're being separated! In the mirror, the two halves also look at themselves, laterally inverted, so that neither knows which half it is.
>
> (Jelinek, 1983/2004, p. 91)

Instead of opening the body, then, Erika performs a peculiar doubling, and what is not one, what mistakes itself for its own reflection, cannot enter into a relationship with another body. A much later act of self-mutilation, undertaken already in the course of the affair with Klemmer, turns out to be characteristically contradictory as a simultaneous act of opening and closing: this time Erika drives sharp pins into her body and inflicts pain on herself by clamping laundry clamps onto her skin.

One might think that the disastrous affair with Klemmer itself represents an attempt at self-opening on Erika's part, and a particularly radical one at that. However, it would be too simple to put it this way, and in the final analysis, simply wrong. It is worth noting that the pupil's name is meaningful – and doubly so. The word *Klemmer* means binoculars, and in this sense the name refers to Erika's voyeuristic inclinations, her attempts to see through her father's binoculars into the meaning of sexuality, and through this, perhaps (but perhaps only: perhaps), into the world of relations with other bodies. The verb *klemmen*, however, in its various modifications, refers back to a field of meaning associated with squeezing and clamping. This ambiguity corresponds quite well with the bizarre topology of the geometrical figure drawn between the novel's three main characters – the teacher, her mother and her student – a figure that can hardly be called a triangle. Klemmer is merely an element in the game Erika is playing with her mother, a prop of perverse procedures that will allow her to act in two contradictory ways at the same time, namely to block her own desire for a relationship with her mother while not pushing her out of the apartment into a relationship with someone else. Her ultimate dream is to transform the flat into a realm where the anxiety and discomfort we feel in the space would be cancelled. Erika would like to rid the *Unheimlichkeit* of space from her apartment once and for all.

That this is her ultimate goal is evidenced by the contents of the sadomasochistic letter that Erika hands over to Klemmer. There is a good deal of gagging and throttling in this letter, but no mention of beating or violent penetration in any form. Essential to Erika's fantasies are strings and ropes with which she would be restrained, and the whole letter reaches its climax in a precisely designed image which eliminates her lover from the scene altogether! Here is the key passage, which speaks for itself:

> Don't worry about my mother. Just ask her for the substitute keys – and there are lots of them! Lock me in with my mother, from the outside! I expect you'll have to leave for some urgent reason, and it's my most fervent desire that you leave me tied up, bound up, roped up, together with my mother. Except that I'll be behind the door of this room. She won't be able to get to me. And leave me like that until the next day. Don't worry about my mother, leave her to me. Take along all the keys to the rooms and the apartment. Don't leave a single key here!
>
> (Jelinek, 1983/2004, p. 225)

Confronted with Erika's deepest desires and fantasies, which aim at a cancellation of the drama of spatial existence, the confused Klemmer discovers in his own mediocre soul the infinite pleasures of aggression, which in his case also seems to be a reaction to spatial and bodily uncertainty and awkwardness (when will this woman finally let me in?!): "The benefits of hatred are finally donated to Klemmer. He is enchanted" (Jelinek, 1983/2004, p. 268). Refusing to fulfill his teacher's elaborate fantasies, he invades her body in an act of aggravated rape. The next day, a battered and humiliated Erika, with a knife in her handbag, goes to the university where Klemmer is studying. Standing in front of the building – dressed in a dress that is far too short, exposed to the mocking stares of the young people and the agony of being flesh in the open – the teacher dreams of someone either taking pity on her or cutting her suffering short:

> Windows flash in the light. They do not open to this woman. They do not open to just anyone. There is no good person, although he is called for. Many would like to help, but do not. The woman twists her neck very far to the side and bares her teeth like a sick horse. No one puts a hand on her, no one takes anything from her. She feebly peers back over her shoulder. The knife should dig into her heart and twist around!
>
> (p. 282)

As no executioner turns up, Erika has to pierce herself; but out of fear or clumsiness, she only cuts her arm. The wound turns out to be harmless and, as the narrator beautifully and painfully puts it, "the world, unwounded, does not stand still" (p. 282).

It is not a secret that this final passage is saturated with allusions to the ending of Franz Kafka's *Trial*: it is there, after all, that just before the execution that the sashes of a distant window open, it is there that the executioners remove K.'s clothes and lay their hands on him, it is there that the condemned man is already close to stabbing himself with his own hands, but in the end it is one of the executioners who carries out the execution and turns the knife twice in the wound (Kafka, 1925, p. 271). Maurice Blanchot has pointed out that the true horror of the endings of many of Kafka's prose pieces lies precisely in the fact that, after the death of the protagonist, the world does not cease to exist, that there is a rebirth of obscene life; death itself proves to be non-final (Blanchot, 1981, pp. 73–74). This is the case in the ending of *Metamorphosis*, where the figure of monstrous, uninterrupted life turns out to be the sister of Gregor Samsa, in *The Hunger Artist* (1922), where this function is performed by the extraordinarily vital panther, and finally in *The Judgement* (1912), where the famous last sentence announces the infinite movement on the bridge. Blanchot also cites the last sentence of *The Trial* as an illustration of his brilliant thesis: "It was as if the shame of it should outlive him" (Kafka, 1925, p. 271).

Is this also how things stand in *The Piano Teacher*? Perhaps. It could even be argued that Jelinek outdoes Kafka in terms of the horror of inconclusiveness, because she denies her protagonist and her readers the purifying pathos associated with the figure of the unknown man looking out the distant window, with the figures of the executioners; finally, in contrast to the actual execution of Joseph K., Erika Kohut is denied everything, even death. The world, unwounded, has not stood still, nothing has changed, and so the wounded Erika sets off again, so that the last sentences of the novel can, in a hellish cycle, connect with the first sentence, in which the heroine rushes into the flat like a whirlwind. The ending reads:

> Erika walks and walks. Her back warms up in the sun. Blood oozes out of her. People look up from the shoulder to the face. Some turn around. Not all. Erika knows the direction she has to take. She heads home, gradually quickening her step.
>
> (Jelinek, 1983/2004, p. 282)

And so, indeed, it seems that nothing has really changed. And yet this strange, clumsy, misplaced cut on Erika's body *is* something new, after all. Performed in a public space, on the street, rather than in the daemonic space of the apartment, it is different from the previous acts of self-mutilation, which, being helpless and misguided, ultimately only perpetuated the closure.

This incision, too, is ineffective, but precisely in its ineffectiveness it proves to be a sign of the unbearable injustice Klemmer has inflicted on Erika. It is an expression of complaint; a clumsy, impotent accusation (and all the more powerful for being so), as well as an act of mourning for the opening that did not occur. It is Erika's lament for a different, inexistent version of herself, one that would be capable of a human encounter. Admittedly, Erika does persist in her lockdown, for this is the only way she can deal with the constitutive anxiety that marks her (and our) spatial existence. But this strange slash can be read as a dislocated, twisted sign, indicating that Erika Kohut at least intuits the existence of an inaccessible path towards the unlocking of the soul, a path towards the open space where we are indeed tormented by terrible vertigo; but where we also try to cope with it in those unstable but sometimes slightly less catastrophic ways that sometimes, sometimes deserve the appellation of love.

References

Barad, K. (2018). On Touching: The Inhuman That Therefore I Am. In S. Witzgall & K. Stakemeier (Eds.), *Power of Material/Politics of Materiality*. Diaphanes.

Blanchot, M. (1981). *De Kafka à Kafka*. Gallimard.

Freud, S. (1941). Ergebnisse, Ideen, Probleme. In *Gesammelte Werke*, Vol. 14. Imago Publishing.

Freud, S. (1961). The Ego and the Id. In *The Standard Edition of the Complete Psychological Works of Sigmund Freud*, Vol. 19 (J. Strachey, Ed. & Trans.). The Hogarth Press. (Original work published 1923.)

Freud, S. (1964). Findings, Ideas, Problems. In *The Standard Edition of the Complete Psychological Works of Sigmund Freud*, Vol. 23 (J. Strachey, Ed. & Trans.). The Hogarth Press. (Original work published 1941.)

Jelinek, E. (2004). *The Piano Teacher* (J. Neuroschel, Trans.). Grove Press. (Original work published 1983.)

Kafka, F. (1925). *The Trial* (D. Wyllie, Trans.). Retrieved from http://www.kkoworld.com/kitablar/Frans_Kafka_Mehkeme-ing.pdf.

Lacan, J. (2014). *Anxiety: The Seminar of Jacques Lacan, Book X* (A.R. Price, Trans.). Polity Press. (Original work published 2004.)

Merleau-Ponty, M. (2002). *Phenomenology of Perception* (C. Smith, Trans.). Routledge. (Original work published 1945.)

Nancy, J.-L. (2008). *Corpus* (R.A. Rand, Trans.). Fordham University Press. (Original work published 1992.)

Pile, S. (1996). *The Body and the City: Psychoanalysis, Space and Subjectivity*. Routledge.

Winnicott, D.W. (1986). *Home Is Where We Start From*. W.W. Norton.

Chapter 6

Love in the Outer Space

On the Spatiality of Being Together

Agata Bielińska

Among various Freudian metaphors, the spatial ones are probably the most famous. From the archaeological metaphor of the unconscious to the displacements and condensations of the dream-work, psychic life is structured spatially in Freud's thought. Furthermore, he also described the object relation – or, to put it simply, love – in spatial terms. In *On Narcissism* the transfer of cathexes from the ego to objects is compared to the relation between a protoplasmic amoeba and "the pseudopodia which it puts out" (Freud, 1914/1957, p. 75). The displacement of libidinal energy is never total: the ego retains a minimal level of cathexis even when it almost completely surrenders to the beloved object. Therefore, a legitimate question arises: why does the ego create its "pseudopodia" in the first place, directing its energy outside? Freud's answer is simple: the ego cathects external objects when it is literally overflowing with libidinal energy, when it must pour itself out because it cannot handle the size of its own narcissism (p. 85). The spatial structure of ego narcissism would be a spherical one – an enclosed "vesicle," sheltered from outside stimuli by a protective envelope with changing boundaries or pseudopods (Freud, 1920/1955, p. 26). According to this model, all libidinal investments move from the inside to the outside, although the inside remains privileged as a source of libidinal energy to which all cathexes eventually return. If the Freudian model is adequate, then in Jacques Lacan's words love "never makes anyone leave himself behind" (Lacan, 1975/1998, p. 47). We merely lean out for a moment from our narcissistic spherical vesicles to release some libidinal tension, always eager to return to the safety of our inner spaces.

The notion of narcissistic enclosure is not to be completely done away with. The development of subjectivity is impossible without the establishment of spatial boundaries between I and not-I. Yet in order to grasp the subtleties of love as a relation – and not only as a transfer of libidinal energy – a different spatial model is necessary: one that would complicate the distinction between the inside and the outside, allowing us to understand how it is possible to actually meet and be together despite inhabiting different psychic spaces. In this chapter, I will try to develop a speculative,

DOI: 10.4324/9781003436188-7

psychoanalytically inspired conception of the spatiality of love. I will refer to and slightly modify the notion of transitional or potential space and the idea of the capacity to be alone introduced by Donald Winnicott. I will address both the advantages and the limitations of applying Winnicott's theory to the problem of erotic love, before combining his perspective with that of other psychoanalytical authors (such as André Green, Christopher Bollas and Jessica Benjamin, among others) to analyze what hinders and what enables lovers' capacity to be together. Emphasis will be given to the role and features of the subject's aloneness, as well as to the nature of the other's spatial presence, that is both disruptive and transformative for the subject. Ultimately, these two aspects will be reconciled in the notion of love as sharing space – a paradoxical communion in which what the lovers share is the rupture in their respective spatial realities produced by the other's presence, and the enjoyment that accompanies it.

I The Place Where We Love

In *The Place Where We Live*, Winnicott reflects on how and where we spend most of our lives, when we are neither engaged in solitary contemplation nor acting in the external world:

> It is not only: what are we doing? The question also needs to be posed: where are we (if anywhere at all)? We have used the concepts of inner and outer, and we want a third concept. Where are we when we are doing what in fact we do a great deal of our time, namely, enjoying ourselves? Does the concept of sublimation really cover the whole pattern?
>
> (Winnicott, 1971/2005, p. 142)

This particular space of enjoyment, neither inside nor outside, would also be the space in which love unfolds, allowing us to step out of our narcissistic vesicle without aiming for the idealized fusion of me and not-me (which is also a narcissistic goal, since it eradicates any otherness in the drive towards oneness). Winnicott suggests that the intermediate area, a transitional space of spontaneous play which provides relief from the constant struggle of reconciling the inner and outer world, is also responsible for the emergence of a certain "electricity" between individuals, "that is a feature, for instance, when two people are in love" (p. 132). He does not develop this idea further, yet one can infer that "electricity," the impression of a highly unique and intimate interplay between two distinct subjectivities, is the erotic equivalent of the primary illusion of omnipotence necessary for the establishment of potential space – an illusion created by the mother who initially adapts to all the infant's needs in order to strengthen his sense of agency and prepare him for later separation (p. 15). Love would then consist not of a real fusion or a "perfect match," but rather of an illusionary fusion that would not blind or mislead the subject. On the contrary, it could be enjoyed precisely because of its illusionary character, allowing it to sustain an intense emotional relation despite the separateness of two individuals. Winnicott's famous description of the transitional object – the first occupant of the transitional space – as that to which the question "did you conceive of this or was it presented to you from without?" simply does not apply (p. 17) also captures the "funny miracle" of reciprocated love (Zupančič, 2003, p. 174). In love, it is impossible to tell "who started it," was love wished into existence or did it fall upon us from the outside. For this reason, even the physical space in which the amorous encounter happens acquires an eerie quality: it does not fully belong to external reality and suspends the distinction between inner and outer world. Although love usually unfolds in quite ordinary spaces, they take on an unreal and dreamlike quality because love as a transitional phenomenon consists precisely in living out a "sample of dream potential" (Winnicott, 1971/2005, p. 69). As the love-relationship progresses (if it is a "good enough" relationship), both parties have to accept the necessity of a certain amount of disillusionment that distinguishes the actual experience of being with the other from fantasy, but the potential space between lovers preserves the vital dreamlike element.

However promising, Winnicott's conception of transitional space is not fully sufficient to capture love's spatial characteristics. First, this space stems from a naturally asymmetric relation between the mother and the dependent infant – a relation that belongs to the vertical axis, not the horizontal one, using Juliet Mitchell's distinction (Mitchell, 2003). The emergence of potential space depends on the mother's ability to adapt to the infant's needs, which, of course, is a sign of love, yet this motherly kind of love cannot be transposed onto horizontal relationships. In the horizontal world of siblings, lovers, friends and enemies, the lack of complementarity is the key feature. The horizontal other always "*exceeds* all expectation" (p. 215; emphasis in the original) and this excess, according to Mitchell, generates an inevitable trauma for the subject, in contrast to the Winnicottian "good enough mother" who gently prepares the infant for separation, shielding him from the acute breakdown of the nascent self. The nostalgia for the reliability of the space between mother and infant appears in love-relationships as a narcissistic wish for the return to the lost paradise of harmonious union, since the horizontal space does not provide this kind of coherence and safety. Granted, in Winnicott's theory the good enough mother gradually diminishes her adaptation to the infant's needs, allowing the child to obtain satisfaction from the transitional object instead. The potential space later becomes an area where the individual can play with other children or, finally, engage in cultural experiences with other adults. Nevertheless, all these transitional objects and phenomena serve as a "symbol of the union of the baby and the mother (or part of the mother)" (Winnicott, 1971/2005, p. 130). In the grown-up world, the pool of culture itself takes the mother's place, becoming the sphere from which one separates through originality and with which one unites through tradition (p. 134). Even among siblings, friends and lovers – neighbors on the lateral axis – the potential space is still modelled on the primary vertical relation, obscuring the inherent trauma of horizontal relationships in which the other turns out to be more than the subject expected and, moreover, threatens to take his place (Mitchell, 2003, pp. 46–47).

The transitional space is devoid of trauma not only because it follows the development of the relationship between mother and infant but also because it excludes the presence of desire and turbulent sexual drives. These two reasons are interconnected: the mother-infant dyad is often considered to be pre-sexual, even if Freud explicitly states the opposite in the *Three Essays on Sexuality* (Freud, 1905/1953, p. 223). When Winnicott describes play, a paradigmatic activity undertaken in the transitional space, he emphasizes that its exciting factor is not at all related to sexual drives, but rather to the magical interaction between inner reality and external objects (Winnicott, 1971/2005, p. 64). The drives, in fact, "are the main threat to play" (p. 70). They distort the transitional space, which is supposed to be a calm, benign haven for the self, free from "excessive instinctual arousal." On the other hand, the space of erotic "horizontal" love – although transitional insofar as it stretches between the internal and external reality – is always twisted and bent by libidinal currents. Winnicott seems to be aware of this, and perhaps that is why he does not elaborate on the subject of the connection between love's "electricity" and the transitional space, instead focusing on other types of attachments. In *The Capacity to be Alone* he distinguishes id-relationships, which are shaped by drives and as such prove to be "a recurring complication" in the life of the self, from ego-relatedness, in which transitional space can flourish:

> Ego-relatedness refers to the relationship between two people, one of whom at any rate is alone; perhaps both are alone, yet the presence of each is important to the other. I consider that if one compares the meaning of the word "like" with that of the word "love," one can see that liking is a matter of ego-relatedness, whereas loving is more a matter of id-relationships, either crude or in sublimated form.
>
> (Winnicott, 1965/1990, p. 31)

If ego-relatedness – the primary example of which is the aloneness of the infant in the unintrusive presence of his mother – sets the stage for id-experiences, creating a holding environment for the self to process libidinal tensions, then the gentle feeling of friendship should set the stage for love's violent ruptures. Only in such conditions can the arriving libidinal impulses be felt not as alienating and destabilizing, like the Lacanian jouissance generated by something enjoying itself at our expense, but as truly belonging to the self. In the transitional space, "the sensation or impulse will feel real and be truly a personal experience," provided that there is someone who will reflect this experience back to the subject, "someone present, although present without making demands" (Winnicott, 1965/1990, p. 34). The problem is that the object of erotic love, the horizontal other, is *always* making demands. Every action of the object is, to use Jean Laplanche's term, an enigmatic message for the subject, completely incomprehensible, yet demanding a response (Laplanche, 1989, pp. 125–130). The love-object does not constitute a transparent mirror, but rather a stubbornly opaque obstacle – that is why love is truly spatial, in a very tangible, non-metaphorical way. In his account of transitional space, Winnicott has surprisingly little to say about actual space and the way it resists the subject's attempts to control it. Spatial resistance can nevertheless prove to be a very useful analogy for the object-relation: the object is in our way, like the physical space that surrounds us (that is why the term "object" is so fitting, despite its impersonal connotation), yet unlike physical space it also pertains to our most inner psychic reality, threatening us from within. André Green, a psychoanalyst inspired by Winnicott who nevertheless developed his own highly original theory, uses the term "trauma-object" to emphasize the destabilizing effect that the object of desire, this "mischief maker," has on the narcissistic ego (Green, 2001, pp. 99–101). The trauma can be described in spatial terms: the object is either too much or too little, too close or too far away, too present or too absent. Moreover, it is in no way permanent, "its moods, states and desires are changing and therefore it forces the ego to make considerable efforts to adjust" (p. 100). The transitional status of the love-object (being both internal and external to the drives) does not minimize its influence – on the contrary, it only enhances its traumatic potential.

Winnicott's ideas about transitional space and the capacity to be alone have many advantages. Together, they create a particularly subtle account of primary narcissism as a relational state, a "two-body relationship" (Winnicott, 1965/1990, p. 30) in which the presence of the other is necessary for the establishment of the ego's sense of its own existence. Winnicott shows the limits of the spatial model of narcissism as an enclosed vesicle, proving that the ego as a closed whole can only come into being by opening itself to a maximum of dependence on the (m)other. Yet his conception must be slightly modified in order to explain not only narcissism and vertical relationships, but also the horizontal love affair with the trauma-object. To capture the complexity of "the place where we love," one has to bring out the disruptive aspects of both the subject's aloneness and the other's presence. I will begin with the problem of aloneness, moving on to analyze the impact of the presence of the object, along with the possibility of its absence, and I will then proceed to outline a spatial account of love as being together through sharing space.

2 Being Alone ...

Winnicott describes transitional space as "the separation that is not a separation but a form of union" (Winnicott, 1971/2005, p. 132). This statement is somewhat true, because separation happens on the ground of dependence, yet it obscures the importance and the reality of separation that truly *is* a separation, that is, a radical loneliness. However, elsewhere he suggests that the "aloneness" in "the capacity to be alone" should be treated absolutely seriously: "I am putting forward and stressing the importance of the idea of the permanent isolation of the individual and claiming that at the core of the individual there is no communication with the not-me world either way" (Winnicott, 1965/1990, pp. 189–190). This fundamental loneliness does not constitute an opposite of dependence. On the contrary, we can experience our isolation so intensely precisely because we are so dependent on one another. Dependence does not make our inner core any more communicable. Indeed, it shields our secret inner life, protecting our solitude, and making our loneliness even more painful.[1]

I suggest that if narcissism as a two-body relationship consists of the capacity to be alone in the other's presence, then love for the other would have to depend on the capacity to be together in the presence of one's radical aloneness. Such a shift, constituting a step further from Winnicott's theory of early mother-infant bonding in the direction of horizontal, non-complementary love, is not easy to conceptualize. Togetherness seems almost impossible since the two individuals literally occupy different spaces, even when they share the same room. As noted by Winnicott, while the external world might be the same for everyone and the inner psychic reality might also be relatively fixed due to environmental factors and early introjections, the third, intermediate area varies greatly between individuals, constituting their singularity (Winnicott, 1971/2005, pp. 143–144). For Winnicott this highly idiosyncratic in-between area has mostly positive qualities, but it can also be seen from a different angle, as a space in which we are trapped, completely alone yet still susceptible to the disturbing influence of the external world: it is neither a safely enclosed inside, nor a shared outside. What if the transitional space does not organize our experiences but rather disorganizes them, leaving a distinctive and often painful mark of the drives on the way we perceive the outside world? According to Eric Santner, the individual's singular self, that which varies between subjects despite similarities in their inner and outer realities, is nothing other than this specific disorganization: "what matters most in a human life may in some sense be one's specific form of disorientation, the idiomatic way in which one's approach to and movement through the world is 'distorted'" (Santner, 2001, p. 39). I suggest that the concept of transitional space can be modified to cover not only the area of vital play and creativity but also that of painful libidinal distortion. After all, to play or to create is to distort the world according to one's own peculiar idiom of desire – and this activity is never completely benign, no matter how much Winnicott would like it to be.

Among psychoanalysts, it is probably Christopher Bollas who has written the most about the role and importance of the individual's spatial idiom, the distorted, crooked way in which one moves through the physical environment: "Indeed, although such movement is too dense to be interpreted, each person senses something of his or her own unique idiom of being as he or she moves freely through space" (Bollas, 2009, p. 40). Our idiom, everything that makes us subjects, is nothing other than a map of our desire, mis-leading us through the world – a map that remains unreadable. As noted by Bollas, the symptomatic way each subject inhabits space reflects the earliest spatial experiences in relationships with the parents: being left behind, put aside, displaced, intruded upon:

> A patient may, for example, indicate through awkward body gait and social ill ease a primary discomfort at having to occupy space in the first place. I can think of one patient whose manner of walking and talking was so arhythmic and hesitant that it became a crucial feature of the analysis, and it is helpful to understand the evolution of this characterological development to see how the patient's way of handling the self as an object may reflect the lack of ordinary spatial-temporal co-ordinates in the parent's handling of the patient when an infant.
>
> (Bollas, 2018, p. 26)

Thus, our spatial idiom is shaped by our most fundamental dependence on the other's presence, but also by loneliness and the ineffaceable lack of the handling other. The way we move through space is the way we make do with this lack, as well as the way the lack itself continues to haunt us. Bollas accurately associates the individual's intrinsic spatial idiom with the process that takes place in dreams: "Without thinking about it much, when we traverse a city – or walk in our district – we are engaged in a type of dreaming" (Bollas, 2009, p. 39). We choose certain paths, often without knowing why, and on these paths we encounter objects that remind us of both our separation and our dependence. During "day dreaming," moving through "day space," not that different from "dream space" (Bollas, 2003, p. 23), the subject is in some way as lonely as one is in an actual dream. Part of the pleasure derived from one's idiosyncratic day dreaming lies precisely in the fact that what one stumbles upon – places, people, objects – is deeply intimate to the point of incommunicability, at the same time remaining objectively external to the subject, unlike in "night dreaming." Yet the darker side of the analogy between the waking and sleep life is that the others we encounter on our way through day space can appear to us as nothing else than "such stuff as dreams are made on"[2]: figments of our dream life, spectres of our previous spatial experiences.

The question one has to answer in order to conceptualize love as a spatial phenomenon is how it is possible for us to meet as more than mere spectres in each other's day dreams – how (if at all) can we experience an encounter that would not be merely a fleeting crossing of two idiomatic paths of desire. The innate spatial division, the incompatibility of the two personal maps and occupied spaces, accounts for one of the most fundamental complaints of a lover:

> When, in love, I solicit a look, what is profoundly unsatisfying and always missing is that – *You never look at me from the place from which I see you.* Conversely, *what I look at is never what I wish to see.*
> (Lacan, 1973/1978, p. 103; emphasis in the original)

The subject will never see how the other sees them from the inside of another spatial idiom. This incongruity in the transitional space between two individuals echoes the previous lack in the space between the mother and infant, the lack experienced no matter how carefully the mother prepares the ground for separation. According to Winnicott, personal isolation protects the individual's fragile identity from outside intrusion, until a style of communication can be established that "does not lead to violation of the central self" (Winnicott, 1965/1990, p. 190). Later, in "mature" intersubjective life, "we wander in and out of each other. We knock, as it were, on one another's doors, and avoid – if we are reasonably balanced – intruding" (Jemstedt, 2000, p. 128). The problem is that since our aloneness is so extreme, every substantial encounter with the proximity of the other becomes a traumatic intrusion. On the other hand, complete acceptance of our spatial estrangement would be simply unbearable. Paraphrasing Winnicott, love is a "sophisticated game of hide-and-seek in which it is joy to be hidden but disaster not to be found" (Winnicott, 1965/1990, p. 186). The only way to be found is to agree to be intruded upon, at least to some extent.

3 ... in the Presence of the Other

To understand the spatial characteristics of love, one must not only focus on the radical aspect of the subject's aloneness, but also treat the second half of the intersubjective situation – the other's presence – equally seriously. As mentioned above, the object, this unavoidable intruder, is "always a cause of disequilibrium for the ego – in fact, it is a trauma" (Green, 2001, p. 97). The traumatic potential derives from the fact that the object, insofar as it is not just a figment of the subject's imagination but a real other, *makes a difference*: and this difference is precisely a spatial one. Winnicott and analysts inspired by his theory, such as Bollas and Jessica Benjamin, criticize psychoanalytic accounts of object-relations that focus only on the intrapsychic phenomena without paying attention to the difference made in the subject's experience by the object's reality. Winnicott proposes to differentiate between object relating – which can refer to the attachment to internal objects – and object usage, which entails that the object "must necessarily be real in the sense of being part of shared reality, not a bundle of projections" (Winnicott, 1971/2005, p. 118). To be used, the object has to be *there*, in objective space, outside the subject's control. According to Jessica Benjamin, a theory of object-relations that does not include this spatial aspect of being truly *there* cannot grasp the reality of intersubjective experience, since it does not distinguish "between *you* as an independently existing subject, and *you* as a fantasy extension of my wishes and desires" (Benjamin, 1988, p. 125). However, it is important to add that the intrapsychic element cannot be separated from the intersubjective one: the object makes a difference because while being *there*, outside, it is nonetheless entangled within the net of inner identifications, memory-traces and libidinal currents. Because we invest so much of our inner lives in outside objects, the tangible, spatial characteristics of these objects in turn influence the shape of our intrapsychic world:

> I have found it rather surprising that in "object relations theory" very little thought is really given to the distinct structure of the object which is usually seen as a container of the individual's projections. Certainly objects bear us. But ironically enough, it is precisely *because* they hold our projections that the structural feature of any one object becomes even more important, because we also put ourself [*sic*] into a container that upon re-experiencing will process us according to its natural integrity.
>
> (Bollas, 2003, p. 4; emphasis in the original)

Since the object is truly outside the subject's control and, moreover, its presence constantly threatens to process the ego according to its own obscure logic, violating the most intimate parts of the subject's inner life, the first reaction to this presence is aggression. The subject attacks the object, setting out to destroy it, partly because they want to protect themselves from its influence, but also because they want to find out whether the object really is external and irreducible to their fantasy: "violation is the attempt to push the other outside the self, to attack the other's separate reality in order finally to discover it" (Benjamin, 1988, p. 68). This discovery can happen only if the other actually survives the aggression. Survival is closely connected to space – to the stubborn resistance of matter in the face of our destructive fantasies, as well as to the fact that the other occupies physical space, which allows them to dodge the attack. When the other survives, they prove that someone is truly there besides the subject, someone to be hated or to be loved: "From now on the subject says: 'Hullo object!' 'I destroyed you.' 'I love you.' 'You have value for me because of your survival of my destruction of you'" (Winnicott, 1971/2005, p. 120). The subject can now use the object that has survived the destruction – not merely relating to it through fantasy but truly cherishing its spatial and bodily characteristics, its closeness and distance, the resistance it puts up and the effort the relationship to it requires. For Winnicott the fact that the other is truly external is both the cause and the result of the process of destruction (p. 21). The object's survival allows the subject to actually appreciate its outwardness, instead of simply considering it a threat to the ego's integrity. When the other fails to survive, giving up to the subject's destructive wishes, the subject becomes deprived of any anchoring in the objective reality: they are "flying off into space" where they find "no limits, no otherness. The world now seems empty of all human life, there is no one to connect with, 'the world is all me'" (Benjamin, 1988, pp. 70–71). I would like to suggest that a complete survival of the object, without any kind of loss, would lead to an equally disastrous outcome. If the other survived the attack completely unscathed, they would seem to be as unreal and devoid of actual spatial presence as the other who did not survive at all. Some degree of loss, a mark of violation left on the other, reminds the subject that the use of the object is always ambivalent and that our aloneness – our idiomatic curve of movement – has profound, often dire, consequences in the outside world.

The traumatic aspect of the encounter with a truly external other is never entirely eliminated: according to Winnicott, the destruction of the object continues in the individual's unconscious fantasy. But so long as the object survives, the subject discovers a completely new source and form of pleasure – they learn to take pleasure from the reality principle itself. As suggested by Jessica Benjamin, this mode of enjoyment is a spatial rather than symbolic one (Benjamin, 1988, pp. 40–41, 126). Far from being a complex metonymic chain of desire, it is a simple affirmation of the fact that the other is *really there*, right next to us. "Probably destruction in fantasy also underlies the joy in the young toddler's constant repetition of 'Hi!' It has something to do with constantly rediscovering that you are there," writes Benjamin (p. 39). In this approach, reality is no longer merely something that limits us, an obstacle which we flee from in our fantasies, but something that can be enjoyed precisely because of its coarseness and grittiness. No fantasy, no matter how pleasant, can provide the subject with this unsurpassed sensation of actually being in space with somebody else, mainly because in fantasies one encounters no resistance and no limitations. Contrary to the narcissistic ideal, in real, "spatial" love, "things don't have to be perfect ... in fact, it is *better* if they are not": the "degree of imperfection 'ratifies' the existence of the world", the fact that we are truly *there* together (p. 47; emphasis in the original).[3]

This particular pleasure that borders on pain – pleasure found in the reality principle – stems from the experience of being used by the object. We are not the only ones who play in the transitional space, "on the shore of endless worlds," manipulating the outside world according to our wishes: sometimes, as Bollas aptly noticed, it is the object that plays upon us (Bollas, 2003, p. 41). Bollas calls these objects that use us "evocative objects," because they evoke unknown aspects of ourselves, processing our inner realities according to their own texture and integrity. They do not constitute a privileged class of objects: on the contrary, every object can potentially play with us, acquiring evocative qualities. Evocative objects inhabit our common, daily space, yet we cannot select them according to our idiomatic script of desire – inasmuch as they are aleatory, they cannot be conjured, we can only come across them by accident: "We have not ... selected the aleatory object to express an idiom of self. Instead, we are played upon by the inspiring arrival of the unselected, which often yields a very special type of pleasure – that of surprise," writes Bollas. "It opens us up, liberating an area like a key fitting a lock" (p. 37). The disruptive (although pleasurable) element of surprise enters into productive conflict with the subject's aloneness, their unique spatial idiom of desire. The object we happen upon is never the one we look for – and even the one we choose for ourselves always includes an unanticipated dimension for which our fantasy has not prepared us. As we move through day space, we experience the struggle between our idiomatic way of being, the net of our "unconscious wishes, needs, defenses, anxieties," and the element of chance "as the environment telephones us, writes to us, weathers us, offers us new books, displays wonderful looking people, and so on" (p. 26).

In love, it is the other's spatial presence that surprises us. Of course, sometimes this presence takes the form of absence, but absence can be perceived as such only if it is preceded by some form of spatial presence. The other's particular way of being there (or not being there – to which I will return in a moment) disrupts the subject's pattern of desire, the map that brings some sense of consistency to their universe. One has to remember that this map already misleads and disorients us, so the other's interference is not merely a disorientation, but a disorientation of a disorientation, or "a disorganization of a disorganization" (Santner, 2006, p. 114), a play upon the way we ourselves play with the outside world. To be with the beloved other – this paradigmatic aleatory object – "is to be played by them" (Bollas, 2003, p. 28), allowing the disruptive element of surprise to challenge our specific form of aloneness. "It is the other side – and better half – of trauma" (Grotstein, 2002, p. 89), an intrusion that, with a bit of luck, can be cherished and enjoyed.

4 If Not All Goes Well. On the Spatiality of Heartbreak

"If all goes well" – as Winnicott often repeats – the fact that the object does not completely adapt to the wishes of the subject becomes a specific source of pleasure and a condition of love's possibility (Winnicott, 1971/2005, p. 14). However, because the object of erotic love is truly aleatory, it is highly unlikely, if not impossible, that everything will go well. Horizontal love, the other half of trauma, gives "more than you bargained for – for better or worse"

(Mitchell, 2003, p. 225). For better or worse, because the joy of the other's presence is always lined with the possibility of absence. "I feel as though I came to meet somebody and they didn't come" (Winnicott, 1971/2005, p. 82), says one of Winnicott's patients, providing a striking summary of the pain that replaces love's delight when the other turns out to be truly external and pushes the subject deeper into their aloneness.

Loss, the reverse side of love's surprising meeting, can be conceived in spatial terms as being lost, not knowing where one is. Like the lucky encounter with the aleatory object, loss disorients the subject, distorting the coordinates of the space they inhabit. However, loss does not evoke the feeling of opening up to new horizons, the sensation of expanding one's idiomatic map of desire. Instead, it creates a void at the very center of this map, provoking what Winnicott called archaic or unthinkable anxiety. Archaic anxiety, which is expressed by particularly unsettling spatial idioms, such as "going to pieces," "falling for ever," "having no relationship to the body" and "having no orientation" (Winnicott, 1965/1990, p. 58), springs from the unreliability of the other in the face of the subject's absolute dependence. Even though it results in psychic disintegration, this anxiety is paradoxically a form of defence and self-integration, because the chaos that accompanies it is produced by the subject themselves, and not by the object they depends upon (p. 61). The encounter with the object's unpredictability – lucky or traumatic – is indeed disorienting, yet, as it turns out, the most painful part of the situation is the subject's attempt to somehow reorient themselves in the aftermath of this event.

In *Life Narcissism, Death Narcissism* André Green outlines a fascinating, spatial conception of psychic pain, which in his account is closely connected to the pain of heartbreak. The subject experiences this pain in the face of unexpected and previously unnoticed changes in the object – the source of pain is not the loss itself but rather that to which the loss testifies, the unpredictable surplus within the other, their "unknown life" (Green, 2001, p. 111). The sudden change in the object (the object's "play" upon us) forces the subject to change themselves and adjust their spatial idiom, the way they relate to the world. According to Green, the subject protects themselves from the necessity of a drastic change through the narcissistic withdrawal from the lost object – a retraction of libidinal cathexes back to the safely enclosed sphere of the ego. However, the object is not that easy to run away from. The reversal of cathexes is accompanied by a "vacuum effect": "Unknown to the subject, the next thing to happen in this deflection of cathexes … is that, without realising it, the ego brings the object back into its net, but it is an empty object, a phantom object" (p. 110). The other – or rather the blank spot, the void in the shape of the lost other – becomes an inseparable part of the subject's inner space. In the light of this theory, the true cause of heartbreak is the attempt to protect oneself from heartbreak. The turning away from the object in the external space results in the object's spectral intrusion into the subject's internal, psychic space. The ego attempts to control the intruder, whereas the imprisoned object seems to be trying to break out of its confinement. But because the object is nothing but its own shadow, the struggling ego simply ends up bruising itself – "like a desperate child banging his head against a wall" (p. 108).

In the pain of heartbreak, the external absence of the other is absorbed and becomes a coordinate of the subject's psychic space. Green describes this phenomenon as a negative cathexis – a libidinal cathexis of the very hole left behind by the object (Green, 2001, p. 110). He follows the conclusions Winnicott drew from the analysis of the case in which, due to the prolonged experience of absence, the patient started to believe that "the only real thing is the gap" (Winnicott, 1971/2005, p. 30). In her desperate search for "something that never goes away" (p. 31) she found the last solace in absence itself. When confronted with the unpredictability of the aleatory object of love, the subject protects the fragile cohesiveness of their universe by weaving the other's absence into the very fabric of their mode of being. For this reason, the absence cannot be properly seen, acknowledged and mourned: getting rid of the phantom object would entail rupturing the self (Green, 2001, p. 110). The empty, absent object within the subject's psychic space conceals the fact that the real object is actually present, only *somewhere else*, outside of one's control, lost in the vast, outer space. Green clearly distinguishes heartbreak from mourning – in his account of psychic pain everything starts when the object "turns away or leaves in search of another object" (p. 109), not when it is completely gone. Despite the immense suffering it produces, internal emptiness left by the lost other becomes a more reliable love-object than the actual other. A new relationship with someone who is truly there (so someone who can also turn away) seems undesirable: as Winnicott's patient noticed, the negative of one person becomes more real than the positive of another (Winnicott, 1971/2005, p. 30).

As Erik Erikson writes, "to be left ... means to be left empty" (Erikson, 1968, p. 278), or rather, to be left with a certain emptiness that becomes the only possible object one can relate to, deepening the subject's sense of loneliness. The only way to render this inner emptiness productive is to merge it with something external – with another form of emptiness, one that is truly outside and thus is always more than just emptiness, a space in which something new can possibly emerge. Ruth Kjär, the painter Melanie Klein wrote about in her famous paper, supposedly discovered her artistic capacities when an empty space on the wall, once occupied by a painting, "in some inexplicable way seemed to coincide with the empty space within her" (Klein, 1929/1984, p. 215). She could only attempt to fill this space after she had noticed its outside manifestation in the form of the empty wall segment. When the internal emptiness overlapped with the empty space outside, the woman became able to turn it into a canvas for images, a "container" for her creativity (using the term introduced by Wilfred Bion [1962/1984, p. 90]).

When one's psychic space has been taken up by the hole left after the object's departure, the only choice other than the ultimately fatal narcissistic struggle to master the inner void is to follow the steps of the lost object and turn away from oneself, facing the vastness and alienness of the outside world. Green notices that "a common defense against psychical pain is the *moving of spatial limits*," a deliberate displacement or "a quest for unknown space" (Green, 2001, p. 108; emphasis in the original). Paradoxically, after the experience of heartbreak – that is, an utter disappointment with any form of outwardness and otherness – one has to turn away from oneself in order to regain oneself. Engagement with the outside space becomes necessary for rebuilding one's vital sense of aloneness: the aloneness that often distorts our world and isolates us from others, but also harbors the potential of its own disruption due to the intrusion of a particularly evocative aleatory object (unlike the morbid, self-enclosed aloneness of narcissistic withdrawal). In her analysis of feminine sexual subjectivity and its spatial metaphors, Jessica Benjamin writes about a woman who "began to dream of rooms":

> She began to look forward to travelling alone, to the feeling of containment and freedom as she flew in an airplane, to being alone and anonymous in her hotel room. Here, she imagined, she would find a kind of aloneness that would allow her to look into herself.
>
> (Benjamin, 1988, p. 128)

It is worth noting that the spaces mentioned (airplane, hotel room) share a very distinct quality: they are both public and anonymous, allowing for privacy, yet are purposely neutral, devoid of any personal particularity.[4] These non-places such as hotels, airports, trains or stations embody a certain form of emptiness, like the blank space on the wall in the story of Ruth Kjär. They provide the sense of aloneness in the presence of otherness, the feeling of liberating solitude accompanied by the experience of being truly there, in the outer space inhabited by fellow wanderers. Moreover, just like the empty canvas, these seemingly blank places (often tellingly associated with travel) give rise to previously unknown potentialities. Most important, they hold a promise that only external space can give us: the possibility of stumbling upon somebody who will be there with us.

5 Being Together – Sharing Space

When writing about free association, Bollas – after Freud – uses metaphors related to train travel. Every day we take a trip "stimulated by desire, need, memory and emotional life" (Bollas, 2009, p. 4) but also by the changing views we observe and the evocative objects that literally stop us in our tracks. As we move through the world as freely associating creatures, we encounter objects and spaces which bear an "ontological potential": they take us back to the moment of birth, evoking the first experience of the immensity of outside space, as we return "to the origin of our being in its first perceptions of the object" (p. 44). Yet, as I would like to suggest, this second birth can only feel truly real when we share the space with someone who is also experiencing their rebirth, next to us, with us and because of us. Winnicott insisted on the importance of the reflecting other in the emergence of the feeling of aliveness. In one of the most striking accounts of his analytical sessions, he quotes a female patient:

> 'I think, you see, I've got to find if there is such a person [*for whom* I matter], someone to matter to *me*, someone who will be able to receive, to make contact with what my eyes have seen and my ears have heard.
> (Winnicott, 1971/2005, p. 80; emphasis in the original)

Without this someone, our daily trip guided by our personal spatial idiom is similar to a fleeting dream, permeated by the sense of total aloneness not distant from death itself: "All sorts of things happen and they wither. This is the myriad deaths you have died" (p. 81). But when the other is there to see "what one's eyes have seen" and reflect it back to the subject, deaths can be replaced by transformative rebirths. Even though Lacan is right that the beloved other can never look at the subject from the place from which the subject sees them, sometimes – and this is what makes love possible – they can both look in the same direction and experience the same space. "[F]or the first time during this session the patient seemed to be in the room with me" (p. 81), writes Winnicott, suggesting that this is not something to be taken for granted. Most of the time, being in the same room is not synonymous with sharing space. The miracle of love consists of this rare instant of spatial communion. Even though what the individuals see and experience always differs due to the differences between their individual maps of desire, in love there is one thing that the two partners have in common: the change of perspective brought about by the presence of the other.

What is actually shared in love is the disruption in the way both subjects experience space. It is the disturbance in our spatial idiom that accounts for the feeling that the other is truly there in the room with us. Unlike the good enough mother who, for Winnicott, facilitates the emergence of the infant's aloneness and selfhood, the horizontal other is not a plain mirror: the beloved person reflects what we have seen but always with a shift, a distortion caused by their own form of aloneness and the way it is, in turn, disrupted by our presence. Precisely for this reason the aleatory object of love is simultaneously a transformative object (Grotstein, 2002, p. 79) – one that brings out in us new ways of being in space, allowing for the experience of rebirth, of discovering the outside world as if for the first time. The potential space shared by lovers includes the workings of sexuality (understood as a polymorphous perversion that shapes the way we move through the universe): it emerges when two distinct sexual idioms disrupt one another, forcing the individuals to break out of their aloneness and open themselves to the presence of the other person. The pleasure that accompanies this experience – the joy of being physically there together, the pleasure stemming from the reality principle – is not an abstract ego-relatedness, devoid of libidinal arousal, but rather is a very tangible, corporeal pleasure of rediscovering space in the conjoined movement of two bodies. Lovers participate in an interplay that resembles a rhythmic dance, and in its most joyful moments "it is as if both partners are following the same score" (Benjamin, 1988, p. 127), despite (or even through) the differences in their respective spatial idioms. In this dance-like movement between inside and outside "resides the possibility to discover something new and to let oneself be surprised, also by oneself" (Jemstedt, 2000, p. 125).

The space which love makes us share extends between the inner and outer realities, as well as between the bodily and linguistic experience. For this reason, it blurs the distinction between the verbal and pre-verbal registers. After all, the free association we engage in is both a free movement – a "train ride" through the world of objects – and a "free talking" (Bollas, 2009, p. 6) that can take place only in the presence of the other who takes the trip with us. So long as the other is truly external, they do not merely accompany the subject in the journey through space, but also change the way space is perceived, allowing the subject to see and hear as if with somebody else's eyes and ears. The communication that allows for this shift of perspective combines language with silent, evocative spatial sensations. In love, "to communicate with one another is to evoke each other … to be scattered by the winds of the primary process to faraway associations and elaborations" (Bollas, 2003, p. 45). Julia Kristeva links the inception of the semiotic disposition – the not-yet linguistic, pre-symbolic form of communication – to the very archaic experience of space: the moment in the child's development when the sensual elements of the environment (light, sound, the mother's breast and face) "become a *there*: a place, a spot, a marker" (Kristeva, 1960/ 1980, p. 283; emphasis in the original). According to Kristeva, the child reacts to this emergence of spatiality with laughter – a nascent seed of language, an imprint that becomes a "place name" (p. 287). Lovers who evoke each other, dancing together through space, communicate precisely with "place names": with laughter, gasps, sighs, as well as "faraway associations," all of which constitute attempts to name the unnameable – the experience of being *there* that is both joyful and overwhelming. This spatio-semiotic transmission that forms a kind of play might be, as Winnicott suggests, a model of the only possible form of communication there is, other than "direct communication, which belongs to psychopathology or to an extreme of immaturity" (Winnicott, 1971/2005, p. 73).

In sharing space and sharing words – the names or markers of spaciousness – we experience truly horizontal love: one devoid both of gentle complementarity and the narcissistic reduction of the other to the ego's self-satisfied wholeness. What was perceived as an intrusion from the standpoint of one's aloneness can be reframed as horizontal being-with, provided that the subject's aloneness – their spatial idiom – is transformed by the presence and perspective of the other, the disruptive, surprising aleatory object. The capacity to be together while experiencing one's aloneness would consist of the ability to sustain the "dance," the crossing of perspectives that produces the unparalleled, head-spinning sensation of being truly *there*, as if entering the world for the first time. Of course, as love forms the "other half of trauma," very little separates this joyful sensation from the dreadful chaos of total disorientation experienced in the face of the other's sudden absence. The risk of heartbreak – the painful way the subject reorients themselves in the emptiness left by the object – is integral to every relation with a truly external and horizontal other. We can never feel entirely safe and at home in the outer space, but it is the only one space where love can be found.

Notes

1 That is why, as Arne Jemstedt aptly states, "[t]he fear of dependency and the fear of loneliness are basically the same thing" (Jemstedt, 2000, p. 130).
2 William Shakespeare, *The Tempest*, Act 4, Scene 1, ll. 156–157.
3 I am deeply grateful to Adam Lipszyc for his remarks on Benjamin's idea of the reality principle as a source of pleasure. I would also like to thank him for the suggestion of this paper's title which perfectly captures the essence of my reflections.
4 I would like to thank Michał Chojnacki for countless conversations about our shared love for non-places, and their ability to contain and transform the subject.

References

Benjamin, J. (1988). *The Bonds of Love: Psychoanalysis, Feminism and the Problem of Domination*. Pantheon Books.
Bion, W. (1984). *Learning from Experience*. Routledge. (Original work published 1962.)
Bollas, C. (2003). *Being a Character: Psychoanalysis and Self Experience*. Routledge.
Bollas, C. (2009). *The Evocative Object World*. Routledge.
Bollas, C. (2018). *The Shadow of the Object. Psychoanalysis of the Unthought Known*. Routledge.
Erikson, E.H. (1968). Womanhood and the Inner Space. In *Identity, Youth and Crisis*. W.W. Norton.
Freud, S. (1953). Three Essays on the Theory of Sexuality. In *The Standard Edition of the Complete Psychological Works of Sigmund Freud*, Vol. 7 (J. Strachey, Ed. & Trans.). The Hogarth Press. (Original work published 1905.)
Freud, S. (1955). Beyond the Pleasure Principle. In *The Standard Edition of the Complete Psychological Works of Sigmund Freud*, Vol. 18 (J. Strachey, Ed. & Trans.). The Hogarth Press. (Original work published 1920.)

Freud, S. (1957). On Narcissism. In *The Standard Edition of the Complete Psychological Works of Sigmund Freud*, Vol. 14 (J. Strachey, Ed. & Trans.). The Hogarth Press. (Original work published 1914.)

Green, A. (2001). *Life Narcissism, Death Narcissism* (A. Weller, Trans.). Free Association Books.

Grotstein, J. S. (2002). "Love Is Where It Finds You": The Caprices of the "Aleatory Object". In J. Scalia (Ed.), *The Vitality of Objects. Exploring the Work of Christopher Bollas*. Continuum.

Jemstedt, A. (2000). Potential Space: The Place of Encounter between Inner and Outer Reality. *International Forum of Psychoanalysis*, 9(1–2), 124–131.

Klein, M. (1984). Infantile Anxiety-Situations Reflected in the Work of Art and in the Creative Impulse. In *Love, Guilt and Reparation and Other Works 1921–1945*. The Free Press. (Original work published 1929.)

Kristeva, J. (1980). *Desire in Language: A Semiotic Approach to Literature and Art* (T. Gora, A. Jardine & L.S. Roudiez, Trans.). Columbia University Press. (Original work published 1960.)

Lacan, J. (1978). *The Seminar of Jacques Lacan. Book XI: The Four Fundamental Concepts of Psychoanalysis* (A. Sheridan, Trans.). W.W. Norton. (Original work published 1973.)

Lacan, J. (1998). *The Seminar of Jacques Lacan. Book XX: Encore: On Feminine Sexuality, the Limits of Love and Knowledge (1972–1973)* (B. Fink, Trans.). W.W. Norton. (Original work published 1975.)

Laplanche, J. (1989). *New Foundations for Psychoanalysis* (D. Macey, Trans.). Basil Blackwell.

Mitchell, J. (2003). *Siblings: Sex and Violence*. Polity Press.

Santner, E.L. (2001). *On the Psychotheology of Everyday Life: Reflections on Freud and Rosenzweig*. University of Chicago Press.

Santner, E.L. (2006). Miracles Happen. In S. Žižek, E.L. Santner & K. Reinhard (Eds.) *The Neighbor: Three Inquires in Political Theology*. University of Chicago Press.

Winnicott, D.W. (2005). *Playing and Reality*. Routledge. (Original work published 1971.)

Winnicott, D.W. (1990). *The Maturational Processes and the Facilitating Environment: Studies in the Theory of Emotional Development*. Karnac. (Original work published 1965.)

Zupančič, A. (2003). *The Shortest Shadow. Nietzsche's Philosophy of the Two*. MIT Press.

Chapter 7

Subject's Position and Subject's Space

A Variation on a Lacanian Theme

Andrzej Leder

1 A Dispute Over the Definition of Subject

I would like to discuss a certain way of understanding subjectivity associated with Lacanian psychoanalysis. My starting point will be the well-known definition of *signifier (signifiant)*,[1] as *the representative of a subject* for another signifier.[2]

This discussion is intended to allow us to resolve the dilemma which reveals itself when we juxtapose the linguistic usage of the word "subject" and its philosophical usage. In the former, a subject is "a noun, noun phrase or pronoun representing the person or thing that performs the action of the verb or, in a passive sentence, that is affected by the action of the verb" (PWN, n.d.a). We will assume that this corresponds to the Lacanian significant or signifier. In the latter philosophical usage, a subject is "the bearer of something (e.g. a property), that in which something resides, to which something is entitled; a synonym of substance" (PWN, n.d.b).

One suspects that the tension between these two definitions is a manifestation of an important issue: the relationship between the necessary singularity of the subject as this-or-that place, distinct from all others, and the potentially all-encompassing power, which is enshrined in the notion of substance.

In the clash between the two definitions mentioned above, we are confronted with the difference between the momentary, instantaneous status of the linguistic subject – being essentially a signifier "representing a person or a thing" – and the philosophical idea of the subject as a substance – the bearer of all possible properties, which can be translated into the bearer of all possible signifiers.

How, in Lacan's post-structuralist terminology, can we name something as being synonymous with substance? Against all the anti-metaphysical rhetoric, can we find an image that captures the intuition carried by this classically metaphysical concept, the notion of substance? Following Deleuze, we could hypothesize that the closest classical philosophical understanding of substance that is located in post-structuralist theories is structure itself. However, we will propose another term: the *subject's space*.

DOI: 10.4324/9781003436188-8

2 What Is Implied by the Lacanian Definition of the Signifier as Representing a Subject to another Signifier?

Lacan has deeply transformed the structuralist concept of signifier.[3] Contrary to the tradition of de Saussure – i.e., the assumption of a close relationship between signifiant and *signifié* – the signifier here does not refer to some *signified* or a referent.

First, the signifier acquires the character of signifier exclusively – Lacan points out that there is no other definition of it (Lacan, 1966, p. 819) – through the relation of representation; the representation of the subject in relation to the Other, which appears as representation by the signifier in relation to another signifier. This marks Lacan's entry into that twentieth-century current of thought, most prominently represented by Emmanuel Lévinas, in which the fact that something signifies, is a signifier, is exclusively linked to the relation of subject to an Other, and not subject to an object.

Second, if subjectivity was defined *only* as the relation of one signifier to another signifier, it would be easy to conceive of their relation as linear, with the addition of further signifiers forming a certain sequence, which could be called time. But a signifier *is not* a subject, a signifier *represents a subject* to another signifier. One signifier "looks" at the other signifier and sees it as a delegate of the subject. So here we have a triangle, or rather a Z-sign (known as graph L), that goes beyond this linear structure of the relationship of two and then many signifiers. The subject can never be identified with them.[4] It is never on a line connecting signifiers into a metonymic sequence.

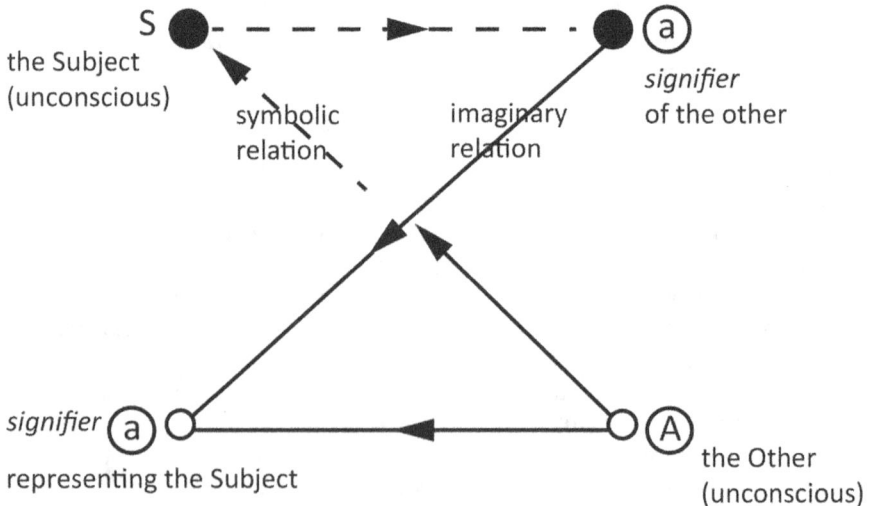

Figure 7.1 Graph L showing that the subject of the unconscious S (Es) is represented by the signifier a (ego) to the signifier a (other) representing the Other (A)
Source: Compiled by the author based on Lacan (2006, p. 40).

But we digress. Let us recall that the very use of the spatial category in relation to subjectivity is not at all obvious. For we know that, despite many revisions and critiques, strategies derived from the temporal metaphor are still dominant in humanistic and philosophical thinking about the subject. National and private histories, dialectics and hermeneutics, designs for the future and memories of the past, are all ways of "stretching" the punctual subject into temporal extension; ways which in the 20th century first signified a breakthrough in thinking, but over time became trivialized and, one suspects, depleted in terms of its capacity to inspire.

Third, Lacan is explicit about the primacy of the signifier: by representing the subject, the signifier determines its position. The subject is ruled by it.[5] Thus, it is not the subject that is the sovereign creator of signifying phenomena here. But precisely given the fact that this signification of the signifier is always, and without exception, a representation of the subject, we are then left to contemplate the clearly stated but obvious assumption[6] that without the *subject* occupying successive *positions* (the subject's position), there would never be a string of signifiers. The subject wanders through the positions that the metonymic chain of correlations of signifier-representer to signifier-sovereign designates. But without the subject, the signifier-representer *would not signify at all*.

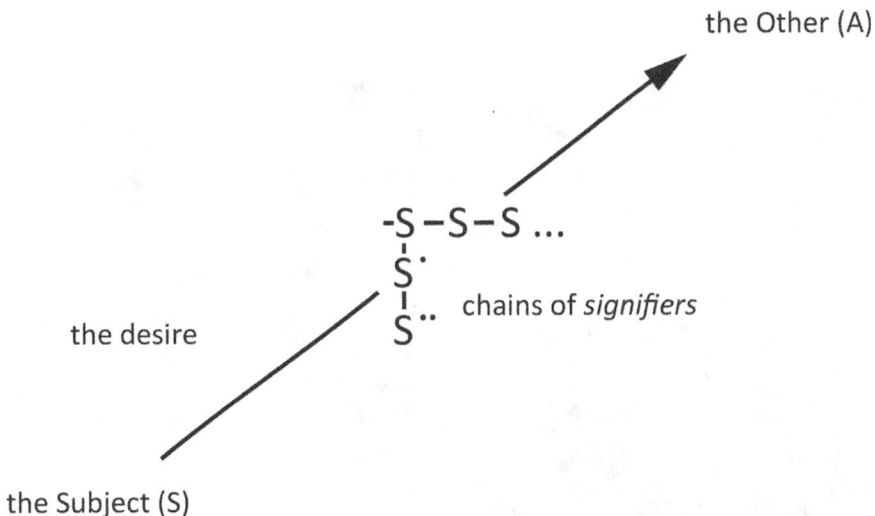

the Other (A)

$$-S-S-S\ldots$$

the desire

chains of *signifiers*

the Subject (S)

Figure 7.2 The Subject, his desire and the Other
Source: Compiled by the author.

The truth of the desire delineates the dimension that, as if from outside the network of signifiers, links in the unconscious the subject S to the sovereign A. But the truth of desire does not appear directly in the consciousness. Rather, it shapes the fantasy, and the subject finds its place there, in this fantasy.

3 Who Is the "Representative"?

This construction, which is surely not entirely intuitive, can be made clearer by referring back to the figure of an ambassador, especially one living in the 18th century, before the invention of the telegraph. An ambassador representing his distant sovereign is himself in direct relationship with that other sovereign, to whom he presents his letters of credence. It is essentially the Other – this foreign sovereign, within arm's reach – who determines the ambassador's most important movements. The influence of the distant subject on the representative, on the other hand, is weak. Rather, the reverse is true: the position of distant sovereign or the *subject's position*, is essentially determined by the ambassador's reports.[7]

We can see this clearly in the famous painting by Jan Matejko entitled *Upadek Polski (Reytan)* (*Rejtan, or the Fall of Poland*). The *signifier* representing the subject of this painting, the revolted nobleman Rejtan, lying on the floor, does not look at his formal *master signifier* – the Polish king,

Figure 7.3 Jan Matejko, *Upadek Polski (Reytan)*, 1866, oil on canvas, 282 cm × 487 cm. Royal Castle in Warsaw, Poland
Source: https://commons.wikimedia.org/wiki/File:Jan_Matejko_-_Upadek_Polski_(Reytan). jpg?uselang=en#Licensing.

Stanisław, dressed in white. His gaze is fixed upon the Russian ambassador, Repnin – sitting between two ladies in the upper left corner of the picture. For Rejtan, this is the true master signifier. However, if we think about the Russian ambassador as the signifier of the subject of the picture, we will see his eyes fixed on the portrait (signifier) of the tsarina, Catherine II, the true Other of this scene.

The whole structure, which is represented here, has the shape of the graph L.

4 The Subject's Position Is a Place-to-be-Held, and the Subject There Is Synonymous with the "Lyrical Subject"

The well-known commentator on Lacanian thought, Joel Dor, expresses the above statement by claiming that the subject is only a *tenant-lieu* (place-holder occupying a position).[8] This place, occupied by the subject S, is just one of many possible positions. We will retain the formulation of the subject's position, understood here as important for further argument.

To put it in more philosophical terms: the signifiers representing the subject are the potential self-consciousness of that subject, which in Lacan's language means that they are located in the imaginary register. This register is always a *semblance* of the truth of desire. However, it is precisely this area of semblance that is most interesting, for it appears to be a necessary illusion. In order for the world to appear as saturated with meaning, the subject's position represented by the signifier is a necessary condition. Viewed in this way, the subject's position has a similar status – as a condition – to Kant's transcendental unity of apperception. It is the transcendental unity of apperception in motion.

Note that in combining the two dictionary definitions of subject that formed our starting point, we had to add a mediating element, namely the subject's position, which is neither the "named word group" close to the signifier, nor the philosophical subject – the bearer of all signifiers and the space of all positions, synonymous with substance. Characteristically, it is this "middle" position that best fits the third dictionary term for subject: the literary subject, this fictional character "from whose perspective the world presented in a literary work is viewed and shaped" (PWN, n.d.c).

This is, of course, only if we deprive this character of their actual biographical identity, and thus treat her as a "lyrical subject" appearing in a logical moment of utterance rather than as an empirically graspable narrator.

5 The Sum of all Possible Subject's Positions Is the Subject's Space – Synonymous with Substance

In the imaginary register, the sum of these items merges into some image of the subject. Joel Dor describes this process as follows: "The *numerous positions* in which the subject is lost tend to meld into an imaginary representation, the only one the subject will be able to give itself, the only one through which it can grasp itself" (Dor, 2002, p. 155; emphasis added).

However, we are interested in the moment that precedes by a hair's breadth this process of condensation, in which the "cast" of the imaginary representation is produced. We want to draw attention to the sum total of subject positions, the sum total of all possible intentional orientations, the sum total of all the "Is" uttered in all sentences possible for a given subject,[9] before these positions are transformed into an imaginative self-image.

This sum of all possible positions that a subject can occupy determines the subject's space. It is now possible to place the subject's position – understood as the "lyrical subject," the subject of the utterance or *tenant-lieu* – in the field of all possible subject's positions, that is, in the subject's space that we have defined. This space then takes on a sense close to the subject of classical philosophy, the *subiectum*: the bearer of all attributes, of all signifiers, representing all subject's positions.

It is a formal space. As for the status of substance, the substance is, after all, a pure negativity, since its existence cannot be, in the words of Kant, "a real attribute." We note this in order to indicate that the subject's position is, in accordance with Lacan's intention, the position of the subject in its negativity; it is the position of the subject of the unconscious, namely S in the graph L.

6 Topology and Trajectory in the Subject's Space

Sometimes Lacan will show us the subject as a Möbius strip.

Obviously, in this representation the subject may be understood as a subject's space. This image offers us other important issues. A subject's space – the space of all subject's positions – has a shape. It also has limits. This means that it has a *topology*; the movement in it will sometimes be easy and will connect some "privileged" positions, sometimes it will be difficult, and sometimes impossible.

For example, if we continue the analysis of Matejko's painting, for Rejtan to jump from the position represented by the signifier "revolted nobleman," representing him directly facing the signifier "treacherous aristocrats," to the one represented by the signifier "citizen of the Nowogród county" representing him face to the signifier "the nobility of Nowogród county" would be rather easy. However, it would be hard for the same subjectivity to find the position of – let us say – an elderly peasant woman in its subject's space. An 18th-century Polish nobleman will hardly imagine himself as a woman, especially a peasant woman. The prospect of being a peasant woman may haunt him in his dreams but disappear when he is awakened. And for some subjectivities it will be completely out of the limits of representation.

A subject's space is thus a certain potentiality. It actualizes itself through a concrete sequence of signifiers, determining the corresponding subject's

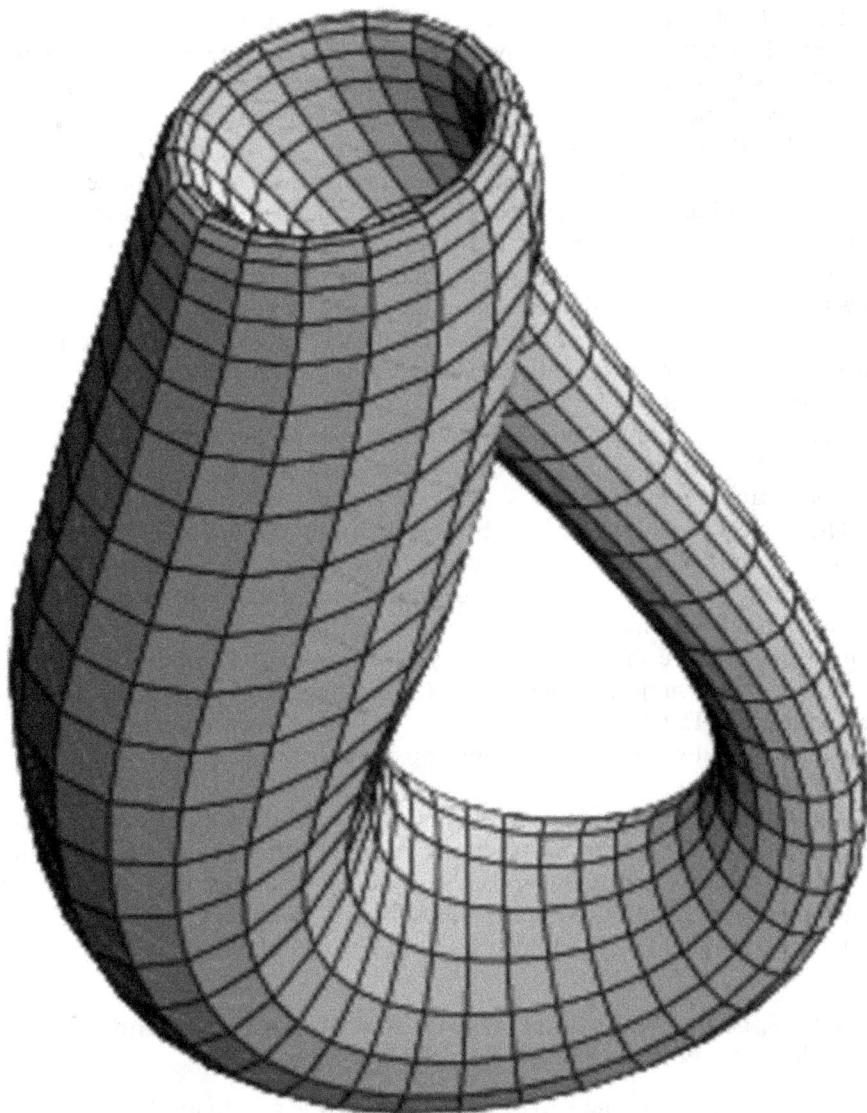

Figure 7.4 Möbius strip appearing as Klein's bottle
Source: https://commons.wikimedia.org/wiki/File:KleinBottle-01.png.

positions in a given field. A parliamentary delegate, a revolted nobleman, a madman with thoughts of suicide – the subject will wander like a vagabond through those positions, *drawing a trajectory in the subject's space*. This trajectory, chain of signifiers, is determined by the topology of this specific subject's space.

The subject – understood here as a subject's space and therefore sub-iectum – is constituted anew in every situation. On the one hand, it is defined by all *possible utterances*, signifiers representing it; every utterance gives to the subject a new position, as in the well-known example of Sartre, who stated that Paul of yesterday is not Paul of today (Sartre, 1943/1977, p. 110–111. On the other hand, however, the limits of possibility of representation, and thus the limits of the subject's space, are defined here precisely by the relation to the master signifier. It is thus the sum total of the *possible* sub-ject's positions at a given moment that can be represented as pointing towards the master signifier, driven be the desire of the Other.

Any chain of signifiers will represent another configuration of the move-ment from one subject's position to another in the subject's space. However, some positions cannot be represented, just as – and here we return to the metaphor of the ambassador – certain distant sovereigns cannot send their representatives to the foreign capital. The road can be too long, or the frontiers can be impassable.

The subject's space organized by the desire of the Other is thus always somehow limited. This means, however, that despite its negative character, the subject's space is not, or indeed cannot be, infinite. For in every structure there are positions which, for the subject, are excluded. Chains of signifiers, i.e., sentences, actualize themselves in the subject's space; or, in other words, the topology of the subject's space generates meanings that determine the sub-ject's position. The subject's space is thus manifold, encompassing all that is possible, but also only the possible positions of the subject for a given structure.

Contrary to the philosophical ideal of substance, the subject cannot be all things, and cannot occupy all positions. Arguably, only in infinite continuity could the subject's space encompass *all possible* positions. One of the most important principles of Western philosophy – Ockham's principle of the economy of thought – is synonymous with this postulation.

7 The Split in the Subject, the Desire of the Other and the Multileveled Nature of the Subject's Space

Like any potentiality, the subject's space is also a negativity. Until a parti-cular subject's position is represented by a particular signifier, and the sub-ject's space by the sequence of them – the trajectory of the signifying chain – it cannot be grasped as this-very-actualizing subjectivity. Hence, the force of Lacan's thesis pointing to the *alterité radicale* (extreme difference)[10] between the signifying chain and the subject. This difference is the difference between the phenomenal positivity of the signifier and the negativity of any subject's position.

The Lacanian lesson on Freud places great emphasis on the question of the rupture inherent in the subject.[11] The unity of the Self is an illusion; there is always a fundamental conflict behind it; a tension of contradictory forces that cancel each other out. This rupture is visible in the very figure of the representation of the subject by one signifier as against the other. As the desire of the subject is the desire of the Other, the signifier, representing the Other, will determine the major orientation of the subject's space – the orientation of the desire-of-the-desire of the Other.

The split in the subject was acutely grasped by Cornelius Castoriadis, who points out that psychoanalysis does not contribute to the "death of man," understood as the final annihilation of the idea of the subject, but rather changes the way the subject is imagined by pointing to the "plurality of subjects contained within the same envelope."[12] An important conclusion arises from this, concerning the subject's space. It is a conclusion that is far from being obvious, and is one that changes our understanding of the individual existence of the subject.

On the one hand, the subject's space is always split, connecting a sum of different fields that are organized by different relations to the Other. On the other hand, it is open to other fields; it can intermingle with them, and can also contain them within itself. In the analytical process the subject's space of the patient will intermingle with the subject's space of the analyst; the patient's space contains the space of the analyst and the analyst's space organizes the patient's space. It gives the analyst the possibility of formulating utterances that represent a patient's unconscious positions. The actual subject of the discourse is thus a double instance, created by the analysand and the analyst. This argument can be extended to more numerous subjectivities: groups, communities, societies, and cultures.

If we read this thesis through the prism of one of the two dictionary definitions of subjectivity, i.e., the subject as a *subiectum*, a substance "tossed" under all possible signifiers, then we must recognize that the structure corresponding to this intuition – whether we are talking about an individual human being, a psychoanalytical dyad, or a discourse, society, or culture as a whole – is defined by the fusing spaces, with the topology belonging to each of them being simultaneously connected and divided by these inner tensions.

As Žižek (1991) notes, it is precisely the attempts to mediatize these tensions that form the timeline. One could also say that surely the subject's space is shaped by attempts to find a kind of stability – to stop the constant collapse under the influence of internal conflict. That is, it strives for a kind of "displacement" of this antagonism. These attempts, always fragile, form a sequence of structurizations that distinguish different types of subjectivity from one another.

Or, in other words, the signifier, while pointing unambiguously to a subject's position, may point to it in different subject's spaces that are contained in a common envelope but are also antagonistic. The ways the signifier refers to other signifiers will then be different, depending on the general structure in which it is considered. Also different will be the sequences of movement – from one signifier to another.

8 Traumatic Encounter: the Placement of the Subject's Position in the Subject's Space

If the transcendental subject, the subject of utterance, finds itself always in a determined position, we can legitimately ask, what is determining it? What places or locates the subject in the particular position in the first place? What makes it so that the subject will be the *tenant-lieu* of this particular position in the space of all possible positions; this particular position and not the other? Yes, we know that the signifier indicates, as the representative, the subject's position. But the signifier doesn't appear in the register of the *real*, in a Lacanian sense. Therefore, we may ask: what is the moment of the *real* that originally locates the subject in its place?

This question can be addressed if we take a look at Lacan's discussion of *tuché* and *automaton* from Seminar XI. He asks: "Where do we meet this real?" (Lacan, 1973, p. 53).[13] The real, we may note, is something met. In this sense, Lacan borrows the Aristotelian concept of tuché, exactly to translate it as the *rencontre du réel* (encounter with the real). And then, developing an important argument where he shows how this encounter is a missed encounter, happening "as if" by chance, he introduces the idea that the encounter with the *real* is always the *traumatic encounter*.[14]

To explain what the traumatic encounter with the *real* means, Lacan chooses the dream of the burning child from Freud's *Traumdeutung*. The father, sleeping after having watched over the body of his dead son, is addressed by him in a dream with the words: "*Vater, siehst du denn nicht, dass ich verbrenne?*" ("Father, can't you see that I am burning?"). We hear the accusation in these words; it may be even stronger in the German formulation than in the English one. All the ethical burden of the repeatedly missed encounters with his son – the missed moment of the fire consuming the dead body seconds ago, the missed moment of the fever some days before, the missed moment of something burning in the child's soul, we don't know when – traumatizes the father and positions him as being the subject of *a traumatic encounter*. This becomes his specific *subject's position*. Lacan comments: "The status of the unconscious, which, as I have shown, is so fragile on the ontic plane, is ethical" (Lacan, 1973, p. 34).

However, the father cannot bear the burden of this subject's position, of the traumatic encounter that occurred in the dream when his son as the Other was admonishing him: "Father!" He awakens and he returns to reality, to the automaton, to the chain of signifiers which will draw the trajectory surrounding the locus of trauma and expanding in the subject's space (Lacan, 1973, p. 58). In this sense, we can speak about the traumatic energy of the encounter with the real, the energy distributed by a chain of signifiers.

In her insightful essay on *Freud, Lacan, and the Ethics of Memory* Cathy Caruth summarizes this discovery:

Lacan resituates the psyche's relation to the real not as a simple matter of seeing or of knowing the nature of empirical events, not as what can be known or what cannot be known about reality, but as the story of an urgent responsibility, or what Lacan defines, in this conjunction, as *an ethical relation to the real*.

(Caruth, 1996, p. 102; emphasis added)

The traumatic encounter with the Other, the moments when the Other came to us with the interpellation, will always stay in our structure of subjectivity. It is the excess energy of this encounter, the energy of the trauma that can never be symbolized, that, at the same time, drives the process of symbolization. It is our *psyche*, the permanent process of the development of trajectories of thoughts, chains of signifiers, which at the same time distribute and dissipate the energy of the traumatic encounter in the subject's space.

The differences of the topologies of particular subject's spaces are determined by the first moments of the symbolization of the traumatic encounter with the real. This phenomenon is sharply captured by Gershom Scholem in one of his essays: "I noticed already, that in such understanding of God that places him in the space of full transcendence, above any designation and excluding any utterance concerning His essence, *a lot depended on the way first steps were comprehended*" (Scholem, 1970, p. 28; emphasis added). The unsymbolizable and thus synonymic traumatic encounters with the *real* will appear in the *symbolic* register as completely different sequences of the movement in the subject's space, generating various chains of signifiers, various trajectories of thoughts, various images of the self.

9 Conclusion

Subject's position, the "lyrical subject," is the mediating term between the concreteness of the subject of a sentence, signifier, and the generality of a substance, a *subiectum*, the carrier of all signifiers. This latter philosophical notion of subject is to be found in the concept of the subject's space. Both terms are a nod to the overwhelming longing inherent in the modern subject to be able to be self-conscious, to actively be one's own helmsman, to have at least a premonition of freedom: a desire unmasked by Lacanian psychoanalysis, yet somehow constitutive of all construction, and perhaps also of all experience of subjectivity.

Let us add one more thing here: the conceptualization introduced here does not lead to the structure of the subject's space itself being "mechanical"; it is not a matter of annihilating the personal character of subjectivity. Rooted in the idea of the traumatic encounter as being the ethical source of subjectivity, and in the spirit of Castoriadis' suggestion, it is rather a matter of extending the way the subject is understood. On the one hand, as it were, "downwards" to the level of the various instances functioning in the individually understood psyche, and, on the other hand, "upwards" to such significant structures as discourse, the political current, the state, the cultural circle, and humanity. Seen from this perspective, psychoanalysis has more in common with the kind of "animism" conceived in Latour's actor-network theory, which assumes a particularly understood agency of each complex social entity over that of reductionist mechanisms.

Notes

1 The words *signifier* and *signifiant* are italicized at first mention in this chapter to underscore their non-intuitive, Lacanian sense. Other terms are thus distinguished too.

2 "Signifier is what represents the subject to another signifier" (Lacan, 2006, p. 820; 1966, p. 819).

3 See Arrivé (1986/1992).

4 "La chaîne des signifiants subsiste dans une altérité radicale par rapport au sujet" (Lacan, 1966, pp. 549–550).

5 Moreover, this primacy is also contained in the fact that it is the *signifiant* lacking-in-Other, the very One towards whom the subject is represented, that gives the signifier the power of meaning. "Le signifiant est prééminent sur le sujet," but on the other hand "S (A/) est le signifiant pour quoi tous les autres signifiants représentent le sujet. Faute du signifiant S (A/), tous les autres ne représenteraient rien" (Lacan, 1966, p. 39 and p. 819).

6 "Le sujet articule la chaîne signifiante" (Lacan, 1966, p. 627).

7 "Le déplacement du signifiant détermine les sujets dans leurs actes" (Lacan, 1966, p. 30).

8 "By presenting himself in the guise of a certain 'taking of a position', the subject can only utter *a discourse of appearances,* if we take into account the truth of his desire" (Dor, 2002, p. 155; emphasis in the original).

9 "Le *je* comme signifiant n'est rien que le *shifter* ou indicatif qui, dans le sujet de l'énoncé, désigne le sujet en tant qu'il parle actuellement" (Lacan, 1966, p. 800).

10 "La chaîne des signifiants subsiste dans une altérité radicale par rapport au sujet" (Lacan, 1966, pp. 549–550).

11 "Le sujet subit une *Spaltung* ou refente de sa subordination au signifiant" (Lacan, 1966, p. 816).

12 "The contribution of psychoanalysis to philosophy need not be sought where it is concerned to reinforce the recently fashionable slogan of the 'death of the subject' …. If psychoanalysis points to anything, it is rather to the multiplicity of subjects contained in the same envelope – and to the fact that each time it is about an instance possessing, in the full sense of the word, the essential attributes of the subject" (Castoriadis, 1997, p. 143).

13 And further: "For what we have in the discovery of psycho-analysis is an encounter, an essential encounter —an appointment to which we are always called with a real that eludes us" (Lacan, 1973, p. 53).

14 "The function of the tuché, of the real as encounter – the encounter in so far as it may be missed, in so far as it is essentially the missed encounter – first presented itself in the history of psycho-analysis in a form that was in itself already enough to arouse our attention, that of the trauma" (Lacan, 1973, p. 54).

References

Arrivé, M. (1992). *Linguistics and Psychoanalysis: Freud, Saussure, Hjelmslev, Lacan and others* (J. Leader, Trans.). John Benjamins Publishing. (Original work published 1986.)

Caruth, C. (1996). *Unclaimed Experience: Trauma, Narrative, and History.* Johns Hopkins University Press.

Castoriadis, C. (1997). Psychanalyse et philosophie: Imagination, imaginaire, reflexion. In *Fait et à faire: Les carrefours du labyrinth.* Le Seuil.

Dor, J. (2002). *Introduction à la lecture de Lacan.* Denoël.

Lacan, J. (1966). *Écrits.* Le Seuil.

Lacan, J. (1973). *Seminaire XI: Les quatre concepts fondamentaux de la psychanalyse.* Le Seuil.

Lacan, J. (2006). *Ecrits: The First Complete Edition in English* (B. Fink, Trans.). W.W. Norton.

PWN (n.d.a). Podmiot. In *Słownik Języka Polskiego PWN.* Retrieved 1 February 2012 from http://www.pwn.pl/?module=multisearch&search=podmiot&submit2=szukaj.

PWN (n.d.b). Podmiot, subiekt, filoz. In *Encyklopedia PWN.* Retrieved 30 May 2023 from https://encyklopedia.pwn.pl/haslo/podmiot;4009554.html.

PWN (n.d.c). Podmiot literacki. In *Encyklopedia PWN.* Retrieved 30 May 2023 from https://encyklopedia.pwn.pl/haslo/podmiot-literacki;3958859.html.

Sartre, J.-P. (1977). *Being and Nothingness. An Essay on Phenomenological Ontology* (H. E. Barnes, Trans.). Washington Square Press. (Original work published 1943.)

Scholem, G. (1970). *Über einige Grundbegriffe des Judentums.* Suhrkamp Verlag.

Žižek, S. (1991). *Looking Awry: An Introduction to Jacques Lacan through Popular Culture.* MIT Press.

Chapter 8

Spacetimeunconscious

Anna J. Secor

1 Water Is Not That Good at Remembering

In the words of Erin Pettit, a glaciologist at the University of Alaska Fairbanks, "[a]s it turns out, water by itself is not actually that good at remembering how to become ice" (Radio Lab, 2017).[1]

What she means is that, as water cools down, as the molecules start to slow their movement, they get a bit closer together, but they don't quite remember how they are supposed to join together into the stable structure of ice. To freeze is not a given.

The very cold molecules need what's called a nucleator, the intrusion of a tiny solid, such as a speck of dust. The solid particle gives the water a structure to mimic. Dropped into the pure, cold water, the nucleator is a reminder and a command: ice.

The best nucleator is ice itself.

There is a remembering and a forgetting. This is not the same remembering and forgetting that might be the property of a human being. Neither does it belong to water. There is knowledge – a matrix, giving rise to what is possible and what is not, what can follow and what must not – and yet there is also a knowledge that does not know itself: the know-how of becoming ice. The nucleator is a molecule whose form itself carries a command (ice!). The knowledge of the angles and relations of solidity that the nucleator conveys is not subjectivized; it is passively registered. When the command comes, it arrives as if from outside (the speck of dust, the snowflake) – but this icing was always possible; it was/is a capacity of water whether known or unknown to it, its past and future.

What is playing out in this drama of the becoming-ice of water? Following feminist quantum physicist and philosopher Karen Barad, we might see in this scene the "ongoing differential articulation of the world" as taking place through a "non-linear enfolding" in which the "past, present and future [are] threaded through one another" (Barad, 2010, pp. 234, 244). This is what Barad calls the "intra-active" becoming of *spacetimematter*, through which the nonlinearity of time is enfolded with the (dis)continuities of space and the responsiveness of matter.

DOI: 10.4324/9781003436188-9

There is also a role for knowledge in this "articulation of the world." Barad's work draws out the philosophical implications of Neils Bohr's epistemological lesson that "our knowledge-making practices are material enactments ... that contribute to, and are part of, the phenomena we describe" (Barad, 2007, p. 247). Matter will be a particle or a wave depending on the apparatus used to measure it. Positions and states are superimposed until observed. The future retrofits the past to correspond with the present. Our knowledge of the world affects the world as we know it. To resituate Lacan's axiom, *there is something of knowledge in the real* (Žižek, 1992).

But there is something funny about the story of water and its icing, for it concerns what water knows, but doesn't know it knows, regarding its own capacities. Not only are water and the nucleator "implicated in various forms of sensing and signalling" (Engelmann & McCormack, 2021, p. 1426; Peters, 2015), but there is something enigmatic in the signal that is transmitted. As Mitch Rose has suggested, signs are "not human constructs organizing the material world into something knowable and meaningful" but enigmatic events that open gaps through which something might pass (Rose, 2021, p. 124; drawing on Kohn, 2013). The nucleator arrives as if from outside to impart what is already known, what has already happened and will not stop happening. The functioning of this unknown knowledge is not reducible to the entanglement of matter and meaning. There is *something else*, not wholly separate from but also not reducible to the discursive-material interplay of observation and measurement: *an unconscious knowledge without a subject.* When the nucleator arrives, the water encounters its own alterity (its capacity for solidity) as a forgotten knowledge that has nonetheless been preserved. The unconscious remembers for – or in the place of – the forgetful substance (Soler, 2014; Lacan, 1975/1998).

Spacetimeunconscious is the parallax between the spatiotemporality of the unconscious (manifest in the psychotopological rotations of dreams and symptoms) and the enfolding of unconscious knowledge with space-timematter (in all its intra-active becoming and quantum indeterminacy). Spacetimeunconscious does not replace spacetimematter or oppose it, but instead arrives as a supplement: "an addition from the outside" that, by "supplying what is missing," is "already inscribed within that to which it is added" (Bernasconi, 2014, p. 19; Derrida, 1967/1997). What follows is an attempt to summon this supplement through a distribution of cuts, a montage of sorts. The result is fragmentary and refers to no totality, lost or to come (Blanchot, 1980/1995). Dreams are folded into other dreams, spaces and times collide and coincide – psychically, molecularly, atmospherically, and traumatically. These fragments are flotsam, skimmed from the surface. We are panning for the unconscious in the real.

2 To Keep Dreaming in Reality

Restage the opening scene. Who will play the water? Who the dust? What will provide the mise-en-scène: a glacier, an asteroid, a myth, a lab?

How about a dream. Let the dream be an asteroid. Let it carry within it a form, a memory, a speck of dust: "The dream waits secretly for the awakening" (Benjamin, 1998, p. 390 [K1a,2]). Maybe we begin dreaming at Auschwitz. Primo Levi recounted his recurrent dream in *The Drowned and the Saved*.

> It is a dream within other dreams, which varies in its details but not in its content. I am seated at the dinner table with my family, or with friends, or at work, or in the countryside – in a surrounding that is, in other words, peaceful and relaxed, apparently without tension and suffering. And yet I feel anguish, an anguish that is subtle but deep, the definite sensation of some threat. And, in fact, as the dream continues, bit by bit or all of a sudden – each time it's different – everything falls apart around me, the setting, the walls, the people. The anguish becomes more intense and pronounced. Everything is now in chaos. I'm alone at the center of a gray, cloudy emptiness, and at once I know what it means, I know that I've always known it: I am once again in the camp, and nothing outside the camp was true. The rest – family, flowering nature, home – was a brief respite, a trick of the sense. Now this inner dream, this dream of peace, is over; and in the outer dream, which continues relentlessly, I hear the sound of a voice I know well: the sound of one word, not a command, but a brief, submissive word. It is the order at dawn in Auschwitz, a foreign word, a word that is feared and expected: "Get up," Wstawać.
>
> (Levi, 1988, pp. 245–255, translation amended;
> quoted in Agamben, 1999, p. 101)

The dream recurs, but it is different every time. The dream does not happen except within another dream, and the dream itself performs a reversal; it turns itself inside out. It is not a question of dream versus reality, but of inner and outer dream. The inner dream crumbles and disintegrates; the pieces of this life (family, flowering, home) are tugged away. These elements are recast as nothing but the hallucinatory satisfactions of a dream; the outer dream to which he must awake is the camp.

As Agamben points us towards in *Remnants of Auschwitz*, this dream recurs in Levi's poem, *At an Uncertain Hour*. It reappears, reversed and redoubled:

> In savage nights, we dreamt teeming, violent dreams with our body and soul: to go back, to eat – to tell. Until we heard the brief and submissive order of dawn: Wstawać. And our hearts were broken in our chests.

Now we have found our homes again; our bellies are full; we have finished telling our tales. It's time. Soon we will once again hear the foreign order: Wstawać.

(Levi, 1988, p. 530; quoted in Agamben, 1999, p. 102)

In the poem, the explicit dream – the one with the full belly, the return home, the telling – first arrives during the savage nights at Auschwitz: its first appearance, a tormented and violent fantasy from which the dreamer is awakened by the morning call of the guards.

But after Auschwitz, the dream doesn't stop arriving, inseparable from the awakening that it precipitates. Blowing across the surface of space and time, the dream encodes the structure of a potentiality, a capacity: a past and a future, a form, an arrangement, a memory, a command. The dream catalyzes an awakening to the dream-structure of (waking) life. Having dreamt at Auschwitz, Levi is subject to the command of the dream – get up – arriving out-of-place and out-of-sequence – and he is commanded to awaken from the inner dream to the outer dream, from the full belly to Auschwitz, once more.

There is also another displacement, after the camp, another awakening. In the passage from *The Drowned and the Saved*, Levi awakens from the inner dream (the dream-within-the-dream) to the outer dream (Auschwitz). But what happens when he awakens from the outer dream, and he is "home"? He awakens in this other room, as the poem implies ("Soon we will once again hear the foreign order"), but what he awakens to is the dream-structure of reality. The full belly, at whatever point it arises, is always a fantasy in the destroyed world after (before, or in the presence of) Auschwitz. Levi wakes, but only to keep dreaming. As Lacan said in his seminar, *The Other Side of Psychoanalysis* (2006/1991, p. 57), "a dream wakes you up just when it might let the truth drop, so that the only reason one wakes up is so as to continue dreaming – dreaming in the real, or to be more exact, in reality."

For Levi, the foreign command continues to awaken him to the potential – the form, the capacity – of the awakening itself. "Wstawać" is the nucleator, the speck of dust that carries the enigmatic message of the substance's own capacity for alterity and displacement: the solid of liquid, the ice of water, the dream of awakening, the outside of the inside of the camp. These are amongst what Marijn Nieuwenhuis and Aya Nassar (2018) might call the perpetual displacements of matter and position that dust manifests and bears witness to. They write: "Dust is the fragment and the fragmented that remains after explosions of established orders and that corrodes the materiality of determined grounds" (Nieuwenhuis & Nassar, 2018, p. 502). What remains after Auschwitz but dust.

3 Spacetimeunconscious, Already There

If psychoanalysis and quantum theory can be made to collide, this is because there is another scene in which they already have. For philosopher and mathematician Arkady Plotnitsky, Bohr and Lacan can be grouped together (alongside Heisenberg and Derrida) as "nonclassical" thinkers who go beyond the "classical" concerns of physics and philosophy to grapple with the manifestations and effects of the unknown and the unknowable. If quantum and psychoanalytical theory converge around the point that "the irreducibly unknowable [is] a constitutive part of knowledge," this interplay is evidence of the contemporaneity of these fields (Plotnitsky, 2002, p. xiv). Without direct connection but exhibiting strange symmetry, Lacan and Bohr orbit the same dense space. Spacetimeunconscious, as a supplement, is an addition of what is already there.

One might also expect to find spacetimeunconscious "already there" in what are now longstanding "more-than-human" concerns for the "redistribution of subjectivity" in the world (Whatmore, 2006, p. 306). But the more-than-human has only rarely been spliced with an unconscious channel (perhaps for fear of a short circuit, given the field's phenomenological underpinnings). Nonetheless, if you listen, there is a hum, like the buzz of a loose or overloaded wire. Incipient passions and alchemical affinities stir the air (Adey, 2015). What is it that buoys the *elemental lure* that Sasha Engelmann (2020) writes of so beautifully? How is something like desire generated in the heating and cooling of molecules, updraft and downdraft, the gathering storm? In his "political ecology of desire," Jared Margulies demonstrates how a more-than-human geography might attune to "the flicker of what would seem to be someone else's speech within our own" (Margulies, 2022, p. 253). Margulies, after all, is interrupted by a cactus, *A. marylanae*. Signalling trans-species extinction anxiety, the cactus (for Margulies) is both a lure for desire and a portent of its end: the thrum of the unconscious in the real.

Yet the parts don't line up neatly, seam to seam. If "more-than-human" suggests an excess (more!), spacetimeunconscious exhibits an affinity for what is *more-or-less*, for the decomposed and the decomposable. Spacetimeunconscious (re)distributes the human and the nonhuman as fragments: unfolds them, flays them, stuffs and stiches them, rearranges them. Composts them.

In this dispersal, spacetimeunconscious is recognizable as a species of the "distributed" notion of the unconscious: an understanding of the unconscious not as submerged in the depths of individual psyches but instead "distributed, spatially, in and beyond the body, and over distance" (Campbell & Pile, 2010, pp. 404, 422; Pile, 1996). As indicated by the Lacanian portmanteau "extimacy" (exterior-intimacy), the unconscious in this sense is not contained or walled off within the bounds of a human or even *the* human

(Kingsbury, 2007; Lacan, 1986/1992; Miller, 1994; Pile, 2014b; Pohl, 2020). Instead, the dislocations and disorientations that are the observable signs of the unconscious are manifest in and through the objects, spaces, and temporalities of the world's unfolding. What enables such a thought of the unconscious, which does not become a "collective unconscious" in the Jungian sense but rather a "distributed" one that is more-than-human? Steve Pile puts forward the argument from Freud's own description of the unconscious as *not only* constituted by repression: "the repressed does not constituted the whole of the unconscious. The unconscious is the more extensive; the repressed is one part of the unconscious" (Freud, 1915/2005, p. 49; quoted in Pile, 2014a, p. 138). From Pile's "distributed unconscious" we arrive at a notion of unconscious knowledge that is not repressed knowledge with reference to a subject, but nonetheless at once "forgotten" and functioning, manifest in its effects in the enfolding of space, time, and matter.

Spacetimeunconscious therefore is none other than a psychoanalytical-geographical understanding of the unconscious. This orientation distinguishes it from other worthy efforts to develop a "preindividual and nonhuman conception of the unconscious" (Lapworth, 2022, p. 3; Searles, 1972). I share Andrew Lapworth's interest in untethering the unconscious from the "individuated substance" or any presumption of enclosure within a matrix of "known identities and dominant representations" (Lapworth, 2022, pp. 3–4). But while Lapworth draws on Gilbert Simondon to elicit an explicitly anti-Freudian concept of "the transindividual unconscious," I begin from the premise that not only are there already grounds for such thought in psychoanalytical geographies, but that, with some gall, this distributed unconscious can be worked over – wedged, pinched, scored and slipped – and moulded into something even less-than-more-than human, the spacetimeunconscious.

To do this, I turn to Lacan's late and less-loved notion of the real unconscious, or the unconscious in the real (Moncayo, 2017; Soler, 2014; Lacan, 1975/1998, 1975/2019a, 2005/2016). I make this turn to the late Lacan because, while the unconscious of spacetimeunconscious remains veined with the extensive Freudian unconscious, a different vocabulary is required to call forth the unconscious in the register of spacetimematter. I find this vocabulary in Lacan's later teachings that elaborate the unconscious not in terms of repressed meaning but as *enigmatic enunciation*: something is articulated in the body that has "a sense beyond meaning" (Moncayo, 2017, p. 57). The nucleator signals, but it is not one in a coherent chain of signifiers. The speck, or even the foreign command, operates without grammar: its effects arise by way of *signifiance* ("signifierness") rather than signification (Fink, 1995). That which has arisen from "the body" (or the material sensorium) but is not directly decipherable to it *returns*, now as its uncanny limit and retro-active cause.[2]

This notion of the unconscious-in-the-real allows us to consider how unknown knowledge outside the symbolic hooks directly into the matter of what happens. While the early Lacan emphasized the unconscious structured like a language, in his later teachings, the real unconscious appears as an "inconsistent multiplicity of differential elements that do not fix meaning ... a vast reserve from which deciphering extracts only some fragments" (Soler, 2014, p. 10). The unconscious is in this sense a knowledge whose effects exceed what is available for interpretation. What emits from the real unconscious (its swarm of unchained signifiers) manifests in the living body and its *jouissance* – that is, its enjoyment as it comes to pass. It is in this sense that Lacan suggests that the signifiers of the unconscious (extracted through the practice of deciphering) do not represent the subject, "but nevertheless affect his *jouissance* as an event of the body" (Lacan, 1975/1998, p. 21). This formulation opens onto the idea of unconscious knowledge without a subject, an unconscious that is manifest (that is, observable) in the body-event (the enigmatic affects) to which its intrusive signifiers (nucleator, Wstawać) give rise. Unknown or unknowable, unconscious knowledge affects the past and arrives from the future, functioning topologically to create folds of time and space (Blum & Secor, 2011). Or to put it another way, spacetimematter enfolds the enigmatic, irreducible message of the unconscious in the real.

4 The Method of the Cut

> The unconscious, in fact, is only ever illuminated and only reveals itself when you look away a little. ... [Y]ou look away and this makes it possible for you to see what is not there.
>
> (Lacan, 1998/2017, p. 15)

There is no (spacetime)unconscious except that there is an interpretive practice that establishes it. Or, as Colette Soler puts it, "[t]he unconscious only responds to the one who summons it" (Soler, 2014, p. xiv). But what is that practice that might summon the spacetimeunconscious? We have close to hand the techniques of psychoanalysis (free association, the interpretation of dreams and parapraxes, and the transference), but it is not all the same between speaking beings and water molecules. A "water clinic" has yet to be invented.

We can experiment. Play around a bit. We do have scissors. "The cut is undoubtedly the most effective mode of psychoanalytical interpretation," said Lacan (2013/2019b, p. 485). One of Lacan's clinical innovations was "scansion," or the practice of breaking off analytic sessions at variable moments. "Cutting, punctuating, or interrupting the analysand's discourse," scansion is a practice of listening for breaks and slips, just as one might scan a verse by listening to its rhythm and marking its meter (Fink, 1999, p. 229). As psychoanalyst Vanessa Sinclair writes in *Scansion in Psychoanalysis and Art: The Cut in Creation*, scansion is not only "another 'royal road' to the unconscious, like free association and dreams," but also a technique of artists and others who use methods of cutting and splicing to disrupt the expected (Sinclair, 2020, p. 6). Sinclair traces "the cut" (including techniques of interruption, collage, montage, and assemblage) across photography, film, poetry, painting, sculpture, music, body art, performance, and digital art forms. Intellectually and aesthetically, scansion and the coming into being of the psychoanalytic unconscious are intertwined, Sinclair shows, with the punctum of the photograph, the de-familiarization practiced in the avant-garde movements of Dadaism and Cubism, and features of uncanniness and derangement within Surrealism and the digital. Cutting, repeating, distorting. Folding in, hollowing out, arraying, layering, inter-splicing.

Perhaps the most proliferating method of the cut in geography is "montage" (Cresswell, 2019; Doel, 1999; Doel & and Clarke, 2007; Pred, 2014; and see *you are here*, issue xvii: *The Montage Effect*, 2014). As James Riding and Carl Dahlman suggest, montage may be especially suitable for representing complex and unsettled "immaterial–material, representational–non-representational, and human–nonhuman spaces" (Riding & Dahlman, 2022, p. 282). Having arisen in film to refer to the cutting and splicing of discontinuous scenes, montage has traversed its origins to become a method for art and writing as well (Willerslev & Suhr, 2013). By disrupting continuity and juxtaposing heterogenous elements, montage both breaks the surface of the world and creates new associations. In the hands of creative geographers, it has been a means to grasp the fleeting time and contracting space of modernity, the overlay of past and present, and the potentialities of place-writing (Hawkins, 2014). For Marcus Doel, montage-and-geography fractures the order of things to "open up a spliced splacing that is twisted and tortuous": a space that is cut from itself, displaced from the place where it appears, an after-effect of its own future (Doel, 2014, p. 12).

Montage offers a way to proceed, to speak without recourse to an established order but instead with the "generative instability" of the cut (McLean, 2013, p. 59). But there is not a simple consensus about what montage generates, and not all versions of montage are suitable for the summoning at hand. For some, montage signals not a cut but a suture: a promise that a new or hidden totality will be revealed. This whole may be presumed to have preceded the tearing up or to be constituted by the montage itself. Indeed, for Allan Pred, "[t]o be for montage/is *not* to be for pastiche/for a jumble of atomistic elements/for a whimsical hotchpotch/to which there is nothing more." Rather, "[t]o be for montage/is to be for a totality of fragments/in which the p(r)o(s)etics of the textual strategy/are the politics of the textual strategy./Consciously, rather than by unreflected default" (Pred, 2014, p. 27). This is a very sensible montage. Strategic. Conscious. It is hard to imagine anything slipping through the cracks.

There are different ways to cut and paste, and different ends. The space-timeunconscious is neither an unrevealed depth nor ground of meaning, but an aspect of how "materialism, in all its forms, exceeds materialism" (Grosz,

2017, p. 5). It is the functioning of unconscious knowledge in the ongoing articulation of the world. The method of its summoning, its *interpretation*, is the cut. Since the (spacetime)unconscious is manifest as its mode of address, *the cut (technique) is itself the locus of the encounter at stake in the cutting.* The cut is "agential": provisionally materializing subject-object, interior-exterior (Barad, 2007). There is nothing to "encounter" except these "cuts that cut (things) together-apart (one move)" (Barad, 2015, p. 406). And on the cutting room floor: scraps of the spacetimeunconscious.

The fragmentary text of spacetimeunconscious "is the pulling to pieces (the tearing) of that which never preexisted (really or ideally) as whole, nor can it ever be reassembled in any future presence whatever" (Blanchot, 1980/ 1995, p. 60). The text as reconfiguring both the past and the future of its "parts" (Barad, 2015). Its fragments are parts that resist totality (Adorno, 1970/1997, as quoted in Hill, 2012). Resistance takes the form of abrupt shifts, refusals, evasions, non-response, whimsy.

In the cracks and gaps between these resisting parts, it may be possible to catch a glimpse of what is enigmatic in how space, time, and matter enfold – that is, to conjure some indications of the spacetimeunconscious. Jacques-Alain Miller maintains that, while the symbolic unconscious might be approached by imitating its own practices (interpretation, punctuation), an analysis approaching the irreducible opacity of the *real unconscious* calls for something other, a post-interpretive practice that "takes its bearings on the cut," functioning against the grain and looping back on itself (Miller, 2007, p. 8). The fragments are events, poetry, literature, and film. The fragments themselves decohere, shedding bits of dust, sparks, floating words, strange feelings. These are the messages. They at once emit from and cause temporal and spatial jolts, twists, sink holes: "What happens when ground gives way?" (Nieuwenhuis & Nassar 2017, n.p.; Kingsbury & Secor, 2021; Landau et al., 2021). In what elapses between fragments, in the *lapsus* of their continuous discontinuity, it may be possible to intercept the signal of the spacetimeunconscious.

5 Rooms Are Haunted by Other Rooms

The unconscious, in its timelessness – in the deathless persistence of its knowledge – is well known to emit breaches into the linearity of time (Freud, 1915/2005; Johnston, 2005; Laplanche, 2017). The ur-case appears in Freud's unpublished 1895 text, *A Project for a Scientific* Psychology (Freud, 1950 [1895]/1966). A young woman, Emma, has come to Dr Freud with a symptom: she will no longer visit shops alone. Her symptom arose following a recent incident in which she entered a shop. The shopkeepers were laughing. She imagined they were laughing at her clothes and found herself inexplicably aroused (Freud calls this scene 1). Scene 1 appears senseless until Freud connects it to something (not repressed but psychically disconnected) that happened to Emma as a child. As a child, she went to a shop alone and was sexually assaulted through her clothes by a shopkeeper. That is scene 2. By the calendar it happened first, but as far as Emma's symptom is concerned, it "happens" (that is, starts to have an effect) *after* the enigmatic incident of laughter in the shop when she is an adult. It is when scene 1 resonates retroactively with scene 2 that the symptom emerges. She did not stop going to shops after the assault in her childhood. She stopped going to shops in the future, when a present event – they laugh (a speck of dust) – called forth a form in the past, a potential arrangement that inhered within the situation but was inchoate, known but unknown. Emma's trauma is not past, present or future, but the resonance between them. This is the action of the *Nachträglichkeit*, translated as *après-coup*, or "afterwardness," in which the chronologically second scene of trauma functions psychically as the first (Laplanche, 2017). The message arrives and we know what we knew all along. Emma jolts awake in order to keep dreaming, Emma doesn't go to shops alone anymore – she dreams on.

The *après-coup* signals the nonlinearity of time, yet the dreamer awakens not only in the folds of time, but in the darkness of a space at once familiar and all wrong (Blum & Secor, 2014). The dreamer fumbles in the dark, crashing into a shrouded object, the implacable obstacle. The dreamer, awakened, stretches out her hands. She feels a wall where the door should be. This is the case for the young Viennese woman known as Anna O. who, in 1881, was being treated by Freud's colleague, Josef Breuer, for symptoms such as paraphasia, paralyses, disturbances in vision and somnambulism. It is Anna O. who names Breuer's method the "talking cure," and it is also she who culminates the treatment: with a phantom pregnancy, Breuer's (non)baby. Until this awkward ending, during the course of her hysteria, Anna O., day by day, was re-experiencing the corresponding events of the year before, of 1880. This folding of time is something that Freud also notes in two other cases, calling it an "abreaction of arrears" (Freud & Breuer, 1893/2000, p. 9). But for Anna O., there is more than a temporal doubling; Anna O. is also lost in space. In 1881, Anna O. is in a new house; her family had moved following the death of her father the previous year. And now, each day, in Breuer's words,

> She was carried back to the previous year with such intensity that in the new house she hallucinated her old room, so that when she wanted to go to the door she knocked up against the stove which stood in the same relation to the window as the door did in the old room.
>
> (p. 33)

Anna O. stumbles in the dark, walking into the stove in search of a door, on the wrong side of her own doubled world.

The shop is another shop; the room contains the contours of another room. Before coming to "embody the mysteries of quantum mechanics"

(Barad, 2007, p. 255), the message of superposition (of times, spaces, states) arrived too early. Superposition refers to how waves (of any number) can occupy the same point in space. It is what makes the finding that particles are also waves – established by the famous two-slit experiment and its modified versions – paradoxical, for it requires accepting the reality of something see-mingly impossible: that particles (matter) *also* occupy the same space at the same time, until their superposition is resolved by observation. And that is only the beginning of how quantum indeterminacy requires rethinking com-monsense notions of time, space, and matter. Think of Schrödinger's cat, hovering in the superposed states of dead and alive until the box is opened. Anna O. lives in two times and spaces. It is 1881, her father has died, and she is being impregnated by words. It is also 1880, and the event of her father's death is unaccomplished, the past is still unfolding in the present and the traumatic event is deferred to the future (Fernando, 2023).

Anna O.'s room is haunted – by another room. How many rooms can haunt a room? Is there a limit? Perhaps not. Certainly, for Marcel Proust, rooms are haunted by a multiplicity of other rooms. In the famous awaken-ing that opens the first volume of *In Search of Lost Time*, it is as though every room in which the body has slept is retained as a kind of corporeal sense-memory. It is only when the waking person settles upon an answer to the question "where am I?" that both the room and thereby the subject are snatched from the multiplicity of places and times within which they circulate to become the singular present of the awakening. Proust writes:

A sleeping man holds in a circle around him the sequence of the hours, the order of the years and worlds. He consults them instinctively as he wakes and reads in a second the point on the earth he occupies, the time that has elapsed before his waking; but their ranks can be mixed up, broken. ... But it was enough if, in my own bed, my sleep was deep and allowed my mind to relax entirely; then it would let go of the map of the place where I had fallen asleep and, when I woke in the middle of the night, since I did not know where I was, I did not even understand in the first moment who I was ... [W]hen I woke thus, my mind restlessly attempting, without success, to discover where I was, everything revolved around me in the darkness, things, countries, years. My body, too benumbed to move, would try to locate, according to the form of its fatigue, the position of its limbs so as to deduce from this the direction of the wall, the placement of the furniture, so as to reconstruct and name the dwelling in which it found itself. Its memory, the memory of its ribs, its knees, its shoulders, offered in succession several of the rooms where it had slept, while around it the invisible walls, changing place according to the shape of the imagined room, spun through the shadows.

(Proust, 1913/2002, p. 5)

There is a memory that is not thought. It inheres in the parts: the ribs, the knees and shoulders, the fatigue, the arrangement. This recalls Ben Anderson and John Wylie's description of the phenomenological enfolding of body, space, and affect: "Corporeal perception and sensation is thus an incorporation of matter into the connective tissues and affective planes of a body subject" (Anderson & Wylie, 2009, p. 324). Ribs, knees, shoulders: the room, the name, the time and place are deduced from these "intimate collections of material sensations where other dreams of presence (dreams of who we are, of where we belong, and of how we get on with life) are consigned" (Rose, 2006, p. 539). These corporeal parts and affects are fragments of differential capacities called forth in their dynamic intra-action not only in the moment, but with a multiplicity of times and places. They are imbued with traces of past forms: with rooms and other rooms that persist in the unthought of their proprioceptive responsiveness. Nothing decays or dies, as if every moment of Rome continued to exist in Rome, unruined.

In Proust's narrative, awakening is like a magnet, pulling in and reassembling the dispersed, re-narrativizing (Get up! Ice!). Awaken to keep dreaming; this dream is reality. Awaken (dream on) in order not to fly to pieces, to put in order what is in fact without a chain, to return dogmatically to an ideal of the wakeful, intentional subject (Harrison, 2009). For Proust, the obsessive bourgeois, the room reassembles itself. Doors and windows and beds and the angle of the light: all of these are recovered and in turn work together to recover the present moment, to resolve the superposition (to collapse the wave function). Discrete positions are established and recorded: x, y, z, and t for time. Objects are reoriented. A determined "reality" is recuperated from the indeterminacy of the real.

For Anna O., this operation proceeds differently, hysterically, and she stumbles about her bedroom of 1880 day after day in 1881 – until she is impregnated by the talking-cure that she has talked into existence. Anna O.'s awakening is not localized in space and time; it extends across different spaces and times, irreducibly. "The past was never simply there to begin with and the future is not simply what will unfold: the past and the future are iteratively reworked through the iterative practices of spacetimemattering," writes Barad (2007, p. 315) in her explanation of the "quantum eraser experiment," in which it is shown that the paths taken by photons are entangled with how they come to be observed – *interpreted* – in the future. As Jacques-Alain Miller puts it, the paradox is that the unconscious *is* its interpretation. The unconscious interprets: Anna O. travels in time and space, Anna O. is pregnant. For Anna O., there is no Bayesian interpretation (probabilistically, it will be this or that). *Her* interpretation knocks up against the real of superposition.

6 The Rotation of the Stars

Inexorable. They always return to the same place. Little cuts in the fabric of the night, these "slits are what allow us to map the real" (Lacan 2013/2019b, p. 480).

Another rotation, another cut. It is the twenty-first century and an awakening. No walls, no ceiling, no room. The one who dreams and wakes is a Syrian refugee, homeless in İstanbul, Türkiye. It is the cold winter of January 2014. The untitled film is a five-minute video in three takes, directed by Ali Ali, who also acts (camera by Imad Hussin and Nour Ali, editing by Markus Schmidt).[3] It was produced as part of a series of workshops called Searching Traces organized by the Goethe-Institut and the cultural initiative Diyalog in İstanbul in December 2014. One of these workshops trained young adults like Ali to make short films documenting or creatively reflecting upon their experiences of displacement in İstanbul.

> The opening shot is of a corner framed by two concrete walls and a patch of scrubby grass, some litter, and the sound of wind.
>
> A few flakes of snow trace wild paths in the air. From the left, a figure shuffles into the frame. With a beige-orange floral blanket pulled around his shoulders, all that is visible of the person are his bare feet in slip-on plastic sandals and his knit cap pulled low over his ears. He settles into the corner, pulling the blanket around himself against the cold.
>
> He has a small plastic bag from which he begins to pull some pieces of something, (perhaps bread) to gnaw on. The camera has not moved, maintaining its gaze at the corner where the man huddles, eats. The bag, now empty, is sucked back under the blanket, which the man pulls ever closer, then up so high that only the top of his cap is visible. When he reemerges, he has lit a cigarette. Propped against the wall as though perhaps in a bed, he holds the blanket across himself with his left hand, smokes with his right. He begins to cough, a racking, rattling deep cough. A couple more shallow puffs through the coughing and he tosses the half-smoked cigarette in the grass. He gets slowly to his feet and the camera follows him as he trudges along the gray wall, which slopes down to reveal that this little patch of grass and concrete is below street level, part of a sloping hill into which another building is cut. There is the sound of traffic horns. The man crawls under the overhanging roof of the building, pulls a big rock over for a pillow, and lies down in a narrow strip of grass against the wall. He coughs convulsively, pulling the blanket around himself, up under his chin, until he settles into sleep.
>
> The cold scene fades to a new, golden-orange pallet (the colors of the blanket). We hear delicate piano music as a new scene comes into focus. Another corner, this one of smooth peach-colored walls. A bed tucked into the corner. A pillow on the bed. The same blanket, with someone under it, on the bed. The man in the knit cap emerges from the blanket.

He sits up. The blanket falls back – he is not cold. Looking around himself in confusion, he strokes the wall, leaving his hand resting flat upon it while the music swells, female vocals. He feels the pillow. And then lies back down, pulling the blanket over himself once more.

There is a sound like a shot (POP) and the bedroom is gone, he is back on the patch of grass, his head on a rock. The snow flurry has picked up. He huddles, writhes, and weeps. He pulls out and lights another cigarette. He whimpers while he smokes and pulls the blanket around himself. But he can only take a few puffs before he starts coughing again. He tosses the cigarette and retreats under the blanket. The screen cuts to black.

Like the dream of the burning child (Freud, 1900), like Levi's dream of the full belly, the untitled video embeds two awakenings: one to a world in which the loss is restored, one to the world in which it is not. The man huddles against the edges of a bordered patch of grass, as though seeking a sense of enclosure, but he is still cold and exposed. In the next take, he wakes to run his hand over the interior wall. He strokes it, feeling its difference, the smooth texture of a dream. A sound (POP) returns him to the cold patch of grass, the stone pillow. The POP (maybe reminiscent of a gunshot) is what is invoked to "entwine materiality and sensibility, the world and the self, things and words, through the forms of a summons, a directive, a questioning – an *imperative*" (Anderson & Wylie, 2009, p. 325; emphasis in the original). But what is summoned, what is imperative, is not just an entwining. There is splitting, dissociation.

The dream of the untitled film is like an inverse of the trauma-dream. The one who is displaced and homeless in İstanbul returns in sleep to a coherence – between blanket, bed, pillow, walls, sleep, subject – that is *no longer* or *not yet*. He awakens not to a reassembling room but to roomlessness. Both seeking and resisting its own coming into being, the unbearable calamity dismembers the present and forestalls future (Fernando, 2023). For the unnamed man of the unnamed film, this calamity is now, and the present moment is breaking down. In the unravelling of processes differentiation and integration in the present, "experience takes on strange qualities, of fragmentation but also of lack of the usual boundaries between self, other, and various features of perception and feeling" (p. 34).

An interruption, a signal: the aural POP both links and separates stone/pillow, here/there, now/then, Ali/Ali, distributing them to the edges of intelligibility: one to each side of a single-sided figure, distinct but not separable. This is the topological figure of the Möbius, familiarly represented as the rotation of a twisted loop, in which whatever moves slips from one side to the other meets itself in reverse. In fact, since the real topology of a Möbius is two-dimensional, the thing that slips (that is, whatever point of the surface) is always the same place as its reversed self. It is a field of doppelgängers. Mathematically speaking, it is a non-orientable surface.

POP – and it is another rotation, disorienting. The Möbius dynamizes the unconscious: "its space start[s] to move, and what's more, doesn't cease to be in movement" (Bursztein, 2017, p. 61). Psychotopology is a spatialization of time: not just of what is timeless in repetition, but also of its durational acting out that circles around the edge of the real and returns something reversed and uncanny, never quite the same (Blum & Secor, 2011, 2014; Friedman & Tomsic, 2016; Kingsbury, 2007). The Möbius rotation circles the split; its torsion is the cut of irreducible difference within the same (Lacan, 1986/1992; Pile, 2014b). The rotation is disorienting. The film is another dream and this telling yet another; each circles the same hole and returns as its own minimal difference. None of this is representable except projected and dissected: snip, splay, pin to the medium.

Distortion is all there is. Objects (stone, pillow, wall, grass, blanket, cigarette, bread) alternate in their presence and absence, transform "from being locatable in reality to being unlocatable in the Real" (Pohl, 2020, p. 81). This is what Lucas Pohl calls an "object-disoriented ontology," in which "the non-place of the object leads to the ontological disorientation of the subject" (p. 74). And it is not only the non-place of the object, but the non-place of place, and the non-time of time, that troubles the one who loops through a nightmare. "The clock is thus also a compass" (Peters, 2015, p. 214). Lost or broken, the objects withdraw, do not give of themselves, become recalcitrant (Rose, 2011); the landscape watches the subject vanish (Wylie, 2007). Displacement, or becoming unlocatable in the real, is the "geo-trauma" (Pain, 2021; Ehrkamp et al., 2019, 2022) that fragments and distributes Levi and Ali across the folds of time and space and in relation to the objects that are supposed to (re)orient them to the here-now.

Not even the stars are where they seem to be. "*LIGHTS ALL ASKEW IN THE HEAVENS*" read the headline of a special cable to the *New York Times* on November 10, 1919, after an eclipse verified Einstein's predictions based on his theory of relativity. "Stars Not Where They Seemed or Were Calculated to Be, But Nobody Need Worry," read the subheading.[4] They are also not *when* they appear to be, what with the time it takes for their light to become visible to us. Some might even be already dead, inverted into black holes. But nobody need worry. Like the dead father in the dream (Freud, 1900; Lacan, 2013/2019b), the light that continues to travel from the star knows nothing of its death. And anyhow from our great distance and from within the blip of our temporal being, they appear not as objects but as cuts, as a map of something real, as wishing wells.

7 The Lightning Knew Nothing of the Ground

The dream is the lighting flash that reveals the darkness, that traces a boundary between what is illuminated and what is not. The lightning is that which conjoins the darkness and the illumination, the sky and the earth, the storm cloud and the ground. It is itself an articulating edge, linking divergent, communicating series, but with a twist:

> Lightning … distinguishes itself from the black sky but must also trail it behind, as though it were distinguishing itself from that which does not distinguish itself from it. It is as if the ground rose to the surface, without ceasing to be ground.
>
> (Deleuze, 1968/1994, p. 28)

Like a foetus in the womb, lightning is a "discontinuity that emerges in the midst of continuity" (Kristeva, 1985, p. 254). This continuous separation initiates the (im)possibility of distinguishing a subject, an object. The lightning bolt emerges as a "response to difference," but the "cut" of differentiation does not separate out an independent or autonomous entity (Barad, 2015, p. 398). What is "on the other side" remains entangled within an intra-action of mutual constitution (Barad, 2007, p. 393). Like the dream and the awakening that it embeds, lightning traces the conjoining edge between contradictory states: "something 'passes' between the borders, events explode, phenomena flash" (Deleuze, 1968/1994, p. 118).

Both Barad (2011, 2015) and Vicki Kirby (2011), drawing upon each other's work, toy with lightning: the play between the build-up of negative charge in a storm cloud, its drive to discharge, and the responsiveness of the ground. They write of the multiple glancing attempts ("stepped leaders") of the charged electrons to find a conductive path to the earth, and the rise of reciprocating filaments from the ground. The lightning bolt is the discharge that happens in the connection For Barad, the story is one of yearning and seduction: "Lightning is an energizing play of a desiring field" (Barad, 2015, p. 38). For Kirby, what transpires is a "sort of stuttering chatter between the ground and the sky" (Kirby, 2011, p. 10). Both authors quote lightning expert Martin Uman when he notes that the stepped leaders (the electrons seeking discharge) do not begin with "knowledge" of the earth; the message comes from a spark traveling upwards, and the lightning bolt is what happens when "'awareness' occurs" (Uman, 1986, 49–50; quoted in Kirby, 2011, p. 11). If the bolt of lightning is the edge of the Möbius (light-dark, sky-ground, negative-positive), the spark called forth from the ground is the twist.

What does it mean to talk about desire and chatter (and stuttering) in the context of charged electrons seeking connection with the ground? Are these just personifications, the projection of human yearnings and repetitions onto things that cannot be thought to desire or to chatter? Or do these observations suggest a crossing over, an "awareness occurring" in between? For Lacan, speaking subjects chatter and desire (and stutter – or repeat) as a way of papering over the twin traumas of alienation and separation (their "cut" from the field of their emergence). But speaking beings aren't the only split entities, reality is "made up of cuts, including and going far beyond the cuts made by language" (Lacan, 2013/2019b, p. 397). Is it so far-fetched to suggest that electrons too are agitated by their own alterity? As Barad explains, blipping and birthing in/of the void, the electron is in a perpetual state of discontinuous continuity: cut and uncut, engaged in an ongoing "encounter with the infinite alterity of the self" (Barad, 2015, p. 399). No wonder it yearns and chatters, gets stuck, repeats and crosses over.

Transit between fields requires experimentation. We can test out the possibilities, gesture towards multiple conductive channels until something sparks. Paths proliferate. Only one needs to work out for the accomplishment of the aim. The spark transmits "awareness" (of the earth, of the possibility of lightening). The flashes of desire and. chatter fade out. The message (spark) that allows lightning (or more accurately, the charged field that will become lightning) to accomplish its discharge (to become a lightning bolt) is a portent that the charged field has itself called forth, unknowingly. It is not just the bolt itself that transits between sky and earth, (re)distributing the darkness and the light, but also the enigmatic affects, unchained signifiers, and looped messages that called it forth and that follow in its wake.

8 Elemental Media, Wonky Transistor

There is chatter. Some of it is empty, but some seems to be part of the unfolding of both matter and meaning across interlocking phenomena, well beyond (and calling into question) what passes for human (Peters, 2015; Barad, 2007). The media of this communication are manifold and more-than-human, fields of transmission that range from the biogenetic or the sedimentary to the atmospheric. As Sasha Engelmann and Derek McCormack write, "[t]his means that sky, sea and fire are message bearing systems of a kind, offering signs, signals or portents of things to come" (Engelmann & McCormack, 2021, pp. 1426–1427). It also means that there is a more-than-human distribution of capacities for the reception and interpretation of these signals. As physicist David Bohm (1990, pp. 284–285) writes, "even an electron has at least a rudimentary mental pole," evident in how it participates in "unfolding the meaning of the information that is implicit in the quantum field."

"We must be careful not to understand" (Lacan, 2013/2019b, p. 424). A form that is comprehensible from one position is not necessarily so from another. Understanding is limited to what is phenomenologically available, what is sensible, from a particular position. "I am trying to get you to go a bit beyond by inviting you to stop trying to understand," says Lacan to his students. "It is in this regard that I am not a phenomenologist" (p. 415). Not even the electron knows what it knows or what it is capable of.

There are gaps. Something doesn't line up. Relays in the elemental field backfire, become twisted and uncanny. It is not only sensible information but unconscious knowledge that is transmitted in and through the message-bearing systems of an unfolding spacetimematter. For Bohr, the electron's "mental pole" emerges as both a cause and effect of how it "unfolds" – interprets or responds to – the enigmatic messages it encounters. But the call comes from inside the house (Walton, 1979). An electron emits a photon, progeny of its self-touching, and then reabsorbs it (Barad, 2012, 2015). Water encounters its doppelgänger and transitions. A swarm of spurting, pooling, charged electrons call forth their own dark precursor (Deleuze, 1994). Like in a time travel film or in analysis itself, the message to the subject is the subject's own (Žižek, 2000). Operating the elemental media, space-timeunconscious is a demonic transistor, working a relay that runs on reversal, estrangement, and misalignment. The disturbance goes both ways. As media studies scholar John Durham Peters muses, "[i]f it is a mistake to think that nature is a subject that speaks intentionally, might it not also often be a mistake to think the same of humans?" (Peters, 2015, p. 318).

While the particle exercises its "mental pole," the dreamer particulates. Theoretical cosmologist and particle physicist Chanda Prescod-Weinstein writes, "I know that my brain is a quark and electron collection. These particles are not just a Black child dreaming," but also "all the things that a Black child is made out of" (Prescod-Weinstein, 2021, p. 18). In response to the quantum physics-derived premise that "knowing is a distributed practice that includes the larger material arrangement" (Barad, 2007, p. 379), the distributed unconscious of psychoanalytical geography improvises. Yes, and there is also a distributed not-knowing of knowledge, a confounding and a dreaming, inherent to this distributed practice of knowing. "The 'mind' is a specific material configuration of the world, not necessarily coincident with a brain," says the physicist (Barad, 2007, p. 379). Yes, and the configuration of the world (of the room or prison or cold stone wall, of the sky or sea or void) is an unconscious-material unfolding that never coincides with itself, rejoins the psychotopologist.

The spacetimeunconscious flickers in the gap between the tense sky and the interested earth, between ice and Auschwitz. It twists (tosses and turns) between the dream and the awakening. It glitches in the blur between Levi and Ali, and hums in the void of (re)birthing electrons and Anna O's phantom pregnancy. The stars (or slits) are dead (or dust), "disjunctive constellations" (Highmore, 2020). The cuts proliferate. Therein dreams a dream without a dreamer.

*

Speck, spark, Wstawać, POP. The shopkeepers laugh, quarks go mental, and Anna O. bumps into her dresser.

These are conjured scraps. They're different in kind and don't add up. Circling the hole where the spacetimeunconscious ex-ists, these are the "equivocations that produce explosions, sudden changes of trajectory" from which analytic work takes its bearings (Brousse, 2019, p. 46). They are intrusive signifiers that have fallen off the chain of meaning but are full of "signifierness." Metaphors that generate no meaning, displacements that bring forth no being, they unleash enigmatic affects: strange yearnings, inexplicable repulsions, uncanny half-recognitions. They are the emanations of an unknown knowledge in the real.

These specks are waves: transmissions of the spacetimeunconcious.

Notes

1 This chapter was first published in *Dialogues in Human Geography* (https://journa ls.sagepub.com/doi/10.1177/20438206231191763) under Open Access Gold, Creative Commons 4.0.
2 See also the "quasi-cause" (Deleuze, 1990), explained topologically in Cockayne et al. (2020).
3 The video can be accessed here: http://streetwalking.inenart.eu/archives/3017.
4 Accessible here from the *New York Times* to subscribers: https://timesmachine. nytimes.com/timesmachine/1919/11/10/issue.html

References

Adey, P. (2015). Air's Affinities: Geopolitics, Chemical Affect and the Force of the Elemental. *Dialogues in Human Geography*, 5(1), 54–75.
Adorno, T. W. (1997). *Aesthetic Theory* (R. Hullot-Kentor, Trans.). A&C Black. (Original work published 1970.)
Agamben, G. (1999). *Remnants of Auschwitz: The Witness and the Archive.* Zone Books.
Anderson, B., & Harrison, P. (2010). The Promise of Non-representational Theories. In P. Harrison and B. Anderson (Eds.), *Taking-Place: Non-Representational Theories and Geography.* Ashgate.
Anderson, B., & Wylie, J. (2009). On Geography and Materiality. *Environment and Planning A*, 41(2), 318–335.
Barad, K. (2007). *Meeting the Universe Halfway.* Duke University Press.
Barad, K. (2010). Quantum Entanglements and Hauntological Relations of Inheritance: Dis/continuities, Spacetime Enfoldings, and Justice-to-Come. *Derrida Today*, 3(2), 240–268.
Barad, K. (2011). Nature's Queer Performativity. *Qui Parle: Critical Humanities and Social Sciences*, 19(2), 121–158.
Barad, K. (2012). On Touching: The Inhuman That Therefore I Am. *Differences*, 23 (3), 206–223.
Barad, K. (2015). Transmaterialities: Trans*/Matter/Realities and Queer Political Imaginings. *GLQ: A Journal of Lesbian and Gay Studies*, 21(2–3), 387–422.
Benjamin, W. (1998). *The Arcades Project* (H. Eiland & K. McLaughlin, Trans.). Belknap Press of Harvard University Press. (Original work published 1972.)
Bernasconi, R. (2014). Supplement. In C. Colebrook, (Ed.), *Jacques Derrida: Key Concepts.* Routledge.

Blanchot, M. (1995). *The Writing of the Disaster* (A. Smock, Trans.). University of Nebraska Press. (Original work published 1980.)

Blum V., & Secor, A.J. (2011). Psychotopologies: Closing the Circuit between Psychic and Material Space. *Environment and Planning D: Society and Space*, 29(6), 1030–1047.

Blum, V., & Secor, A.J. (2014). Mapping Trauma: Topography to Topology. In P. Kingsbury and S. Pile (Eds), *Psychoanalytic Geographies*. Routledge.

Bohm, D. (1990). A New Theory of the Relationship of Mind and Matter. *Philosophical Psychology*, 3(2–3), 271–286.

Brousse, M-H. (2019). What is Real? A Dialogue between Quantum Physicists and Psychoanalysts on Real and Matter. *The Lacanian Review*, 7, 11–64.

Bursztein, J-G. (2017). *The Unconscious, Its Space-Time: Aristotle, Lacan, Poincaré* (R. Klein, Trans.). Hermann.

Campbell, J., & Pile, S. (2010). Telepathy and its Vicissitudes: Freud, Thought Transference and the Hidden Lives of the (Repressed and Non-repressed) Unconscious. *Subjectivity*, 3(4), 403–425.

Cockayne, D. G., Ruez, D., & Secor, A.J. (2020). Thinking Space Differently: Deleuze's Möbius Topology for a Theorisation of the Encounter. *Transactions of the Institute of British Geographers*, 45(1), 194–207.

Cresswell, T. (2019). *Maxwell Street: Writing and thinking place*. University of Chicago Press.

Deleuze, G. (1990). *The Logic of Sense* (M. Lester, Trans.) Columbia University Press. (Original work published 1969.)

Deleuze, G. (1994). *Difference and Repetition* (P. Patton, Trans.). Columbia University Press. (Original work published 1968.)

Derrida, J. (1997). *Of Grammatology* (G. Chakravorty Spivak, Trans.). Johns Hopkins University Press. (Original work published 1967.)

Doel, M.A. (1999). *Poststructuralist Geographies: The Diabolical Art of Spatial Science*. Rowman & Littlefield.

Doel, M.A. (2014). Montage *and* Geography, or Splicing Splace. *you are here: The Journal of Creative Geography, Issue XVII: The Montage Effect*, 17, 7–13.

Doel, M.A., & Clarke, D.B. (2007). Afterimages. *Environment and Planning D: Society and Space*, 25(5), 890–910.

Ehrkamp, P., Loyd, J.M., & Secor, A.J. (2019). Embodiment and Memory in the Geopolitics of Trauma. In K. Mitchell, R. Jones, & J.L. Fluri (Eds.), *Handbook on Critical Geographies of Migration*. Edward Elgar Publishing.

Ehrkamp, P., Loyd, J.M., & Secor, A.J. (2022). Trauma as Displacement: Observations from Refugee Resettlement. *Annals of the American Association of Geographers*, 112(3), 715–722.

Engelmann, S. (2020). *Sensing Art in the Atmosphere: Elemental Lures and Aerosolar Practices*. Routledge.

Engelmann, S., & McCormack, D. (2021). Elemental Worlds: Specificities, Exposures, Alchemies. *Progress in Human Geography*, 45(6), 1419–1439.

Fernando, J. (2023). *A Psychoanalytic Understanding of Trauma: Post-traumatic Mental Functioning, the Zero Process, and the Construction of Reality*. Routledge.

Fink, B. (1995). *The Lacanian Subject: Between Language and Jouissance*. Princeton University Press.

Fink, B. (1999). *A Clinical Introduction to Lacanian Psychoanalysis: Theory and Technique*. Harvard University Press.

Freud, S. (1953). The Interpretation of Dreams. In *The Standard Edition of the Complete Psychological Works of Sigmund Freud*, Vols. 4–5 (J. Strachey, Ed. & Trans.). The Hogarth Press. (Original work published 1900.)

Freud, S. (1966). Project for a Scientific Psychology. In *The Standard Edition of the Complete Psychological Works of Sigmund Freud*, Vol. 1 (J. Strachey, Ed. & Trans.). The Hogarth Press. (Original work published 1950 [1895].)

Freud, S. (2005). The Unconscious. In *The Unconscious*. Penguin Books. (Original work published 1915.).

Freud, S., & Breuer, J. (2000). *Studies in Hysteria* (J. Strachey, Trans.). Basic Books. (Original work published 1893.)

Friedman, M., & Tomsic, S. (Eds.). (2016). *Psychoanalysis: Topological Perspectives: New Conceptions of Geometry and Space in Freud and Lacan*. Transcript Verlag.

Grosz, E. (2017). *The Incorporeal: Ontology, Ethics, and the Limits of Materialism*. Columbia University Press.

Harrison, P. (2009). In the Absence of Practice. *Environment and Planning D: Society and Space*, 27(6), 987–1009.

Hawkins, H. (2014). Montage/Collage: Art-making, Place-making. *you are here: The Journal of Creative Geography, Issue XVII: The Montage Effect*, 17, 53–60.

Highmore, B. (2020). Disjunctive Constellations: On Climate Change, Conjunctures and Cultural Studies. *New Formations*, 102(102), 28–43.

Hill, L. (2012). *Maurice Blanchot and Fragmentary Writing: A Change of Epoch*. A&C Black.

Johnston, A. (2005). *Time Driven: Metapsychology and the Splitting of the Drive*. Northwestern University Press.

Jones, M. (2009). Phase Space: Geography, Relational Thinking, and Beyond. *Progress in Human Geography*, 33(4), 487–506.

Kingsbury, P. (2007). The Extimacy of Space. *Social & Cultural Geography*, 8(2), 235–258.

Kingsbury, P., & Secor, A.J. (Eds.). (2021). *A Place More Void*. University of Nebraska Press.

Kirby, V (2011). *Quantum Anthropologies*. Duke University Press.

Kohn, E. (2013). *How Forests Think: Toward an Anthropology Beyond the Human*. University of California Press.

Kristeva, J. (1985). Stabat Mater. *Poetics Today*, 6(1–2), 133–152.

Lacan, J. (1992). *The Seminar of Jacques Lacan Book VII: The Ethics of Psychoanalysis, 1959–1960* (D. Porter, Trans.). W.W. Norton. (Original work published 1986.)

Lacan, J. (1998). *Encore: The Seminar of Jacques Lacan: Book XX: On Feminine Sexuality, the Limits of Love and Knowledge, 1972–1973* (B. Fink, Trans.). W.W. Norton. (Original work published 1975.)

Lacan, J. (2006). *The Seminar of Jacques Lacan: Book XVII: The Other Side of Psychoanalysis, 1969–1970* (R. Grigg, Trans.). W.W. Norton. (Original work published 1991.)

Lacan, J. (2016). *The Seminar of Jacques Lacan Book XXIII: The Sinthome* (A.R. Price, Trans.). Polity Press. (Original work published 2005.)

Lacan, J. (2017). *The Seminar of Jacques Lacan, Book V: Formations of the Unconscious* (R. Grigg, Trans.). Polity Press. (Original work published 1998.)

Lacan, J. (2019a) The Third Address Given at the 7th Congress of the Ecole freudienne de Paris, Rome, 1 November 1974 (P. Dravers, Trans.). *The Lacanian Review*, 7, 83–109. (Original work published 1975.)

Lacan, J. (2019b). *The Seminar of Jacques Lacan, Book VI: Desire and its Interpretation, 1958–1959* (B. Fink, Trans.). Polity Press. (Original work published 2013.)

Landau, F., Pohl, L., & Roskamm, N. (Eds.). (2021). *[Un]Grounding: Post-Foundational Geographies* (Vol. 34). Transcript Verlag.

Laplanche, J. (2017). *Après-coup* (J. House & L. Thurston, Trans.). The Unconscious in Translation.

Lapworth, A. (2022). Thinking the Unconscious Beyond the Psychoanalytic Subject: Simondon, Murakami, and the Transductive Forces of the Transindividual. *Social & Cultural Geography*, 1–18.

Levi, P. (1988). *The Drowned and the Saved* (R. Rosenthal, Trans.). Summit Books.

Margulies, J. (2022). A Political Ecology of Desire: Between Extinction, Anxiety, and Flourishing. *Environmental Humanities*, 14(2), 241–264.

Martin, L., & Secor, A.J. (2014). Towards a Post-Mathematical Topology. *Progress in Human Geography*, 38(3), 420–438.

McLean, S. (2013). All the Difference in the World: Liminality, Montage, and the Reinvention of Comparative Anthropology. In C. Surhr & R. Willerslev (Eds.), *Transcultural Montage*. Berghahn Books.

Miller, J.-A. (1994). Extimite. In M. Bracher, M.W. Alcom, R.J. Corthwell, & F. Massardier Kenney (Eds.), *Lacanian Theory of Discourse: Subject, Structure, and Society.* New York University Press.

Miller, J-A. (2007). Interpretation in Reverse. In V. Voruz & B. Wolf (Eds.), *The Later Lacan: An Introduction.* SUNY Press.

Moncayo, R. (2017). *Lalangue, Sinthome, Jouissance, and Nomination.* Karnac.

Nieuwenhuis, M., & Nassar, A. (2017). *Losing Ground: On Holes and Other Absences.* University of Warwick Workshop and Exhibition, 19–20 May. Available at: https://sinkholesworkshop.wordpress.com/.

Nieuwenhuis, M., & Nassar, A. (2018). Dust: Perfect Circularity. *Cultural Geographies*, 25(3), 501–507.

Pain, R. (2021). Geotrauma: Violence, Place and Repossession. *Progress in Human Geography*, 45(5), 972–989.

Peters, J.D. (2015). *The Marvellous Clouds: Toward a Philosophy of Elemental Media.* University of Chicago Press.

Pile, S. (1996). *The Body and The City: Psychoanalysis, Space and Subjectivity.* Routledge.

Pile, S. (2014a). A Distributed Unconscious: The Hangover, What Happens in Vegas and Whether It Stays There or Not. In P. Kingsbury & S. Pile (Eds.), *Psychoanalytic Geographies.* Routledge.

Pile, S. (2014b). Beastly Minds: A Topological Twist in the Rethinking of the Human in Nonhuman Geographies Using Two of Freud's Case Studies, Emmy von N. and the Wolfman. *Transactions of the Institute of British Geographers*, 39(2), 224–236.

Plotnitsky, A. (2002). *The Knowable and the Unknowable.* University of Michigan Press.

Pohl, L. (2020). Object-Disoriented Geographies: The Ghost Tower of Bangkok and the Topology of Anxiety. *Cultural Geographies*, 27(1), 71–84.

Pred, A. (2014). *Recognising European Modernities: A Montage of the Present.* Routledge.

Prescod-Weinstein, C. (2021). *The Disordered Cosmos: A Journey into Dark Matter, Spacetime, and Dreams Deferred.* Hachette UK.

Proust, M. (2002). *Swann's Way* (L. Davis, Trans.). Penguin Classics. (Original work published 1913.)

Radio Lab (2017). *Super Cool*, 5 December. Available at: https://www.wnycstudios.org/podcasts/radiolab/articles/super-cool-2017.

Riding, J., & Dahlman, C.T. (2022). Montage Space: Borderlands, Micronations, Terra Nullius, and the Imperialism of the Geographical Imagination. *Dialogues in Human Geography*, 12(2), 278–301.

Rose, M. (2006). Gathering "Dreams of Presence": A Project for the Cultural Landscape. *Environment and Planning D: Society and Space*, 24(4), 537–554.

Rose, M. (2011). Secular Materialism: A Critique of Earthly Theory. *Journal of Material Culture*, 16(2), 107–129.

Rose, M. (2021). The Void and its Summons: Subjectivity, Signs and the Enigmatic. In P. Kingsbury & A.J. Secor (Eds.), *A Place More Void*. University of Nebraska Press.

Searles, H. F. (1972). Unconscious Processes in relation to the Environmental Crisis. *Psychoanalytic Review*, 59(3), 361–374.

Simondon, G. (2017). *On the Mode of Existence of Technical Objects*. Univocal Press.

Sinclair, V. (2020). *Scansion in Psychoanalysis and Art: The Cut in Creation*. Routledge.

Soler, C. (2014). *Lacan – The Unconscious Reinvented: The Unconscious Reinvented*. (E. Faye & S. Schwartz, Trans.). Routledge.

Soler, C. (2016). *Lacanian Affects: The Function of Affect in Lacan's Work* (B. Fink, Trans.). Routledge.

Uman, M.A. (1986). *All About Lightning*. Dovers.

Walton, F. (Director). (1979). *When a Stranger Calls* [Film]. Columbia Pictures; Melvin Simon Productions.

Whatmore, S. (2006). Materialist Returns: Practising Cultural Geography in and for A More-Than-Human World. *Cultural Geographies*, 13(4), 600–609.

Willerslev, R., & Suhr, C. (2013). Introduction: Montage as an amplifier of invisibility. In C. Surhr & R. Willerslev (Eds.), *Transcultural Montage*. Berghahn Books.

Wylie, J. (2007). *Landscape*. Routledge.

Žižek, S. (1992). *Looking Awry: An Introduction to Jacques Lacan through Popular Culture*. MIT Press.

Žižek, S. (2000). *The Ticklish Subject*. Verso.

Chapter 9

Spatial Disorientation

Psychoanalysis, Labyrinth and Architectural Representations

Gabriela Świtek

"What protects the sane man against delirium or hallucination is not his critical powers, but the structure of his space: objects remain before him, keeping their distance and, … touching him only with respect" (Merleau-Ponty, 1945/1994, p. 291). Maurice Merleau-Ponty's interest in the space of hallucinations and dreams is a thread of his philosophy that opens up the possibility of finding the tangents between phenomenology, psychoanalysis, and psychiatry (Benvenuto, 2015, p. 177). Not only in the *Phenomenology of Perception* did the philosopher undertake the search for this kind of tangency. His celebrated comment, contained in a preface to Angelo Hesnard's book on Freud, is also a testimony of these explorations: "Phenomenology and psychoanalysis are not parallel; much better, they are both aiming toward the same *latency*" (Merleau-Ponty, 1969/1982–1983, p. 67; emphasis in the original).

Merleau-Ponty's reflection on the unconscious in Freud's writings is not a new direction of philosophical investigations. Nor is a correspondence between phenomenology and psychoanalysis a new field of inquiry. Thomas Csordas elaborates, for instance, a table of binary juxtapositions between phenomenology and psychoanalysis, emphasizing that phenomenology is focused on describing everyday-experience structures. In contrast, psychoanalysis is fixed on the therapeutic explorations of the unconscious (Csordas, 2012, p. 57). There are also attempts at revealing a coherent understanding of Freud in Merleau-Ponty's *The Structure of Behaviour* or *The Visible and the Invisible* (Olkowski, 1982–1983).

There is no doubt that Merleau-Ponty was an attentive reader of Freud. Direct references to Freud's writings are present not only in his *Phenomenology of Perception*, in the paragraphs on the sexual body (Merleau-Ponty, 1945/1994, pp. 158–162), but also in other publications, such as *Indirect Language and the Voices of Silence*. In the latter, the philosopher alludes to Leonardo da Vinci's painting, a subject of Freud's essay of 1910, including his (and Oskar Pfister's) misinterpretation of St. Anne's cloak as a vulture. Criticizing André Malraux's *Musée imaginaire* for promoting the cult of artists as if they lived beyond history, beyond everyday life, and without the

DOI: 10.4324/9781003436188-10

body, Merleau-Ponty warns against the other extreme, i.e., psychoanalytic interpretations understood as the only explanation of art. In other words, Leonardo is not just a victim of "an unhappy childhood." At the same time, the phenomenologist gives the psychoanalyst his due: "Besides, Freud never said that he explained da Vinci by the vulture; he said in effect that analysis stops where painting begins" (Merleau-Ponty, 1952/1974a, p. 61).

Discussing the psychologists' debt to Husserl and Heidegger in a lecture titled *Phenomenology and the Sciences of Man*, Merleau-Ponty enumerates Ludwig Binswanger, Berlin Gestaltists, such as Kurt Koffka, Wolfgang Köhler, Max Wertheimer, and Kurt Goldstein. In this context, the phenomenologist mentions Freud:

> Psychoanalysis, though in many respects it represents a very different mode of thought, has felt these phenomenological tendencies in its recent development. Nothing in the writings of Freud reveals the least knowledge of, or the least sympathy with, the phenomenological litera- ture. But the exigencies of his own problems led him to a dynamic con- ception of psychoanalysis and elicited from Freud himself a revision of the theoretical framework, which he had first used. One can see the joining of these two currents in a psychologist like Lewin, who was strongly influenced by phenomenology.
>
> (Merleau-Ponty, 1958/1974b, p. 231)

We may also refer to the illustration in Rudolf Arnheim's *The Dynamics of Architectural Form* to find common ground for the phenomenology of per- ception, Gestalt psychology, architecture, and psychoanalysis. In his medita- tions on the "architectural organization of thought," Arnheim comments on Freud's famous diagram of the interrelations between the id, the ego, and the superego. As he argues, the drawing

> depicts the upsurge of buried energy from the depth of the id toward the liberating realm of consciousness. It shows the horizontal barrier that blocks this upward motion. It also shows the opening provided by the superego, which acts as a bridge. Underlying the construct of shapes, just as in architecture, is a configuration of forces.
>
> (Arnheim, 2009, p. 274)

It is no surprise that the psychologist of perception reads the writings of Freud and Jung. However, knowing Arnheim's skepticism towards psycho- analysis (Ferrari, 1988, p. 83), it is remarkable that the comments on Freud's drawing are the concluding lines of the Gestaltist's book on architecture. Arnheim describes the picture in the language of his interpretations of architectural space, e.g., using terms omnipresent in *The Dynamics of Archi- tectural Form*, such as "shapes," "relations," and "forces." So perhaps we should assume that Arnheim's notion of forces in architecture owes something to Freud's ruminations on conflicting forces of the conscious, the unconscious, and the preconscious mind. For reflection on psychoanalysis and architectural representations, the concluding sentence of *The Dynamics of Architectural Form* turns out to be particularly fruitful: "Since all human thoughts must be worked out in the medium of perceptual space, architecture, wittingly or not, presents embodiments of thought when it invents and builds shapes" (Arnheim, 2009, p. 274).

Merleau-Ponty's thoughts on space and Arnheim's reflections on architectural forms are an inspiration that links Gestalt principles of visual perception and some concepts of space in psychoanalysis with the phenomenology of architecture. It is to the latent structure of architectural space and architecture as an "embodiment of thought" that I will turn in this chapter. I will examine a number of representations of spatial disorientation, including the archetypal image of the labyrinth with which Jungian psychoanalysts often describe the unconscious and the individuation process.

*

The structure of his space protects the sane man against delirium or hallucination. What does it mean that his sanity is structured? Does it mean that his sanity depends on the spatial structure of his experience? Is the structure of his space intersubjective, communicable, and shared as everyday life experience? Is the structure of his/our space architectural? How do we "possess" the structure of space? It is not an accident that I suggest moving from Merleau-Ponty's usage of a singular possessive pronoun ("his") to a plural possessive pronoun ("our"). A telling replacement of the pronouns occurs in Dalibor Vesely's book *Architecture in the Age of Divided Representation*:

> Merleau-Ponty writes, "what protects us against delirium or hallucinations are not our critical powers but the structure of our space." … The structure of space has its source in the depth of culture and coincides with the overall coherence of our cultural world.
>
> (Vesely, 2004, p. 40)

Following this line of argument, let us discuss an architectural image of the structure of "our" space that is communicable as an archetype.

"The unconscious is often symbolized by corridors, labyrinths, or mazes" (von Franz, 1964, p. 171). Marie-Louise von Franz includes this remark in a caption under the drawing representing three mazes: "a Finnish stone maze (Bronze Age); a 19th-century British turf maze; and a maze (in tiles) on the floor of Chartres Cathedral" (p. 171). In her essay, included in the volume *Man and His Symbols*, von Franz follows the path of Jung's reflection on the pattern that he calls the process of individuation. The three labyrinths support her interpretation of a 48-year-old man's dream about his explorations of a large townhouse:

> I didn't yet know all its different parts. So I took a walk through it and discovered, mainly in the cellar, several rooms about which I knew nothing and even exits leading into other cellars or into subterranean streets. I felt uneasy when I found that several of these exits were not locked and some had no locks at all.
>
> (p. 169)

This dream serves von Franz to explain the concept of the shadow, an unconscious part of the personality in Jungian psychoanalysis. What is paramount for my considerations is a comparison of this imaginary architectural promenade to an archetypal maze. Von Franz suggests that "the maze of strange passages, chambers, and unlocked exits in the cellar recalls the old Egyptian representation of the underworld, which is a well-known symbol of the unconscious" (p. 170).

The intention is not to challenge von Franz's analytical explanation of the dreamer's personality (e.g., of his repression of pleasure and spontaneity) but to point to the persistence with which the image of a labyrinth, an archetypal/architectural structure reappears in Jungian psychoanalysis. A similar reference can be found in Aldo Carotenuto's interpretation of a dream by a man called Arion who explores a town in a car with a friend:

> In the town there are many little intersecting streets, as well as some difficult thoroughfares, and I suffer from dizziness. A space that looks wide enough to pass through becomes narrower as we approach. We do not know whether to keep going or to turn back.
>
> (Carotenuto, 1985, p. 48)

Carotenuto recalls here "the archetypal image of the labyrinth, which fundamentally expresses the path of life." He is more precise than von Franz in defining the source of this image, namely the myth of the Cretan labyrinth (pp. 48–49).

In *Approaching the Unconscious*, an essay included in the volume *Man and His Symbols*, Jung defines archetypes as being without "known origin," reproducing themselves "in any time or in any part of the world" (Jung, 1964, p. 69). However, let us recall that the popularity of the labyrinth myth in the humanities is also part of a historical phenomenon named Cretomania. Induced by the archaeological excavations and reconstructions at Knossos, beginning in 1900, Cretomania is manifest in different visual forms and cultural practices, including Freud's psychoanalysis. Modern reception of the Minoan material culture involved architecture, the visual, and the performative arts; ranging from Frank Lloyd Wright's early architectural designs to Mariano Fortuny's luxury Knossos scarves and Léon Bakst's set and costume designs for the 1923 production of *Phèdre* (Momigliano & Farnoux, 2017). In a 1901 letter, Freud mentions an excavated palace in Crete, which is considered "the authentic labyrinth of Minos" (Freud, 1955, p. x), while his patient, Hilda Doolittle, planned to present the psychoanalyst with a Minoan snake goddess figurine (Momigliano, 2020, pp. 1–2). In one of his 1930s lectures, *Revision of the Theory of Dreams*, Freud famously equates the space of the mythical labyrinth with the human body: "the twisting paths are the bowels and Ariadne's thread is the umbilical cord" (Freud, 1933/1964, p. 25).

Hypotheses identifying Knossos with the labyrinth of Minos (e.g., in Arthur Evans's archaeological publications) must be understood as the effect of sometimes obsessively combining Greek myths with historical and archaeological realities (Momigliano, 2020, p. 72). Researchers repeat the argument that we owe the word "labyrinth" to the Palace of Minos. The etymology of "labyrinth" has been associated with "labrys," a double-axe decorative motif found on the walls and other architectural elements of the palace (Graham, 1972, p. 28). Moreover, a Knossos tablet inscription mentioning the "Lady of the Labyrinth" has been associated with the myth of Ariadne and Daedalus. This connection was assumed, for example, by Karl Kerényi in his influential study *Dionysos: Archetypal Image of Indestructible Life*. What is intriguing in this story is not an abundance of archaeological and historical hypotheses but a presumption that the architecture of the Palace of Minos is an embodiment of the myth.

In *The Vertical Labyrinth: Individuation in Jungian Psychology*, Carotenuto describes the labyrinth as a representation of the "fragility and uncertainty of consciousness" (Carotenuto, 1985, pp. 49, 128). Interestingly, his understanding of the myth is influenced by Giorgio Colli's ruminations on the Lady of the Labyrinth as part of his essay *La nascita della filosofia* (1975), where the philosopher perceives the geometrical form of the labyrinth as a "perverse game of intellect" (Colli, 1975/1992, p. 36). As the editor of the first complete edition of Nietzsche's writings, Colli reads the labyrinth myth in the spirit of Nietzsche's duality of the Dionysian and the Apollonian as two forces of human nature. The Dionysian character of the myth is, for instance, Ariadne, the wife of Dionysus, the woman-goddess, and the Lady of the Labyrinth. The creator of the labyrinth – Daedalus – belongs to the Apollonian world (Świtek, 2012, p. 22). He is an inventor, a genius craftsman, and a builder whose creativity is the product of the mind, "nascent reason" (Colli, 1975/1992, p. 35).

In the history and philosophy of architecture, Daedalus is considered the mythical first architect. In the narratives about the origins of architecture, he competes with the biblical Adam, the first gardener (assuming that Paradise needed to be cultivated) and the first architect who had to build a shelter after the expulsion; it was also investigated whether Adam needed a hut in the Garden of Eden (Rykwert, 1972). Indra Kagis McEwen begins her study *Socrates' Ancestor: An Essay on Architectural Beginnings* by reflecting on a Platonic dialogue. "My ancestor, Daedalus" and "the wisdom of Daedalus" [*Daidalou sophia*] are the notions uttered by Socrates in Plato's dialogue *Euthyphro* (McEwen, 1997, p. 1). But what do the myths say about the architecture of Daedalus's labyrinth? Did it have a roof or a front door? How was it planned? What materials were used to build it? (Świtek, 2012, p. 20)

From Diodorus of Sicily we learn that Daedalus acquired the art of building, carving statues, and working with stone, wood, and other materials. He constructed a wooden replica of a cow for Queen Pasiphae, glued the wings with wax for himself and Icarus, and after escaping Crete, he erected the city walls on a steep rock and made a golden ram for Aphrodite. One of the words appearing in Greek sources and related to the name of Daedalus is *daidalon*, which translates as a "cunningly crafted" thing (McEwen, 1997, p. 53). Diodorus of Sicily writes about Daedalidae, the artisans who claimed to be descendants of Daedalus (ca. 30 BCE/1994b, p. 59), and about Daedaleia, the wonderful works that Daedalus created in Sardinia (ca. 30 BCE/1994a, p. 437). The Knossos labyrinth would then be one of the *daidala*, and therefore a construction that testifies to the extraordinary abilities of Daedalus.

The space of the mythical labyrinth is also associated with the notion of *choros*, usually denoting dance. However, in Book 18 (590) of the *Iliad*, Homer mentions Daedalus and his dancing floor, which he was to build for Ariadne in Knossos after Theseus had entered the labyrinth and killed the Minotaur. As we read in the description of Achilles's shield, which contains the only Homeric reference to Daedalus: "the famed god of the two strong arms [Hephaestus] cunningly wrought a dancing-floor [*choros*] like unto that which in wide Knossos Daedalus fashioned of old for fair-tressed Ariadne" (McEwen, 1997, pp. 57–58). Arthur Evans argued that two archaeological discoveries in Knossos, the "Dancing Lady fresco" and the "Theatral Area," refer to Homer's mention of Ariadne's *choros* (Momigliano, 2020, p. 57). Indra Kagis McEwen identifies the Homeric dancing floor [*choros*] with the image [*eidos*] of the labyrinth (McEwen, 1997, p. 60). Other experts in Greek mythology, such as Karl Kerényi, consider the meander ornament, which appears in the Attic vase painting, to be one of the representations referring to the myth of the labyrinth; Tondo of an Attic Red-Figure Kylix by Aison, depicting Theseus killing the Minotaur in the presence of Athena (Madrid, Museo Arqueológico Nacional), the scene surrounded by a meander, is a case in point (Kerényi, 1976/2022, p. 117). As a geometric meander reminiscent of a building plan (and not a section or another form of architectural representation of space), the labyrinth appears on Cretan and Roman coins, mosaics, and floors of Gothic cathedrals, or as mazes in early modern European gardens.

Let us now compare Daedalus's labyrinth in Knossos, the Homeric *choros*, and the meander as an image of the labyrinth with the spaces of dreams interpreted by the Jungian psychoanalysts. Von Franz's remarks about the process of individuation open with an image of a "meander"; it is a decoration in a seventh-century manuscript whose serpentine lines differ from a Greek geometrical ornament. Von Franz introduces the symbolic image of "a meandering pattern" not to recall the space of Daedalus's labyrinth but to describe the dreams in which the "process of psychic growth" is revealed (von Franz, 1964, p. 160). The space of dreams as the subject of psychoanalysis does not have to follow the historical and archaeological sources of the labyrinth myth. Moreover, von Franz's and Carotenuto's case studies differ in what concerns the space of the dreams under analysis: one narrative takes place in the interior of a house, the other in a town. An intriguing link, however, can be traced between the psychoanalytic accounts of these two dreams and some ancient descriptions of the labyrinth. In the cases discussed by von Franz and Carotenuto, a feeling of uneasiness, a spatial uncanny disorientation, accompanies the dreamers' wanderings. "I felt uneasy," confesses von Franz's patient (p. 169). "I suffer from dizziness. ... We do not know whether to keep going or to turn back," admits Arion of Carotenuto's narrative (Carotenuto, 1985, p. 48). To be at a loss which way to choose is an aporetic situation, resembling the spaces of the mythical labyrinth. *Apeiros* is the word Diodorus of Sicily uses to describe Daedalus's work (McEwen, 1997, p. 59). Its passages were "so winding that those unfamiliar with them had difficulty in making their way out" (Diodorus of Sicily, ca. 30 BCE/1994b, p. 61).

*

"I seemed every night to descend – not metaphorically, but literally to descend – into chasms and sunless abysses, depths below depths, from which it seemed hopeless that I could ever re-ascend" (De Quincey, 1821/1994, p. 235). One of the famous literary images of spatial disorientation experienced in a delirious dream appears in Thomas De Quincey's *Confessions of an English Opium-Eater* (1821). The *Confessions* are one of his autobiographical works describing the growth and effects of the poet's opium addiction. In the early nineteenth century, opium's addictive properties were not profoundly understood, but De Quincey was not alone in prizing the power of a narcotic drug to facilitate poetic imagination. His friend and poet, Samuel Taylor Coleridge, claimed to write a part of *Kubla Khan* (1816) in a "sort of Reverie brought on by two grains of Opium" (Ford, 2007, p. 229).

In my search for the affinities between the space of psychoanalysis and architecture, I invoke De Quincey's narrative for several reasons. First, in *Thomas De Quincey: Bicentenary Studies*, the writer is placed together with Sigmund Freud as a forerunner of psychoanalytic psychology (Proudfit, 1985, pp. 88–108). Second, contemporary scholars, referring to the *Oxford English Dictionary*, point out that the first use of the word "subconscious" is credited to De Quincey (Porter, 1980, p. 603; Perry, 1993, p. 823).

Interpreters using psychoanalytic theories are also interested in other meta-phors and remarks, i.e., concerning the nature of memory, which is a key concept for Freud. As we read in *Confessions*:

> [T]here is no such thing as ultimate *forgetting* traces once impressed upon the memory are indestructible; a thousand accidents may and will interpose a veil between our present consciousness and the secret inscriptions on the mind. ... whether veiled or unveiled, the inscription remains for ever; just as the stars seem to withdraw before the common light of day, whereas, in fact, ... they are waiting to be revealed.
>
> (De Quincey, 1821/1994, p. 238)

Third, some scholars juxtapose De Quincey's writings with *The Interpretation of Dreams* (and its two key concepts – condensation and displacement) and Freud's essay *Creative Writers and Day-Dreaming* (Ford, 2007, p. 243). As to the latter, it discusses "psychological" novels that often result from the writer's self-observation (Freud, 1908/1959b, p. 150). The *Confessions* would fit into this category, but De Quincey's work was never the subject of Freud's meticulous focus. In contemporary interpretations, De Quincey's auto-biographical works are sometimes seen as self-therapeutic attempts to keep his nightmares under control (Crawford, 2011, p. 231). Last but not least, De Quincey's celebrated description of Giovanni Battista Piranesi's *Carceri* (*Imaginary Prisons*), included in the final pages of *Confessions*, finds its place in the history of architecture as "the first romantic meditation on what might be called the spatial uncanny" (Vidler, 1999, p. 37).

> Many years ago, when I was looking over Piranesi's *Antiquities of Rome*, Coleridge, then standing by, described to me a set of plates from that artist, called his *Dreams* and which record the scenery of his own visions during the delirium of a fever.
>
> (De Quincey, 1821/1994, p. 239)

For many decades, De Quincey's remarks on Piranesi influenced art his-torical interpretations of the architect's sets of etchings, even though the writer had never personally seen them (Tschudi, 2017, p. 150). Moreover, De Quincey's account contains some inaccuracies and errors. While the *Anti-quities of Rome* corresponds to the Italian publication *Le Antichità Romane* (1756), the title of another set of etchings – *Dreams* – is De Quincey's invention. Piranesi printed the so-called *Carceri* in two editions. The first series is entitled *Invenzioni Capric di Carceri* (as inscribed on the 1745 edi-tion's title page). The second is called *Carceri d'Invenzione* as written on the 1760–1761 edition's frontispiece (Gavuzzo-Stewart, 1999, p. 5). The writer's remark that the etchings' scenery represents Piranesi's delirium is considered a misinterpretation in contemporary art historical studies. Nevertheless, De

Quincey's celebrated passage could have contributed to the fact that Piranesi's sixteen plates of *Carceri* have received more scholarly and literary attention than the rest of his graphic work, which – as a Piranesi scholar, John Wilton-Ely estimates – amounts to over 1,000 separate items (Wilton-Ely, 2001, p. 229).

In some of Piranesi's *Carceri,* described "only from memory of Coleridge's account," De Quincey sees "vast Gothic halls" (De Quincey, 1821/1994, p. 239). De Quincey's meditations on the *Carceri* are preceded by his remarks on Livy's *Consul Romanus* (pp. 238–239). It is a paradox that this ardent reader of Livy prefers to see "Gothic halls" rather than appreciate Piranesi's profound and archaeological knowledge of Roman antiquities. In his time, Piranesi wanted to be considered a serious and sensible architect who achieved mastery in archaeological illustration. As he writes in the dedication to *Campo Marzio dell'antica Roma* (1762):

> I am rather afraid that parts of the Campus which I describe should seem figments of my imagination [*inventate a capriccio*] and not based on any evidence. ... But before any one accuses me of falsehood, he should, I beg, examine the ancient [marble] plan of the city.
>
> (Wilton-Ely, 1978, p. 76)

Like the authors of the English Gothic novels, such as Horace Walpole and William Beckford, De Quincey contributed to inscribing *Carceri* into a series of interpretations also present in the literature of French Romanticism (Keller, 1966, pp. 13–46; Vidler, 1999, pp. 37, 232). This cultural phenomenon of *Carceri*'s reception in Romantic literature can be described as a distortion by displacement. With this notion, I allude to Freud's remarks on delusions and dreams in Wilhelm Jensen's *Gradiva* (Freud, 1907/1959a, p. 58). I do not mean, however, to compare the archaeologist Piranesi to *Gradiva*'s protagonist, the archaeologist Norbert Hanold and his story of the return of a repressed eroticism, but to draw attention to the displacement in time made by De Quincey. His "poor," "delirious," and "hopeless" Piranesi (De Quincey, 1821/1994, p. 240) laboring up the stairs of "Gothic halls" is the stereotypical image of a Romantic artist, having little in common with the eighteenth-century archaeologist of ancient Rome.

It must be emphasized, however, that the two series of *Carceri* differ from Piranesi's archaeological publications. They are experiments with the *capriccio* as a form of architectural representation and inspired by the so-called prison scene characteristic of eighteenth-century stage design, often represented through the *per angolo* perspective (Gavuzzo-Stewart, 1999, pp. 62–74). At the same time, the *Carceri* contain many antique references, architectural and sculptural, as well as literary. For example, Plate XVI of the 1761 edition includes a Latin inscription *Impie tati et malis artibus*, which is today interpreted as an ironic allusion to Piranesi's patron, Lord

Charlemont, who had failed to finance *Le Antichità Romane* (Gavuzzo-Stewart, 1999, Fig. 32, pp. 39, 105–136).

Setting De Quincey's inaccuracies aside, his meditations on the *Carceri* provide us with intriguing descriptions of spatial disorientation, including the projection of his dreams and the states of mind into the space of Piranesi's etchings. There is no evidence that Piranesi intended to portray himself in the plates of *Carceri*; one may only conclude that he "speaks" through the Latin and Italian inscriptions as evidence of his erudition. And yet, in the etchings' spatial ambiguity, De Quincey perceives the architect's silhouette: "Creeping along the sides of the walls, you perceived a staircase; and upon this, groping his way upwards, was Piranesi himself" (De Quincey, 1821/1994, p. 240). Ascending stairs is an image predominant in De Quincey's account:

> [R]aise your eyes and behold a second flight of stairs still higher, on which again Piranesi is perceived, by this time standing on the very brink of the abyss. Once again elevate your eye, and a still more aerial flight is described; and there, again, is the delirious Piranesi, busy on his aspiring labours: and so on, until the unfinished stairs and the hopeless Piranesi both are lost in the upper gloom of the hall.
>
> (p. 240)

In Freud's *Interpretation of Dreams*, walking up or down staircases, steps, or ladders is considered a representation of the sexual act. As the psychoanalyst argues: "staircases (and analogous things) were unquestionably symbols of copulation. ... the rhythmical pattern of copulation is reproduced in going upstairs" (Freud, 1900/1953, p. 355). It is unknown which plates of the *Carceri* did Coleridge describe in detail to his friend; however, the stairs appear in almost all the etchings.

In the history of architecture, a juxtaposition of De Quincey's meditation on the *Carceri* with Freud's *Uncanny* is a more critical trope than Freud's remarks on the sexual connotations of staircases. One of the aspects of the uncanny – according to Anthony Vidler – is its relation to the spatial and environmental; that of the "orientation," of "knowing one's way about" (Vidler, 1999, p. 23). What fascinates the architectural historian in De Quincey's descriptions of space is not the passage from the homely to the haunted house but the lack of spatial orientation in the labyrinth-like interiors. According to Vilder, De Quincey describes "the vertical labyrinth": it "images the artist, Piranesi, caught in a vertigo *en abîme* of his own making, forever climbing the unfinished stairs in the labyrinth of carceral spaces" (p. 37).

*

I have only sketched the labyrinth's complex symbolism in Jungian psychoanalysis as an image of the unconscious and the "game of intellect." If we accept the argument that the *Carceri* represent "vertical labyrinths," this is not to say that their sole meaning is an image of the unconscious. Like the mythical Daedalus, Piranesi seems an Apollonian master of architectural representation. The "labyrinths" of the *Carceri* appear as images (etchings) but not as meanders reminiscent of a building's plan. As Ulya Vogt-Göknil notes, they seem to represent the interiors, but we can see the crossings of bridges and arcades, and at the same time, the bridges, stairs, and ladders do not lead to any particular place (Vogt-Göknil, 1958, p. 21). This architectural complexity fascinates De Quincey, who compares it to the spaces of his dreams: "With the same power of endless growth and self-reproduction did my architecture proceed in dreams. In the early stage of the malady, the splendours of my dreams were indeed chiefly architectural" (De Quincey, 1821/1994, p. 240).

What does it mean that dreams are architectural? Or is De Quincey's narration architectural? In what ways does it reflect the space represented in the *Carceri*? Is it labyrinthine? Does the structure of the writer's space protect him against his opium-induced hallucinations? In parts containing a reference to the *Carceri*, De Quincey's narration loses its compactness and becomes fragmented into short paragraphs. A recollection from his childhood interrupts the descriptions of his dreams, followed by the memory of reading Livy's *Consul Romanus*. At this moment, Coleridge and Piranesi enter the narration. One of the paragraphs relating to the writer's experiences precedes the comments on the *Carceri*:

> The sense of space, and in the end the sense of time, were both powerfully affected. Buildings, landscapes, etc., were exhibited in proportions so vast as the bodily eye is not fitted to receive. Space swelled, and was amplified to an extent of unutterable and self-repeating infinity.
>
> (De Quincey, 1821/1994, p. 236)

As Curtis Perry aptly argues, De Quincey introduces himself as "the opium-eater" and "the confessing subject," but the description of Piranesi's etchings at the end of *Confessions* questions the "distance established between that narrator and his tale." In other words, the *Carceri* suggest "a structure of repetition in place of a simpler architectural model proposed by the narrator" in the preface to *Confessions* (Perry, 1993, pp. 811–812). It could also be argued that in the final pages of his *Confessions*, the writer finds the images of the labyrinth-like architectural space impressed upon his cultural memory; images with which he tries to domesticate and analyze his personal, opium-induced, and spatially disoriented dreams. Theseus emerged from the labyrinth with the help of Ariadne's thread. Also, Daedalus, as the architect, must have known the way out. But De Quincey's Piranesi could not escape the passaged prisons he had created.

References

Arnheim, R. (2009). *The Dynamics of Architectural Form*. University of California Press.

Benvenuto, S. (2015). Merleau-Ponty and Hallucination. *American Imago*, 72(2), 177–196.

Carotenuto, A. (1985). *The Vertical Labyrinth: Individuation in Jungian Psychology* (J. Shepley, Trans.). Inner City Books.

Colli, G. (1992). *Narodziny filozofii* [*The Birth of Philosophy*] (S. Kasprzysiak, Trans.). Oficyna Literacka. (Original work published 1975.)

Crawford, J. (2011). The Haunting of Thomas De Quincey. *The Cambridge Quarterly*, 40(3), 224–242.

Csordas, T.J. (2012). Psychoanalysis and Phenomenology. *Ethos*, 40(1), 54–74.

De Quincey, T. (1994). *Confessions of an English-Opium Eater*. Wordsworth Editions Limited. (Original work published 1821.)

Diodorus of Sicily (1994a). *The Library of History, Books II.35–IV.58* (C.H. Oldfather, Trans.). Harvard University Press. (Original work published ca. 30 BCE.)

Diodorus of Sicily (1994b). *The Library of History, Books IV.59–VIII* (C.H. Oldfather, Trans.). Harvard University Press. (Original work published ca. 30 BCE.)

Ferrari, S. (1988). Freud and Arnheim: Psychoanalysis and the Visual Arts. *Salmagundi*, 78/79, 83–96.

Ford, N. (2007). Beyond Opium: De Quincey's Range of Reveries. *The Cambridge Quarterly*, 36(3), 229–249.

Franz, M.-L.von. (1964). The Process of Individuation. In C.G. Jung (Ed.), *Man and His Symbols*. Anchor Press.

Freud, S. (1953). The Interpretation of Dreams. In *The Standard Edition of the Complete Psychological Works of Sigmund Freud*, Vol. 5 (J. Strachey, Ed. & Trans.). The Hogarth Press. (Original work published 1900.)

Freud, S. (1955). Totem and Taboo, Editor's Note. In *The Standard Edition of the Complete Psychological Works of Sigmund Freud*, Vol. 13 (J. Strachey, Ed. & Trans.). The Hogarth Press.

Freud, S. (1959a). Delusions and Dreams in Jensen's Gradiva. In *The Standard Edition of the Complete Psychological Works of Sigmund Freud*, Vol. 9 (J. Strachey, Ed. & Trans.). The Hogarth Press. (Original work published 1907.)

Freud, S. (1959b). Creative Writers and Daydreaming. In *The Standard Edition of the Complete Psychological Works of Sigmund Freud*, Vol. 9 (J. Strachey, Ed. & Trans.). The Hogarth Press. (Original work published 1908.)

Freud, S. (1964). New Introductory Lectures on Psycho-Analysis. In *The Standard Edition of the Complete Psychological Works of Sigmund Freud*, Vol. 22 (J. Strachey, Ed. & Trans.). (Original work published 1933.)

Gavuzzo-Stewart, S. (1999). *Nelle Carceri di G.B. Piranesi*. Northern Universities Press.

Jung, C.G. (1964). Approaching the Unconscious. In C.G. Jung (Ed.), *Man and His Symbols*Anchor Press.

Graham, J.W. (1972). *The Palaces of Crete*. Princeton University Press.

Keller, L. (1966). *Piranèse et les romantiques français: Le mythe des escaliers en spirale*. J. Corti.

Kerényi, K. (2022). *Dionizos: Archetyp życia niezniszczalnego* (I. Kania, Trans.). Wydawnictwo Aletheia. (Original work published 1976.)

McEwen, I.K. (1997). *Socrates' Ancestor: An Essay on Architectural Beginnings*. MIT Press.

Merleau-Ponty, M. (1974a). Indirect Language and the Voices of Silence. In J. O'Neill (Ed.), *Phenomenology, Language and Sociology: Selected Essays of Maurice Merleau-Ponty*, Heinemann. (Original work published 1952.)

Merleau-Ponty, M. (1974b). Phenomenology and the Sciences of Man (J. Wild, Trans.). In J. O'Neill (Ed.), *Phenomenology, Language and Sociology: Selected Essays of Maurice Merleau-Ponty*. Heinemann. (Original work published 1958.)

Merleau-Ponty, M. (1982–1983). Phenomenology and Psychoanalysis: Preface to Hesnard's *L'Oeuvre de Freud*. *Review of Existential Psychology and Psychiatry*, 18 (1–3), 67–72. (Original work published 1969.)

Merleau-Ponty, M. (1994). *Phenomenology of Perception* (C. Smith, Trans.). Routledge. (Original work published 1945.)

Momigliano, N. (2020). *In Search of the Labyrinth: The Cultural Legacy of Minoan Crete*. Bloomsbury Academic.

Momigliano, N., & Farnoux, A. (2017). *Cretomania: Modern Desires for the Minoan Past*. Routledge.

Olkowski, D. E. (1982–1983). Merleau-Ponty's Freudianism: From the Body of Consciousness to the Body of Flesh. *Review of Existential Psychology and Psychiatry*, 18(1–3), 97–116.

Perry, C. (1993). Piranesi's Prison: Thomas De Quincey and the Failure of Autobiography. *Studies in English Literature, 1500–1900*, 33(4), 809–824.

Porter, R.J. (1980). The Demon Past: De Quincey and the Autobiographer's Dilemma. *Studies in English Literature, 1500–1900*, 20(4), 591–609.

Proudfit, C.L. (1985). Thomas De Quincey and Sigmund Freud: Sons, Fathers, Dreamers – Precursors of Psychoanalytic Developmental Psychology. In R.L. Snyder (Ed.), *Thomas De Quincey: Bicentenary Studies*. University of Oklahoma Press.

Rykwert, J. (1972). *On Adam's House in Paradise: The Idea of the Primitive Hut in Architectural History*. The Museum of Modern Art.

Świtek, G. (2012). *Aporie architektury*. Zachęta Narodowa Galeria Sztuki.

Tschudi, V.P. (2017). Piranesi, Failed Photographer. *AA Files*, 75, 150–151.

Vesely, D. (2004). *Architecture in the Age of Divided Representation: The Question of Creativity in the Shadow of Production*. MIT Press.

Vidler, A. (1999). *The Architectural Uncanny: Essays in the Modern Unhomely*. MIT Press.

Vogt-Göknil, U. (1958). *Giovanni Battista Piranesi: Carceri*. Origo.

Wilton-Ely, J. (1978). *The Mind and Art of Giovanni Battista Piranesi*. Thames & Hudson.

Wilton-Ely, J. (2001). Piranesi's "Carceri." *Print Quarterly*, 18(2), 229–231.

Chapter 10

Place and Psychoanalysis

Building a Bridge between Heidegger and Aristotle

Tomasz Drzazgowski

We know that there are many spaces: the virtual space, the therapeutic space, the space of relationship, the space of the mind. Recent events have drastically reminded us of the space where we are physically present: exposed to cold, plague, and war. Psychoanalysis can help us to understand our relationship with this space; because – according to Thomas Ogden (2010) – as a theory and practice it is increasingly interested not only in *what* we think, but also in *how* we think. The purpose of this chapter is to use a psychoanalytic approach to explore the meaning of one specific place, which extends to the way in which we experience and understand space.

Figure 10.1 Gdańsk Shakespeare Theatre

DOI: 10.4324/9781003436188-11

The Gdańsk Shakespeare Theatre was founded in 2008. Its creation was guided by the idea of reconstructing an English Renaissance theatre (also known as the Elizabethan theatre) within a Polish city. The word "reconstruction" is significant since the builders of the theatre referred to the striking resemblance of one of Gdańsk's buildings to the Fortune Playhouse founded in London in 1600 (Limon, 2011, 2022). What they meant was the Fencing School, a multi-functional building where not only exercises and various shows took place, but which also served as a municipal theatre between the seventeenth and nineteenth centuries. It was here that Shakespeare's plays were staged during his lifetime. The newly built Elizabethan theatre was to have the same shape and was to stand in the same place as the former Fencing School (Limon, 2022). During the Prince of Wales' visit to Gdańsk in 1993 (the Prince was the patron of the reconstruction project), the ground plan of the future theatre was actually painted on the asphalt – in its full size, and in the location of the former Fencing School.[1]

This shape of a square physically placed in a space refers to the features of a place distinguished by Aristotle (ca. 350 BCE/1961). He devoted the fourth book of his *Physics* to this very issue. Aristotle noted that "place is what directly contains any body" (209b1–2). He further stated that place could not

Figure 10.2 Fencing School in Gdańsk
Source: Peter Willer draft dated 1650.

Figure 10.3 Reconstruction of the Fortune Playhouse
Source: *Encyclopaedia Britannica* (1911).

be either form or matter because they "cannot be dissociated from that to which they belong, as place can … so that the place of any body is not any of its parts or any of its states but is distinct from it" (209b21–28). First, there was the Fencing School, which ceased to exist. It left a place, which a few centuries later (in 1993) was marked with a white line on the asphalt. This was exactly the spot where the Gdańsk Shakespeare Theatre would be built.

The white square, delimitating both the building that existed in the past and the one that was to be created, is a good illustration of Aristotle's

Figure 10.4 The ground plan of the theatre painted on the asphalt, Gdańsk 1993
Source: Photograph by unknown author; see Limon (1997).

thought that place is a border. He linked the existence of places to the possibility of movement and concluded that place must be "the limit of the surrounding body (at which this body is in contact with the body it surrounds), provided that the surrounded body is capable of local motion" (212a5–7). Although "both form and place are limits. Yet form and place do not limit the same thing: form is the limit of the thing circumscribed; place is the limit of the circumscribing body" (211b12–15). For example, the form of a book on a shelf is its limit and the place of the book is the boundaries (surfaces) of two books standing on both its sides (and the shelves). Aristotle believes that a place not only surrounds and adheres to the body or thing, but also precedes it. He agreed with Hesiod's "judgment, that beings must first of all have location … everything is somewhere, that is, in a place … [And] place does not perish with the perishing things in it" (208b34–39, 209a1–2).

Seen from this perspective, the plan to rebuild the Gdańsk Shakespeare Theatre would involve the thought that the building itself had not survived; the tradition and skill of staging performances may or may not have survived. However, what definitely did survive was the place, marked with a white square on the ground. The place could become the leaven from which the theatre would be created. Or would it, in fact, be reborn?

Aristotle distinguished "'place' considered generally, in which all bodies are, from the specific 'place' in which a body is directly" (209a34–35). Therefore, a book has its place on a shelf, a shelf – in a room, a room – in a house, a house – on the street, a street – in the city... And all these *specific* places are in the *general* place that Aristotle thought was the cosmos. This distinction appears to be intuitive and to chime with common sense, as do the conclusions that follow from it. One of them is the hierarchy of places that seem to be contained in one another. They are all in the cosmos, which would be the reservoir for all beings. Similarly, intuitive is the conclusion that the place precedes the thing that will be in it, and that it remains when the thing disappears.

Let us return to the Gdańsk Shakespeare Theatre. An article was published in 2009, which questioned the historical existence of an Elizabethan theatre in Gdańsk (Rekść, 2009). Certainly, the author claimed, it was not present during Shakespeare's lifetime. Of course, there were English theatre companies in Gdańsk, but they staged their performances in many different places. None of them could be called a permanent Elizabethan theatre. The Fencing School itself was built twenty years after Shakespeare's death. Apparently, it was a small building unsuitable for theatrical performances, which were, in fact, staged elsewhere, e.g., in the main town hall.

Initially, a very intense discussion seemed to ensue. For if the theatre was not a reconstruction, it would not necessarily have to be built in this particular place in the main city, where its huge structure would have a negative impact on the historic neighborhood, as its detractors believed would be the case. In fact, the discussion did not really start, and I have neither the intention nor the means of settling it here. The more important question is, if it was not the place that preceded the theatre, then where did it come from?

We can also refer to a simpler, more everyday situation. When I put a book on a shelf, it takes its place. The place precedes the presence of the book. Most of us, however, are probably familiar with situations when we try to stuff a new book onto a shelf that has its full complement. Sometimes we even manage to squeeze the book into an imperceptible gap, "the place." In this situation, did the place also precede the book? Or maybe I created it by inserting the book?

Similar questions were formulated at the beginning of the twentieth century by phenomenologists, especially Edmund Husserl and Martin Heidegger. The latter analyzed what things were. For Heidegger, things do not matter in themselves; they matter because of their participation in human existence. This applies especially to tools or other *things-at-hand* (*Zuhandene*), but not only to them. According to Heidegger (1927), it is not the place that precedes the thing, but rather the thing conditions and creates the place. A place exists only because of the thing it houses. The garden is not just a patch of land, it is a place of plants, a place for plants. The bookshelf exists because of the books that stand on it. It is not that it gives them space, but that the books create it.

Heidegger deprived things of their intrinsic meaning as physical bodies, relativizing their existence to participation in human beings. It was a

Copernican revolution, because as a result of this move, places became secondary to the beings they contained, and began to be created by them. Finally, space was no longer a physical reservoir, but rather "a relationship produced between things or between human mind and the world surrounding it" (Buczyńska-Garewicz, 2006, p. 10).

These two perspectives – i.e., Aristotelian and Heideggerian – seem extremely distant, even opposite. The Polish philosopher and phenomenologist Hanna Buczyńska-Garewicz (2006, p. 25) wrote that "the attempt to build a bridge between Aristotle and Heidegger seems rather impossible to achieve." However, I think many of us have the intuition that both theories in certain respects describe reality, just as some features of light are better explained when the light is thought to be a wave, others when the light is perceived as composed of particles. Sometimes it is easier for us to understand the world according to one perspective, sometimes according to the other. It is still one world though. A world where thought and intent are needed to make a fragment of space a place for a book. But if it does not fit physically there, I will not create this place. Because the world is physical and mental at the same time. If we manage to live in it, it means that somehow we have had to combine these two aspects – to build bridges between Aristotle and Heidegger.

This bridge is built over and over in the psyche, in the inner world. In this sense, it is never the case that only man is in the world, because at the same time the world is always in man. This interaction is made possible by fantasizing. Its role in mental life was strongly emphasized by the peer of phenomenology – psychoanalysis. Sigmund Freud, and then his successors, emphasized that parts of the personality (such as the superego) are not simple introjections of parental characters or even their attitudes or values, but are always distorted by the child's mental activity. Hanna Segal, describing Melanie Klein's understanding of the internal objects that make up the human inner world, emphasized that they are by no means "'objects' situated in the body or the psyche, [rather they are] unconscious phantasies which people have about what they contain" (Segal, 1964/2002, p. 12).

This, I think, applies also to things in our environment, both those created by nature and those made by man. Finally, the same can be said about space. Its fragments can also become the subject of fantasy. We know sacred mountains, trees used as symbols, haunted houses, suicide bridges, lovers' alleys ... However, apart from individual fantasies about fragments of space, we also have ideas about what they can be used for. About what needs can be met in them; what they afford. The latter word is the source of the term *affordance*, which is used in environmental psychology to describe the potential ways an organism reads the use of a given fragment of space (Gibson, 1972; Bańka, 2002). This concept is very important because it connects what is internal, subjective and psychic with what is external, objective and physical. It is a bridge between Aristotle and Heidegger –

precisely that: a bridge. The impulse and the decision to build it comes from the inner psychological world of humans. However, it is the river – as a part of the physical and external reality, with its shape (width, depth, availability of shores, distance from human settlements, etc.) – that determines the construction of the bridge in this specific location. Another example is a wooden bench in a park. It is used in many ways, many of which give designers and city officials a headache. Teenagers sit on the backrest with their legs on the seat, homeless people sleep on it, at night hooligans destroy the seat. There can be many ways – *affordances* – to use the bench, but human ingenuity is limited or determined by its shape, construction and material.

From this point of view, development consists in the fact that fantasies about a given space are gradually replaced by the perception of affordances. Thinking develops in exactly the same way; indeed, according to Hanna Segal, "thinking could be viewed as a modification of unconscious phantasy, a modification similarly brought about by reality testing" (Segal, 1964/2002, p. 23).

The experience of space is therefore not continuous and unchanging, but consists of moments of varying intensity. The space itself is not only a reservoir containing me and other beings, but a constellation of objects with which I enter into relationships of various natures and intensity. These objects are places.

From a certain perspective, we may even assume the existence of a hierarchy, or a continuum of places. At one end of the spectrum, there are those that are used to meet one-off needs, such as an ATM, hotel or airport. At the other end, we can put the whole world, and even the universe, because it was the cosmos that Aristotle called the "'place' considered generally, in which all bodies are" (Aristotle, *Physics*, ca. 350 BCE/1961, 209a34). It is not only physical, material – as phenomenology and psychoanalysis make us realize. It is not an infinitely large reservoir for beings, but a space that gives a containing and a holding, "a field saturated with existential meanings and objects" (Lipszyc, 2021, p. 107).

Let us note how similar this approach is to the transitional phenomena identified by Donald Winnicott (1953). These occur when an infant attaches external objects such as the corner of a blanket or quilt to an autoerotic activity such as thumb sucking. It can become important for a child as an object, on the one hand, of strong feelings of love and hatred, but also as a source of soothing, thereby bringing about a calming effect. Winnicott used the term *transitional object* in this context. He believed that in a child's experience everything which belongs to the category of transitional phenomena does not come only from the outside, nor is it purely a hallucination.

> In the course of years it becomes not so much forgotten as relegated to limbo … It loses meaning, and this is because the transitional

phenomena have become diffused, have become spread out over the whole intermediate territory between "inner psychic reality" and "the external world as perceived by two persons in common," that is to say, over the whole cultural field.

(Winnicott, 1971/2009, p. 7)

Winnicott enumerates here "play ... artistic creativity and appreciation ... religious feeling, ... dreaming ... fetishism, lying and stealing" (p.7). I believe that this dispersion of transitional phenomena can also be extended to human existence in space. I do not only mean situations such as visiting a historic city, admiring the sunset by the sea or hiking in the mountains. I think that just about any space in which humans are present is Winnicott's "potential space, one that can become an infinite area of separation" (Winnicott, 1971/2009, p. 146). In the course of development, it is possible to distinguish the inner world from the outer world. However, as Winnicott contends, complete separation is not possible. In fact, the internal (infant) and external (mother) worlds are not separated, but a third sphere is created between them, tangential to both. These words can be understood as follows: I never completely leave my mother's arms, but over time, they widen more and more to eventually cover the whole world. The area between them and me is precisely the potential space.

Perhaps transitional phenomena that are most saturated are those fragments of space that are neither specific places nor the "general" ones. Here I mean places that are more than simple locations for things, but remain much more concrete and tangible than entities such as universe, planet, continent or country. These are the places par excellence, for example, a favorite armchair by the window; my home; the corner shop; the school I am walking my child to; an office building; a characteristic landmark church; a dangerous neighborhood that I avoid; the city I live in; the city that I plan to visit during the summer holidays; the city where I was born; the tree under which I first kissed my beloved; my mother's grave, etc. It seems that the more easily and the more I experience a given fragment of space as a place, the less it is separated from my inner world and the more susceptible it becomes to projections and introjections, shifting between fantasizing about and perceiving affordances.

Perhaps it is the beginning of each place – the need and the possibility of incorporating some fragment of the outside world into a personal or group pattern of behavior. It is people who give meaning to some area as a place. The problem is that they often do so unconsciously. In particular, cities, as Christopher Bollas emphasized, are "rather unconscious processes. There are so many competing functions, aesthetics, local interests, and economics, each element influencing the other, that a city is more like the seeming chaos of the unconscious mind" (Bollas, 2000, p. 32). We can add transitional phenomena to the factors mentioned by Bollas. Our environments are always the resultant of intentional, conscious factors and *unconscious forms of thinking*;

and, of course, their interaction with what is found in space, with present matter and form. This applies to both the city as a whole and the places that constitute it. Places such as the Gdańsk Shakespeare Theatre, for example.

After all the above considerations, let us return to this theatre one last time. The creation and form of this place largely resulted from the conscious decisions of its creators. Let us recall that the main idea was to reconstruct in the city an Elizabethan theatre. A less conscious motive could have been the need to express the feeling that, as Poles, we were not so much entering Europe as returning to it. We were not building a theatre, but rebuilding the theatre, restoring a connection with the cultural community, which half a century of being in the Soviet camp had weakened, but not broken.

Of course, we can never be sure what the unconscious motives are, and whether they are not just another configuration of a given place. Moreover, it should not be assumed that there is one single interpretation. You can look at a place, just like a dream, from many perspectives, each of which will be equally real. However, it is definitely worth not stopping at the conscious layer, but looking for unconscious meanings. In this we shall be guided as always, by our feelings and associations. According to the official interpretation of the creators of the Gdańsk Shakespeare Theatre, the black color of its brick is supposed to refer either to gothic Dutch brick or to hard coal, which is the most common natural resource in Poland. The inaccessibility of the building, in turn, is to refer to the mask behind which the actor hides during the performance, while the shape of the theatre and its enormity (several times larger than the volume and surface of the supposedly recreated Fencing School) is to create a dialogue with St. Mary's Basilica, i.e., the most important church in Gdańsk. It is a conscious layer. On the other hand, for me, as for some other people, the black color and the scale of the Shakespeare Theatre are reminiscent of a tomb. I even encountered the term *sarcophagus* that, in this context, certainly refers not only to a decorated coffin, but also to the massive structure covering the nuclear reactor building of the Chernobyl power plant. Following this lead, we could ask what the theatre's black tombstone actually covers. Well, in this place there was not only the Fencing School, but also the Great Synagogue. It was built at the end of the nineteenth century as the largest synagogue in the city. The building was demolished by the Nazi-dominated authorities of the Free City of Gdańsk in May 1939.

Thus, we are dealing with a multi-level, complex interaction of the psyche and a certain area of the world; an area that is not a blank page, but one that is steeped in a history, which includes emotions, needs, desires and values. This area has housed various institutions. The psyche is also full of content. Some of them are conscious, such as the will to recreate a certain tradition. Others are less conscious, such as the desire not to recreate another, Jewish tradition.[2] It is a desire to refer to "phantasmatic constructions from the mythical past," as Andrzej Leder (2014, p. 93) wrote, in order not to "look into the mirror of the present day."

Figure 10.5 Aerial photograph of the Great Synagogue in Gdańsk taken ca. 1920
Source: National Archives and Records Administration.

Thinking about emotions and the fears it evokes, the black color of the brick allows me to think – or hope – that somewhere at the deepest unconscious level, the sarcophagus of the Gdańsk Shakespeare Theatre also expresses a mourning for the deaths of millions of Jews, our fellow citizens, whose extermination caused a breach in Polish society; a tragic "disappearance" that continues to influence our present.

In sum, the theatre I have recalled is a product of external and internal factors, some of them deeply unconscious. Every place is such a construct. Each place is a transitional object. It can be seen more as a product of the human spirit, as Heidegger would have it; it can also be seen in an Aristotelian manner, as being truly external. However, as Winnicott argued concerning the transitional object, the question of whether it comes from the outside or the inside should never be posed.

Notes

1 To be exact, the square was to mark the heart of the theatre: the place where in the past there used to be the stage and where it was to be built in the future.
2 Indeed, along the sides of the square where the Great Synagogue was located, the non-existent outline of its walls was recreated (using a different color of paving stones). It is very striking to see how the line disappears under the black bricks of the theatre.

References

Aristotle (1961). *Physics* (R. Hope, Trans.). University of Nebraska Press. (Original work published ca. 350 BCE)

Bańka, A. (2002). *Społeczna psychologia środowiskowa.* Wydawnictwo Naukowe Scholar.

Bollas, C. (2000). Architecture and the Unconscious. *International Forum of Psychoanalysis*, 9(1), 28–42.

Buczyńska-Garewicz, H. (2006). *Miejsca, strony, okolice: Przyczynek do fenomenologii przestrzeni.* Universitas.

Gibson, J.J. (1972). The Affordances of the Environment. In E. Reed & R. Jones (Eds.), *Reasons for Realism: Selected Essays of James J. Gibson.* Lawrence Erlbaum Associates.

Heidegger, M. (1927). *Sein und Zeit.* Max Niemeyer Verlag.

Leder, A. (2014). *Prześniona Rewolucja: Ćwiczenie z logiki historycznej.* Wydawnictwo Krytyki Politycznej.

Limon, J. (1997). Theatrum Gedanense. *Projekt*, 92–103, 204–207.

Limon, J. (2011). The City and the "Problem" of Theatre Reconstructions: "Shakespearean" Theatres in London and Gdańsk. *Actes des congrès de la Société française Shakespeare*, 28, 159–183.

Limon, J. (2022). *Gdański teatr "elżbietański."* Wydawnictwo słowo/obraz terytoria.

Lipszyc, A. (2021). Inne gmachy. O kilku budynkach u Bernharda. In W. Charchalis & A. Żychliński (Eds.), *Korekty Bernharda: Szkice krytyczne.* Wydawnictwo Naukowe UAM.

Ogden, T. (2010). On Three Types of Thinking: Magical Thinking, Dream Thinking, and Transformative Thinking. *Psychoanalytic Quarterly*, 79, 314–347.

Rekść, W. (2009, March 12). Teatr elżbietański w Gdańsku mistyfikacją? *E-teatr.* https://e-teatr.pl/teatr-elzbietanski-w-gdansku-mistyfikacja-a67512.

Segal, H. (2002). *Introduction to the Work of Melanie Klein.* Karnac. (Original work published 1964.)

Winnicott, D.W. (1953). Transitional Objects and Transitional Phenomena: A Study of the First Not-Me Possession. *International Journal of Psycho-Analysis*, 34(2), 89–97.

Winnicott, D.W. (2009). *Playing and Reality.* Routledge. (Original work published 1971.)

Chapter 11

"There Are No Empty Rooms"

Toward Literary Psychotopographies

Antoni Zając

In *The Secret Life of Puppets* Victoria Nelson (2003) developed a conceptual framework for analyzing the ghostly, supernatural, and artificial phenomena in modernist literary fiction. One of the terms she introduced seems particularly useful and calls for further development, since the author discussed it only briefly. Nelson uses the concept of literary psychotopography to describe the network of interactions between the unconscious psychic life of the writing subject, the outside world they live in, and the literary world they create:

> To these interior psychic regions as we find them projected onto an outer landscape I would like to give the name psychotopography. A psychotopographer is the artist who devotes herself to describing – with varying degrees of awareness about the true nature of the subject – the images of these inner regions as she discovers them in an imagined exterior landscape. Working backward from the sum of these details, the reader gains a picture not of what lies without but of what lies within. ... The contents of the psyche are cast like a net in ever-widening circles, first onto immediate surroundings – furniture, rooms, houses – then onto the larger natural landscape, finally even onto the globe itself.
>
> (Nelson, 2003, pp. 110–111)

The writing self as a psychotopographer can confront previously hidden phenomena of their internal life by projecting their experiences onto the world of the text. Nelson reaches beyond the conventional literary representation and portrays literature as an intermediary realm that breaches the most general spatial categories, creating a new arrangement for autobiographical explorations. A platform for place-writing (*topographia*) emerges, combining the elements of internal and external existence into a new textual lifeworld, in which the self is both as a creator and an actor. Thus, the writer multiplies themselves in the distorting mirror of the text. However, instead of opting for a singular representation, they choose to disseminate the traces of their life throughout the whole narrative. These crypto-

DOI: 10.4324/9781003436188-12

autobiographical allusions concern not only the conscious experiences, but also the unconscious conflicts and complexes. They surface in the text only as an enigmatic linguistic objects, created and re-created at the same time. Psychotopography generates an infrastructure that enables the subject to develop an autobiographical insight by externalizing and inscribing the phenomena of the inner life into the world of literary fiction, albeit in their distorted and misshaped version.

In this chapter, I aim to expand Nelson's concept. I believe that it could be particularly useful if referred to certain literary genres that combine the autobiographical confession (sometimes deeply buried in the seemingly fictional narrative) with the experimental modes of autoreferentiality. I am interested in the ways the subject reimagines themselves in the literary psychotopography. Rather than desperately striving for full biographical truth and full self-knowledge, they portray the structure of their experience like the Cubist paintings. By multiplying and reshaping the self in the literary narrative, they seek to perceive themselves as if they were someone different. By looking at themselves as if from the outside, they gain a fresh perspective on the most intimate and clandestine phenomena of their inner life. The idea of the self-divided and spatialized subject is the first element of the psychotopographic model I aim to outline in this chapter. The second entity that calls for further analysis is the world of the text, onto which the subject projects their experiences. I would like to describe the spatiotemporal characteristics of this universe by referring to the notion of chronotope introduced by Mikhail Bakhtin. Although Bakhtin claims that the chronotopes of the real and the represented world firmly resist fusion, he also argues that

> they are nevertheless indissolubly tied up with each other and find themselves in continual mutual interaction; uninterrupted exchange goes on between them, similar to the uninterrupted exchange of matter between living organisms and the environment that surrounds them. … The work and the world represented in it enter the real world and enrich it, and the real world enters the work and its world as part of the process of its creation, as well as part of its subsequent life, in a continual renewing of the work through the creative perception of listeners and readers.
>
> (Bakhtin, 1981/2008, p. 254)

Thus, I will present the writing subject as a "synchronically anachronical" self that recreates the spatiotemporal incoherence of their existence in the fractured chronotope of their narrative. This aspect of the literary psychotopography may be crucial for psychoanalytical literary theory, as well as the psychoanalytical theory of space. This field has been shaped by psychoanalytic geographers such as Steve Pile, Paul Kingsbury (Pile & Kingsbury, 2014) Vicki Blum or Anna Secor (Blum & Secor, 2014) who write about physical spaces susceptible to the psychic projections and introjections, and inhabited by spectres of the past. Drawing on Sigmund Freud, Jacques Lacan, and Henri Levefebre, these scholars focus on the spatial intersections between the realms of the inside and outside, past and present, intimate and sociopolitical. In this chapter, however, I will take a different path by focusing solely on the literary space; instead of referring to Freud or Lacan, I offer a discussion of a conceptual framework outlined by Donald Winnicott (1971/2005) in his *Playing and Reality*. This discussion will involve a reconsideration of Winnicott's most important notions, such as potential space, transitional object, and cultural experience.

I am interested not only in the theoretical model of the writing subject, but also in specific narrative structures that could be ascribed to this model. In the subsequent section of this chapter, I consider metalepsis as the most distinctive psychotopographical trope. Metalepsis involves a sudden, surprising disruption of ontological hierarchies and the narrative orders of the text; for example, an intrusion of the writer into the chronotope of their own text, or the fact that the character of the novel we read is suddenly disclosed as its author.

I conclude this chapter with a close reading of a poem by the Polish author Barbara Klicka. I consider this poem to be a psychotopographical metacommentary on the complex relationship between the spaces of life and the spaces of the literary text. In my analysis of this poem, I pay special attention to its rhythm and repetitions, both linguistic and figural.

Winnicott was particularly interested in the proxemics of the mother-child[1] relationship and its spatiotemporal characteristics. He drew attention to the positive process of gradual distancing – both physical and emotional – between the mother and the child, in which the child becomes an independent subject. However, before this final separation happens, it is first rehearsed in a safe environment, thus preventing the subject from experiencing this detachment as a traumatic event. During this part of the process, the child grows to learn that they and their mother are two different entities. This discovery leads the child to the realization of a fundamental difference between Me and Not-Me. In the next step, the child becomes aware of the existence of the outside world, and thus, the original firm mother-child union is replaced – not by the subject's narcissistic sense of omnipotence, but rather by relationships with various external objects established by newly individuated subject.

According to Winnicott, the process of transition from the realm of purely internal to the realm of relational is enabled by the third element which transcends the Me/Not-Me binary:

> Transitional object is *not an internal object* (which is a mental concept) – it is a possession. Yet it is not (for the infant) an external object either. ... The transitional object may therefore stand for the "external" breast, but *indirectly*, through standing for an "internal" breast.
>
> (Winnicott, 1971/2005, p. 13; emphasis in the original)

Nearly anything can become a transitional object – or "Me-extension" (p. 135) – a toy, a rug, a gesture, a word. The most interesting example, however, would be a piece of string, with which one of Winnicott's young patients joined various objects, like chairs. Winnicott writes:

> [I]n the example I gave of a boy's use of string ... I referred to two objects as being both joined and separated by the string. This is the paradox that I accept and do not attempt to resolve. The baby's separating-out of the world of objects from the self is achieved only through the absence of a space between, the potential space being filled in the way that I am describing.
>
> (p. 145)

Hence, transitional objects might be generally described as phantom threads between the mother and the child. Although these threads still partially connect the child to the mother, they also allow the child to discover the outside world which is a space filled with beings and phenomena that are neither the child nor the mother, but "the third party." These objects serve as a metonymy for both the internal and external world, and therefore, as Jean-Bertrand Pontalis (1981, pp. 45–46) interprets them, they mark both the mother and her absence.

In the above-quoted passage, Winnicott uses another of his groundbreaking terms, "potential space." He coined it to describe the paradoxical spatial dimension that enables both the distance and the contact between Me and its extensions, and the outside world:

> From the beginning the baby has maximally intense experiences in the potential space between the subjective object and the object objectively perceived, between me-extensions and not-me. This potential space is at the interplay between there being nothing but me and there being objects and phenomena outside omnipotent control.
>
> (Winnicott, 1971/2005, p.135)

Winnicott goes even further by saying that the potential space is a sort of playground, in which experimental play is both "immensely exciting" (p. 64) and risky for the subject. One experiment is quickly followed by another, but its results are never completely forgotten. Each object and each creative interaction are remembered, and so they enrich and pluralize the subject, who gradually becomes less self-contained and stops narcissistically perceiving itself as an omnipotent entity. From now on, the subject exists only as related to someone or something, and thus, it becomes spatialized within the de-centered network of libidinal investments.

I find it important to mention that Winnicott focused mainly on the reparative value of the transitional object. He underlined its ability to draw the subject out of the separation anxiety, and into the new possibilities of the external world. However, it is worth remembering that in Winnicott's theory and its subsequent reinterpretations, the transitional object only partially replaces the mother. Furthermore, it also stands for the distance and absence of the only object hitherto known to the child. Although the transitional object serves as the phantom thread, it also introduces the child to the ambivalent feeling of mediation and its spatiotemporal implications – someone was *there*, but it is not *anymore*, so *for the time being* this new thing will be *here* with me. The subjects also learn that their affects might connect them to someone or something absent, at least in this moment. The child's interaction with the transitional object during this absence might be joyful or soothing, but only if it does not last too long, because "there is [a] time-limit to frustration" (Winnicott, 1971/2005, p. 14); it might, however, also feel melancholic, especially considering that the child is unsure whether the mother will ever come back:

> The feeling of the mother's existence lasts x minutes. If the mother is away more than x minutes, then the imago fades, and along with the baby's capacity to use the symbol of the union ceases. The baby is distressed, but this distress is soon *mended* because the mother returns in $x+y$ minutes. In $x+y$ minutes the baby has not become altered. But in $x+y+z$ minutes the baby has become *traumatized*. In $x+y+z$ minutes the mother's return does not mend the baby's altered state. Trauma implies that the baby has experienced a break in life's continuity, so that primitive defenses now become organized to defend against a repetition of "unthinkable anxiety" or a return of the acute confusional state that belongs to disintegration of the nascent ego structure.
>
> We must assume that the vast majority of babies never experience the $x+y+z$ quantity of deprivation. After "recovery" from $x+y+z$ deprivation a baby has to start again permanently deprived of the root which could provide *continuity with the personal beginning*. This implies the existence of a memory system and on organization of memories.
>
> (Winnicott, 1971/2005, pp. 131–132, emphasis in the original)

Here, Winnicott differentiates between only two kinds of maternal disappearance: the "normal" one and the "traumatizing" one. I believe, however, that he overlooks the melancholic, and not traumatic, nature of each absence. When the child interacts with the transitional object, it does not forget about the mother; rather, it waits for her to come back, so that its loss turns out to be only momentary, though the child cannot be sure of that. Hence, the transitional object helps the child to sustain his/her affects in hope of the mother's reappearance. This way, the child learns about the temporal nature of experience and discovers the realm of memory, an internal spatiotemporal dimension that marks a partial presence of an absent object. Thus, the playground of potential space filled with transitional phenomena is also an environment that allows to learn the proxemics of memory, loss (including an irreversible one) and grief. It serves a vital role in preparing the child for being alive in the dynamic and incoherent outside world where nothing lasts forever. The life itself is an interplay of continuity and discontinuity.

Margaret Gibson argues that "There are dead objects and then there are objects of the dead – those spectral, melancholy objects mediating, and signifying, an absence. As part of mourning and memory, objects function as … traces of corporeal absence" (Gibson 2004, p. 285). Transition enabled by the transitional object does not result in disappearance of the past events. It allows the subject to loosen the attachment with the lost object so that it might finally be perceived as unattainable in its entirety, but prone for a reminiscence. The subject might therefore not only move on, but also look back on, rather than come back to, what has been lost. In Winnicott's words, the subject might finally "use" the lost subject by "destroying" the idea of its eternal presence:

> [A]fter "subject relates to object" comes "subject destroys object" (as it becomes external); and then there may come "object survives destruction by the subject." But there may or may not be survival. A new feature thus arrives in the theory of object-relating. The subject says to the object: … "Hullo object!" "I destroyed you." "I love you." "You have value for me because of your survival of my destruction of you." "While I am loving you I am all the time destroying you in (unconscious) fantasy." Here fantasy begins for the individual. The subject can now use the object that has survived.
>
> (Winnicott, 1971/2005, p. 120)

The object, then, is not fully destroyed, but rather perseveres in its afterlife, represented in the subject's memory. However, it is not as neatly stored and preserved in the subject's mind as Winnicott would suggest. Some objects appear to haunt us with their uncanny reappearances, as if they were trying to regain a palpable presence in the subject's life. It is also important to notice that as time goes by, the image of the past is prone to distortions and its original shape becomes uncertain. The original scene of loss becomes unattainable and the subject cannot be sure whether they remember each detail correctly. In consequence, they have to come up with a new version of this scene. Since they lose direct insight to their own past, they have to become unreliable narrator of their own lives.

The subject might develop different responses to this realization. One of the methods they might adopt to face their own narrative unreliability is to confront their inner conflicts, uncertainties and glitches of memory by engaging in what Winnicott calls "cultural experience" (Winnicott, 1971/2005, pp. 128–140). This sort of "secondary level potential space" allows the subject to engage in autobiographic play with ambivalent attachments and the unruly objects of the past by means of its creative representation. Here is what Winnicott writes about a domain of cultural experience:

> I have used the term "cultural experience" as an extension of the idea of transitional phenomena and of play without being certain that I can define the word "culture." The accent indeed is on experience. ... The place where cultural experience is located is in the *potential space* between the individual and the environment (originally the object). The same can be said of playing. Cultural experience begins with creative living first manifested in play.
>
> (Winnicott, 1971/2005, pp. 133–135)

Cultural experience is a post-individuational remainder of potential space which does not disappear as soon as the child grows up and goes out into the world. This realm of possible events, unexpected relationships, and liminal experiments perseveres as a structure within the subject and the way they relate to the external world. Thus, the cultural experience is a sideways space, a heterotopia where previously undiscovered, alternative relationships happen on the verge of the inner and outer dimensions.

Here, I am particularly interested in modes of the subject's active participation in the cultural experience. They become a writer who projects their own experiences, encrypted within their mental topography, onto the chronotope of the literary text.[2] As Freud (1908) stated in his paper titled "Creative Writers and Daydreaming,"

> The psychological novel in general no doubt owes its special nature to the inclination of the modern writer to split up his ego, by self-observation, into many part-egos, and, in consequence, to personify the conflicting currents of his own mental life in several heroes.
>
> (Freud, 1908, p. 150)[3]

Literature, which I would like to call a "metalevel potential space," activates a new way of relating to one's own life. It is particularly true in regards to experimental literature that occurs on the intersection of fiction and life-writing (see Smith & Watson, 2016), and involves complex rhetorical devices such as intertextuality, fictionalization, or metalepsis, the use of which I will discuss later in the chapter. Furthermore, these devices also emulate the dynamics of memory, with special attention paid to the melancholic, spectral presence-absence of life's past phenomena. Max Saunders (2010) offers a fascinating account of autoreferential and metaliterary narratives he calls "autobiografictions":

Autobiografiction is "real" autobiographical experience (the "spiritual experiences") turned into fictional form. But it isn't just the form that is fictionalized, but the autobiographical experience itself; either because it has been altered, or because it has been attributed to someone else; reinvented as another's imaginary experience.

...

To argue that autobiografiction expresses a sense that one's spiritual experiences have a fictional dimension, is tantamount to adopting a psychoanalytic view of the self as self-divided, partly unconscious, a site of repression, fantasy, and the disturbing and elusive affects of transference. Autobiografiction, that is to say, also expresses a sense of the self as "other"; that its narratives are not simply reducible to the facts of one's formal biography or autobiography.

...

Autobiography recognizes itself as having a fictional dimension. Fiction recognizes itself as having an autobiographical dimension. Autobiografiction is not only where these two recognitions coincide, but is also the recognition that they are inseparable; and that they have been since the beginning.

(Saunders, 2010, pp. 171, 206, 526)

Winnicott stated that

Of the transitional object it can be said that it is a matter of agreement between us and the baby that we will never ask the question: "Did you conceive of this or was it presented to you from without?" The important point is that no decision on this point is expected. The question is not to be formulated.

(Winnicott, 1971/2005, p. 17)

However, after taking Saunders's argument into consideration, I would argue that the transitional phenomena of literature are not only created in response to this question, but they also prompt to investigate upon the stability of this very differentiation. Literature, therefore, blurs the boundaries between "what is conceived," i.e., the products of imagination, and what is "presented from without," i.e., the faithful representation of the actual phenomena. Thus, in literary fiction, and in autobiografiction in particular, the transitional objects are indefinitely, and not temporarily, transitional. It is so because their paradoxical overdetermination is tolerated and unresolved by authors. In consequence, the subject of autobiografictional narrative is indeed an unreliable narrator of their own life.

Although it might feel distressing, this inconvenience could also be productive and even fortunate, if considered as an invitation for autobiografictional play in the potential space of literature. Various scenarios of the past might be considered within this space, as it allows the writing self to explore more than one of them. The subject might as well seek to play with a number of life-scenarios by creating their own non-identical doppelgängers, such as narrators, characters, or lyrical speakers. This spatialization enriches the subject who therefore distances themselves from their own experiences. Thus, they realize that they should treat the events of their life more loosely, as something to play with, and prone to the potentialities of fiction which could enrich the narrative account of one's own life. Instead of desperately striving for full biographical truth and full self-knowledge, they might rather seek to portray – both consciously and unconsciously – the structure of their experience and the events taking part in their mental topography by re-presenting them via formal and spatiotemporal arrangements of their narratives.

I would like to go even further by suggesting that it is not only the characters who represent certain parts of the subjective topography. The subject's affect could be spatially projected onto the text as a specific mood or attunement that sets its tone, or as a scene of the subject-object interaction that does not faithfully recreate the "real-life biographical events," but rather depicts affective dynamics of those events. I therefore agree with Saunders, who writes that "You don't have to have actually turned into an insect to be able to write 'Metamorphosis'; but you probably have to have felt alienation, or abjection. Fiction can be 'autobiographical' in many different ways" (Saunders 2010, p. 8). Moreover, I claim that the effect of psychotopographic spatialization transcends the author-character projection, as the features of the writing subject might be dispersed within the multiple regions of the chronotope, thus becoming a literary psychotopography. This way, the subject's experiences and affects become secretly encrypted within various arrangements, passages and compartments of the text. Dusty attics, claustrophobic corridors, stormy seas or small provincial towns, names of which sound weirdly familiar – all of these spatial phenomena could be quite revealing, if read inquisitively enough, as a literary constructs that metaphorically or metonymically resemble the subject's affects, unconscious conflicts and attachments in their inner topography. Thus, the subject extends themselves sideways within the potential space of a psychotopographic narrative. This process also incorporates a metaliterary and autoreferential discourse of revisiting, distorting, and overwriting the past.

The most important narratological device of literary psychotopography is called "metalepsis," and Gerard Genette describes it as "any intrusion by the extradiegetic narrator or narratee into the diegetic universe (or by diegetic characters into a metadiegetic universe)" (Genette, 1980, pp. 234–235). Metalepsis involves a surprising disruption of ontological hierarchies and narrative orders of the text; for example, an intrusion of the writer into the chronotope of their own text, or a sudden reveal that the novel we are reading was actually written by a character in this novel. Although normally levels of narrative are supposed to be clearly separated and distinguishable, metalepsis unexpectedly traverses these structures, thus proving that the proxemics of various dimensions of literary narrative are relative and onto-logically unstable, which gives another meaning to the notion of the transitional in regards to literary objects. It also means that "the one who tells" might become spectrally present in the various phenomena of "the world of which one tells" as Genette puts it (p. 236). Thus, metalepsis activates the constant psychotopographical oscillation between the inner-outer spatio-temporal arrangements of the writing subject, and the chronotope of the text. Since it serves as a paradoxical rupture that creates a mediation (or as a glitch that makes the narrative orders collapse into each other), metalepsis might be compared to the idea of caesura developed by Wilfred Bion in one of his last papers: "investigate the caesura; not the analyst; not the analy-sand, not the unconscious, not the conscious, not sanity; not insanity. But the caesura, the link, the synapse, the counter-transference, the transitive-intransitive mood" (Bion, 1977/1989, p. 56).

One of the most famous examples of metalepsis as a violent (see Malina, 2002) caesural intervention comes from Julio Cortazar's (1978) short story titled *Axolotl*:

> My face was pressed against the glass of the aquarium, my eyes were attempting once more to penetrate the mystery of those eyes of gold without iris, without pupil. I saw from very close up the face of an axo-lotl immobile next to the glass. No transition and no surprise, I saw my face against the glass, I saw it on the outside of the tank, I saw it on the other side of the glass. Then my face drew back and I understood.
>
> …
>
> I am an axolotl for good now, and if I think like a man it's only because every axolotl thinks like a man in his rosy stone semblance. … I console myself by thinking that perhaps he is going to write a story about us, that, believing he's making up a story, he's going to write all this about axolotls.
>
> (Cortazar, 1978, pp. 8–9)

The topography of the self is connected to the topography of the diegesis, and this arrangement might be imagined as a topological figure of Möbius strip (Waller, 1987, p. 2). Metaleptic transfer between these realms constantly jams the linear and hierarchic structures of the text, thus turning it into an interlocking system of gaps, loops, and delays. This system seems to resemble the dynamics of subjectivity which are also shaped by metaleptic intrusions, deferrals, and glitches which are omnipresent in the warped logic of the Uncanny (Malina, 2002, pp. 119, 123–124) or the Afterwardness (Edelman, 1994, p. 176). Disruptions caused by these narrative devices and/or psycho-analytical tropes of experience act to loosen the most severe ties of the fixed spatiotemporal arrangements, thus turning all of its elements into transitional and transitive ones. Hence, the most radical and daring response to the problem of narrative unreliability might be to not only accept it, but also to take it even to another level by creating an effect of an onto-epistemological vertigo in the potential space of the literary psychotopography.

The subjective/textual dynamic I seek to describe here is particularly prevalent in the modernist and postmodernist literary prose, for example in works of Bruno Schulz (Nelson, 2003), Ingeborg Bachmann (Krylova, 2009), Vladimir Nabokov (Lipszyc, 2016; Nakata, 2019), Thomas Bernhard (Krylova, 2010), W.G. Sebald (Pieldner, 2013), or lesser known modernist writers such as Max Blecher (Glăvan, 2014), Zygmunt Haupt (Niewiadomski, 2018), and Andrzej Kuśniewicz (Zając, 2021). It is also worth noting that the scholars who research the topic of metalepsis, including Genette, also tend to focus on novels or short stories rather than any other genres. Although one might argue that the psychotopographic model of reading requires the multi-level narrative structure, and the complex world-making, and that these two features are significant only for prose, I believe that contemporary poetry might also be prone to such an interpretation. Poetry as a genre is particularly invested in the study of the self-reflective and the self-reflexive. In this special kind of literary playground, endless possibilities for inventive description of subject-object relationships unravel; the poem allows for a complicated play of transitions and discontinuities between the writing subject and the textual self, rhetorically and ontologically designed as a specific lyrical speaker. By constantly distorting and reinventing the linguistic idioms of lyric, poetry strives for the singularity of the subjective expression and the speculative metacommentary on the self. It always comments, reconstructs, and deconstructs, and not only portrays the internal-external spatiotemporal arrangements. Moreover, one of the distinctive formal features of the poem is that it involves rhythmical ruptures that also serve as respiratory pauses, such as verse caesuras, or line breaks, and they also contribute to the meaning of the text.

In order to validate my hypothesis regarding the psychotopographic potentialities of contemporary poetry, I would like to conclude my analysis with a close reading of the poem which offers a fascinating metaperspective on potential spaces of text which are seemingly interconnected to the potential spaces of life. The poem titled "Allel" ("Allele") was written by Barbara Klicka (2021), one of the most prominent contemporary Polish poets,[4] about whom Agnieszka Waligóra (2018) aptly remarked that

> Klicka's poems almost always involve a synopsis, an event, a situation … and thus seem to diverge towards prose. However, this eventfulness or epic character is constantly shattered by the structure of the text which goes from the abstract to the concrete, from the general to the individual perspective, from description to impression. If movement or characters are involved, … the reader expects an ending, a resolution as to who goes where and why. The author, however, never concludes her story; she

ruptures and disperses the phrase by introducing another topic completely unrelated to the previous ones. Thus, her poetry becomes a fractured, non-linear novel, comprised of a series of smaller pieces.

(Waligóra, 2018, p. 260)

Allel was published in Klicka's most recent poetry collection of the same title. I quote this poem in its entirety, in Joanna Piechura's translation:

With dirt in your belly button, with a stone – go.
Barely even city green – poor lure –
and yet the way back is hardly there. From l a y
down to day it rushes, is all.
Here, let it mutate, here, pass pneumothorax: oxygen
in the body's cavities that doesn't serve the breath.
Doesn't serve at all, yet clings to the conviction
that there are no empty
rooms, animals live everywhere. It is
believed, they believe, it is after how we will be consoled.
After the crash, after the full moon, after the warm month.
With dirt,
with a stone in your belly button,
a steep foot into two graves – go.
Look, already one.

(Klicka, 2021, p. 7; emphasis in the original)

The title of the poem itself refers to a state of potentiality. An allele is "one of two or more versions of DNA sequence (a single base or a segment of bases) at a given genomic location" (National Human Genome Research Institute, 2023). Usually, there are two different alleles in each cell, though only one of them is selected during the process of meiosis which determines various physical features, such as eye or hair color. Before meiosis, however, both alternatives are still possible. The word "allele" seems to be very accurate in describing this phenomenon of suspended potentiality, because it is etymologically derived from two Greek words: the first one is *allos*, which means "other," and the second one is *allelo*, which means "mutual" or "reciprocal." The noun *allelomorph*, on the other hand, literally means "other shape." Thus, the other form of a single feature always exists before the division that is lethal to one allele, but vital for the survival of the other.

The poem starts with a sort of wake-up call for the subject. It is worth noting that here, instead of the conventional lyrical I, the self is strangely impersonal and spatialized which means that the poem instantly stages a link between the subject and the outside world. Therefore, instead of the confessional voice of the lyrical speaker, there is a voice from without that animates the body and provokes it to enter the external space. This body, however, is already marked with an existence of something seemingly external and foreign – it is dirt and a stone in the belly button. This Not-Me object is placed in a very specific cavity. A belly button is, after all, a scar that reminds us of the separation of the child from the mother. Here, the division between the Me and the Not-Me is even more problematic, because there exists a medical condition called "navel stone." It occurs when dead skin cells and dirt accumulate in the belly button for so long that they form a hardened mass, which is comprised of the excessive matter from both our bodies and from the outside world. It is not obvious whether the poem speaks of this condition or not. What matters, however, is that this weird extimate object kept in the belly button has been there even before the events presented in the poem emerge. The temporal element is introduced into the already complicated psychospatial arrangement and therefore the reader starts to wonder about the past of the subject and their body. For instance, it could be that the belly button is filled with dirt, because the body lay on the ground or in the ground, especially since a grave is mentioned in the last lines of the poem.

I want to stress the fact that the dirt stays with/within the subject when they enter the "city green" space. Its "poor lure" is effective, because the subject gets lost or even trapped in the external realm. They are unable to find their way back to their former existential condition, of which we know virtually nothing. The transition between the old and the new form of life is described in the following words: "From lay / down to day it rushes, is all." In the original, the word used for the expression "lay down" is "dna," or "bottoms, depths," a word composed of the same letters as DNA. This homonym has two important meanings: first, it means that the subject hit the rock bottom of their life and second, it refers to the DNA polymer as the very basis of existence that constantly changes throughout one's lifetime and, therefore, it is loaded with potentiality. I believe that this dialectic oscillation between depressed disillusionment ("dna") and persistent seeking of enrichment ("DNA") is at the core of this poem.

The next stanza starts with another call for action: "Here, let it mutate, here, pass pneumothorax." Metaphorically, this is a call for creativity akin to the one I sought to describe with regards to the autobiografictional playground of literature. This call, therefore, invokes us to search for potential remixes, alterations, and modifications of reality, which is what literature does best. However, a dialectic approach is needed here as well. By referring to mutation, the poem once again revisits the field of genetics, in which such mutations are not always fruitful, as many of them may cause fatal diseases. Some of these mutations are triggered by mutagens, physical or chemical agents from the outside world such as viruses, bacteria, or even tobacco smoke. These mutagens permanently change the DNA of the organism, and thus they "metaleptically" intrude into the most fundamental structure of biological life. Subsequently, in this line of the poem Klicka refers to another act of breaching which might refer both to the human's body and to the body of the text, namely she mentions a severe medical condition called pneumothorax. It stands for a pathological lung condition that is often caused by smoking tobacco or by physical trauma such as penetrating injury. Pneumothorax is an abnormal collection of air in a so-called pleural space which surrounds each lung and serves as a border between the lung and the chest wall (Bintcliffe & Maskell, 2014). Air fills up the pleural space and generates pressure which causes the collapse of the lung. To name such spaces in the human body as the pleural space, human anatomy scientists use the notion of the "potential space"[5] (see Dalley, 2008). It designates a space that exists in-between two adjacent structures in the body, normally pressed together tightly. If the body is healthy, these spaces barely exist, but they might enlarge drastically under pathological conditions, for instance, as a result of illness. We might compare these potential physiological spaces to an unopened plastic bag or a balloon that has not been inflated. What brings these spaces into existence is an intrusion of air or fluid caused by an injury or fracture. Until such intrusion, their presence is only a potentiality.

Although to the best of my knowledge Winnicott did not know that the anatomic concept of potential space exists, it feels almost uncanny to reread the passage about the boy's string from *Playing and Reality* having learned about this coincidence: "The baby's separating-out of the world of objects from the self is achieved only through *the absence of a space between, the potential space being filled in*" (Winnicott, 1971/2005, p. 145, emphasis added). Our bodies are filled with unknown spaces and areas, hidden in-between the organs and the tissues, but their discovery is only possible as a result of an eventful, though dangerous, encounter of the internal organs, and the external objects or pathogens. Thus, the body can also be portrayed as prone to metaleptic activations and animations.

Now I would like to resume my close reading of Klicka's poem by once again reexamining the notion of "pneumothorax." As per Greek etymology, "thorax" means chest, and "pneuma" stands for the air that enters the pleural space, which is why Klicka writes about a special kind of oxygen inhabiting the cavities of the body which is not used for breathing. This "other oxygen" extends into all of the cavities in the subject or in the outside world, so they become apparent for the very first time, thus enabling an inquiry into these previously invisible spaces. The dialectical figure of aeration (which may or may not be equal to breathing) is, I believe, a sort of psychotopographic envisionment of the precarious creativity that is both melancholic and quite optimistic in its vigorous, if doubting, striving for a different mode of existence. The oxygen "clings to the conviction" that in fact there always is an alternative, here portrayed as a space inhabited by yet unknown objects. The image of unspecified animals living "everywhere" is ambiguous, bringing not only hope, but also a vague sense of uncertainty or even danger, because as we seek the change in our lives, we do not know whether it will have a positive or negative outcome. Nevertheless, these potential spaces are not devoid of presence; at least the (impersonal) speaker says "it is believed, they believe, it is after how we will be consoled." The subject themselves has yet to determine whether this belief in deferred consolation is in vain. According to the logic of "allelic" potentiality, such side realms might or might not ever be attainable for the subject, because another scenario could be in play instead.

The final part of the poem begins with a repetition of the first two verses, as if the poem performed only one lap of an ongoing process that will never be completed. However, a new image, and a new call from without, is presented at the very end: "a steep foot into two graves – go. / Look, already one." Only one of the two alleles will survive the cellular division that determines the future. One form of life could be lost irreversibly, although the second one perseveres, at least so long as the next lap of the "strangely looped" poem begins.

I would argue that although Klicka's poem considers the vitalizing potentialities of creation and creativity, it is not overly optimistic. Rather, it presents a complex network of affects and libidinal investments which fuel a never-ending dialogue between hope and disenchantment. The speaker strives for new possibilities, but they also realize that the presence of these possibilities will mark the absence of the other ones, including those that never came into being. They might be envisioned as paradoxical undead objects buried in the spaces of our psyche that also serve as the crypts of our past (see Török & Abraham, 1986). Therefore, the literary play of psychotopography is melancholic rather than reparative, but at least it allows us finally to reflect upon the losses we have experienced.

I believe that the development of a literary psychotopography might be metaphorically compared to a kind of medical examination that serves to assess the condition of a patient with pneumothorax (see Winter & Smethurst, 1999). "Percussing"[6] is an act of tapping the body's surface in its various places. The method is used to examine the liminal spaces between organs and the presence of fluid or air in the body. I would argue that in the autobiografictional prose, and in the "strange loops" of the self-reflexive poems, the subject can percuss both their own psyche and the outside world. This way, they search for potential spaces, hidden in the caesura between the inside and the outside. It is a melancholic search for the undisclosed potentialities of life; they might be discovered from the perspective of the literary playground, although their presence is only transitional and ephemeral. They might be found, but only as those who are already irreversibly lost.

Notes

1 It is important to remember that when Winnicott uses the word "mother" he always refers not only to an infant's natural mother, but to any person serving as a mother figure to this infant (see Winnicott, 1971/2005, p. 13).

2 For a Winnicottian interpretation of act of reading as a cultural experience in potential space see Winsworth (2008); Coles (2022). These approaches seem very useful; however, in this chapter I wish to describe a different process, in which the writer perceives the act of writing as a creation of a specific kind of potential space that enables the spatialization of their experiences and their mental topography.

3 It is important to remember that in that same paper Freud states the following: "The child's best loved and most intense occupation is with his play or games. Might we not say that every child at play behaves like a creative writer in that he creates a world of his own, or, rather, rearranges the things of this world in a new way which pleases him. It would be wrong to think he does not take that world seriously; on the contrary, he takes his play very seriously and he invests a lot of emotion in it. The opposite of play is not what is serious but what is real. In spite of all the emotion with which he constructs his world of play, the child distinguishes it quite well from reality; and he likes to link his imagined objects and situations to the tangible and visible things of the real world" (Freud, 1908, pp. 144–145).

4 For more English translations of Klicka's poems, see Klicka (2017).

5 Dalley (2008, p. 393) states that "Potential anatomical spaces are vital to normal, pain-free function of the heart, lungs, and locomotor system. They are also the basis for extraluminal endoscopic procedures. However, understanding potential spaces can be challenging. In dissection, potential spaces such as bursae and tendon sheaths are usually unnoticed. Others, such as the pleural and pericardial sacs, are viewed only after they have been opened, making them into realized spaces more representative of pathological states." See also DeBonis (2021).

6 For an interesting ethnographic study of percussing as a multisensory practice, see Harris (2016).

Acknowledgements

I am incredibly grateful to Joanna Piechura who was so kind as to translate Barbara Klicka's poem specifically for this chapter. During our numerous discussions she has also encouraged me to think about metalepsis as a fundamental trope of literary topographies.

References

Bakhtin, M. (2008). *The Dialogic Imagination by M.M. Bakhtin. Four Essays* (M. Holquist, Ed. & Trans., & C. Emerson, Trans.). University of Texas Press. (Original work published 1981.)

Bintcliffe, O., & Maskell, N. (2014). Spontaneous Pneumothorax. *BMJ*, 348, Article g2928.

Bion, W. (1989). *Two Papers: The Grid and Caesura*. Karnac. (Original work published 1977.)

Blum, V., & Secor, A. (2014). Mapping Trauma: Topography to Topology. In P. Kingsbury & S. Pile (Eds.), *Psychoanalytic Geographies*. Routledge.

Coles, E.S. (2022). D.W. Winnicott and the Finding of Literature. In S. Bar-Haim, E. S. Coles, & H. Tyson (Eds.), *Wild Analysis: From the Couch to Cultural and Political Life*. Routledge.

Cortazar, J. (1978). *End of Game and Other Stories* (P. Blackburn, Trans.). Harper & Row.

Dalley, A.F. (2008). These Spaces Have Great Potential: Teaching Students About Anatomical Potential Spaces. *The FASEB Journal*, 22(1), 393.4.

DeBonis, K. (2021). Potential Space. *Academic Psychiatry*, 45, 122–123.

Edelman, L. (1994). *Homographesis: Essays in Gay Literary and Cultural Theory.* Routledge.

Freud, S. (1959b). Creative Writers and Daydreaming. In *The Standard Edition of the Complete Psychological Works of Sigmund Freud*, Vol. 9 (J. Strachey, Ed. & Trans.). The Hogarth Press. (Original work published 1908.)

Fuchs, A. (2016). Psychotopography and Ethnopoetic Realism in Uwe Tellkamp's Der Turm . *New German Critique*, 39(2), 119–132.

Genette, G. (1980). *Narrative Discourse: An Essay in Method.* Cornell University Press.

Gibson, M. (2004). Melancholy Objects. *Mortality* 9(4), 285–299.

Glăvan, G. (2014). Mapping the Unreal: Max Blecher in the Shadow of the Avant-Garde. *Arcadia*2014, 49(1), 1–20.

Harris, A. (2016). Listening-Touch, Affect and the Crafting of Medical Bodies Through Percussion. *Body & Society*, 22(1), 31–61.

Harris, W.C. (1997). Undifferentiated Bunnies: Setting Psychic Boundaries in the Animal Stories of Beatrix Potter, Jack London, and Ernest Seton. *Victorian Review*, 23(1), 62–113.

Hofstadter, D. (2007). *I Am a Strange Loop.* Basic Books.

Klicka, B. (2017). *Bankiet i skóra: Banket i koža. Banquet and leather* (⊠. Čilić Škeljo & D. Malcolm, Trans.). Versopolis.

Klicka, B. (2021). *Allel.* Wydawnictwo J.

Krylova, K. (2009). Melancholy, Topography, and the Search for the Origin in Ingeborg Bachmann's Drei Wege zum See . *German Life and Letters*, 62(2), 157–173.

Krylova, K. (2010). "Eine den Menschen zerzausende Landschaft": Psychotopography and the Alpine Landscape in Thomas Bernhard's "Frost." *Austrian Studies*, 18, 74–88.

Lipszyc, A. (2016). Spectre of the Author, a Double with a Flaw: Photographies in Nabokov's Autobiography. *View. Theories and Practices of Visual Culture*, 13. http s://www.pismowidok.org/en/archive/2016/13-auto-photo-biographies/spectre-of-the-author-a-double-with-a-flaw.

Lipszyc, A. (2019). *Freud: Logika doświadczenia. Spekulacje marańskie.* Wydawnictwo IBL PAN.

Litchfield, R. (2010). *(Re)Imagining Los Angeles: Five Psychotopographies in the Fiction of Steve Erickson.* Doctoral dissertation, University College London.

Malina, D. (2002). *Breaking the Frame: Metalepsis and the Construction of the Subject.* Ohio State University Press.

Nakata, A. (2019). Memories Trick – Memories Mix: Transparent Things. In I. Księżopolska & M. Wiśniewski (Eds.), *Vladimir Nabokov and the Fictions of Memory.* Fundacja Augusta Hrabiego Cieszkowskiego.

National Human Genome Research Institute. (2023). *Allele.* https://www.genome.gov/genetics-glossary/Allele.

Nelson, V. (2003). *The Secret Life of Puppets.* Harvard University Press.

Niewiadomski, A. (2018). Przestrzenie Zygmunta Haupta (rekonesans). *Roczniki Humanistyczne*, 66, 159–178.

Pieldner, J. (2013). The Topography of Memory in W.G. Sebald's Austerlitz. *University of Bucharest Review*, 3(2), 45–52.

Pile, S., & Kingsbury, P. (2014). Introduction: The unconscious, Transference, Drives, Repetition and Other Things Tied to Geography. In P. Kingsbury & S. Pile (Eds.), *Psychoanalytic Geographies*. Routledge.

Pontalis, J.-B. (1981). *Frontiers in Psychoanalysis: Between the Dream and the Psychic Pain* (C. Cullen & P. Cullen, Trans.). The Hogarth Press and the Institute of Psycho-Analysis.

Richter, G. (2010). *Thought-Images: Frankfurt School Writers' Reflections from Damaged Life*. Stanford University Press.

Saunders, M. (2010). *Self Impression. Life-Writing, Autobiografiction, & the Forms of Modern Literature*. Oxford University Press.

Soja, E.W. (1996). *Thirdspace: Journeys to Los Angeles and Other Real – and – Imagined Places*. Basil Blackwell.

Smith, S., & Watson, J. (2016). *Life Writing in the Long Run: A Smith & Watson Autobiography Studies Reader*. Michigan Publishing.

Török, M., & Abraham, N. (1986). *The Wolf Man's Magic Word: A Cryptonymy* (N. Rand, Trans.). University of Minnesota Press.

Waligóra, A. (2018). Poezja anestetyczna – *nice* Barbary Klickiej. *Poznańskie Studia Polonistyczne. Seria Literacka*, 33, 257–267.

Waller, M. (1987). Academic Tootsie: The Denial of Difference and the Difference It Makes. *Diacritics*, 17(1), 2–20.

Winnicott, D.W. (2005). *Playing and Reality* (2nd ed.). Routledge. (Original work published 1971.)

Winsworth, B. (2008). The Potential Space of Reading: The Text as a Holding Environment. In C. Alexandre-Garner (Ed.), *Frontières, marges et confins*. Presses Universitaires de Paris Ouest.

Winter, R., & Smethurst, D. (1999). Percussion: A New Way to Diagnose a Pneumothorax. *Br J Anaesth.*, 83(6), 960–961.

Zając, A. (2021). Between History and (Distorted) Memory. Hidden Monograms of the Past in *The King of Two Sicilies* by Andrzej Kuśniewicz (G. Ronge, Trans.). *Forum of Poetics*, 23, 126–145.

Chapter 12

Three Membranes of Delusion

Schreber, Malebranche and the Financial Market

Marta Olesik

In this chapter, I want to weave a short tale of three different substances, or extended membranes consisting of three different trains of thought intertwined in an argument which will build towards a single, layered spatial form. Each of the membranes consists of a case of schizophrenia, a (linguistic) space of delusion. We will be considering a linguistic membrane of erotic stimulation (with which God persecutes judge Daniel Schreber); a tactile membrane of intelligible extension, the substance of pure creation (the experience of matter as an eternally renewed act of God who persecutes an oratorian priest and ardent dualist, Nicolas Malebranche); and a market membrane of decoded financial conjectures (an eerie shroud whose logic persecutes global history).

These are indeed strange forms of extension, to be sure, and yet they are perfectly consistent with the Cartesian idea which posits matter as a conceptual thing, a physicality coextensive with the matrix of geometry. The three cases of schizophrenia which will be my focus here – one of them being an extreme case of Cartesian dualism – share the same sense of materiality. Each, in their own convoluted way, is a reflexive meditation on extended substance, one which needs to do its own thinking in order to exist. How is this thinking done in each case? How does language *turn* delusional? These two questions will propel the argument here. Each membrane comes with its own transcendental structure whose constitution – both the process of formation and material consistency – I will attempt to examine. My interest lies in a shared form of causality, an internal movement, process and pattern of categories which build into the membranes of delusional experience.

The method attempted here will take its cue from a self-definition of nervous illness given by a patient quoted by Valentina Cardella: "Schizophrenia is a disease of information. And undergoing a psychotic break was like turning on a faucet to a torrent of details, which overwhelmed my life" (Weiner, 2003, cited in Cardella, 2017, p. 69). It is this linguistic disease, this derangement of information, whose causality I will be tentatively tracing below. The patient's self-observation continues as follows:

> In psychosis, nothing is what it seems. Everything exists to be understood beneath the surface. A bench remained a bench but who sat there

DOI: 10.4324/9781003436188-13

became critical. Like irony, the casual exchange of words between a stranger or a friend meant something more than what was being said. The movies, TV, and newspapers were alive with information for those who knew how to read. Without warning my world became suffused with meaning like light. In response, I felt as if I had been only half conscious before, as ignorant of reality as a small child. Although my sense of perception remained unaffected, everything I saw and heard took on a halo of meaning that had to be interpreted before I knew how to act. An advertising banner revealed a secret message only I could read. The layout of a store display conveyed a clue. A leaf fell and in its falling spoke: nothing was too small to act as a courier of meaning.

(p. 877)

Before this torrent carries away the overheated nerves, however, there is an earlier phase of the illness, an opposite logical moment when meaning is suddenly and, it seems, irrevocably detracted from the world of external experience. Cardella observes that schizophrenia begins with a loss of sense of reality, due to the unraveling of the symbolic structure defining the world-context inhabited by experience (2017, p. 67). The signifying relation is being dissolved which, in turn, frees the energy harnessed by the connection. In a second logical phase of the disease, this energy is turned into a surplus sense which yields the phenomenological torrent described by the patient. It is the production of this energetic surplus whose mechanisms I look to explore below.

In order to elicit the spatial dimension of the three systems of delusion, I will superimpose the definition of informational disease and de Saussure's model of linguistic masses:

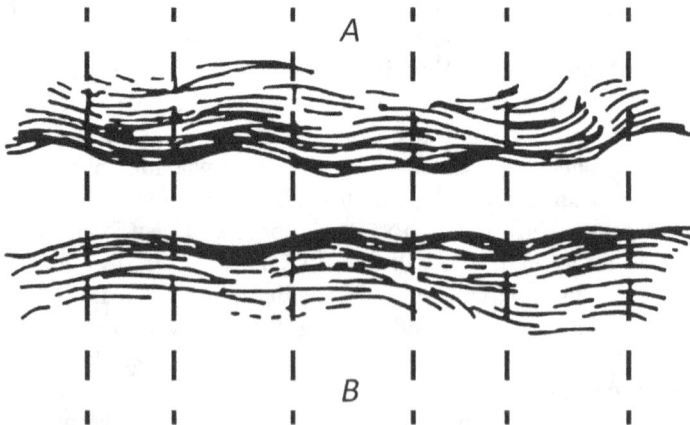

Figure 12.1 De Saussure's diagram
Source: Ferdinand de Saussure (2011). *Course in General Linguistics* (translated by Wade Baskin, edited by Perry Meisel and Haun Saussy.). Columbia University Press, page 112. (Original work published 1916.)

The model, as de Saussure conceives it, is arranged vertically, delineating the composition of representative relation organized by the arbitrariness of the sign. There are two linguistic masses involved, that of undifferentiated sound and thought. Signs, linking concrete *signifiants* and *signifiés*, are constituted as morsels of these two masses which are divided to create corresponding units. The dotted lines cut through both of the surfaces, thus associating words and (experiences of) things.

It is this arbitrary link that is being severed in the first logical moment of the disease of information. The dotted lines cutting through the model are dissolved. The masses uncouple, forming a dualist relation with two irreconcilable substances and no signifying structure, drained of the stability of meaning organizing the sense of reality. We need to take note of this logical irreconcilability, the inability of the masses to interconnect. The languages of nerve-rays, intelligible extension and market flows – all three are cleaved in half and it is precisely around this painful, logical slit that the text will organize.

In each case, the two clashing substances nevertheless develop a forbidden logical liaison, creating a charged syntax which spreads horizontally, along unusual lines – around the space of formal separation. We now move to the spatial interpretation of the second logical moment of the disease of information – where the sudden emergence of surplus sense drowns the loss of the reference relation. In each of the discussed cases, the spatial/logical distribution is the same – separated masses reconnect horizontally. "In psychosis, nothing is what it seems. Everything exists to be understood beneath the surface" (Weiner, 2003, p. 877). The surface that the patient speaks of will be interpreted spatially. The torrent of linguistic stimuli disturbs it, as one membrane moves against the other. Surplus sense is born of this conceptual intimacy, accumulating beneath the surface, at the tipping/tickling point of a different, irreconcilable idiom. Reinterpreted horizontally, the model becomes that of a caress and de Saussure's design exposes a nervous tissue. The masses consist of fibers of formal relations. A visual paradigm of experience, which organizes the vertical reading of the model, changes into a tactile one. This allows us to reorganize the entire economy of the model so as to experience the erotic charge of abstraction circulating within the three systems of delusion. This bizarre formula will drive the investigation into an economy of surplus linguistic production constituting structures outside the regime of signification.

Touch will not function as a model of immediacy here. On the contrary, the masses remain alien. Surplus sense travels *along* their surfaces which are responsive but impenetrable. The model organizes around a line of their separation and its causality and dynamic resides here, inside the slit which opens up between the two linguistic blocks. A simple change of direction of interpretation allows us to uncover the world of resistances, tensions and intensities circulating within this cleavage, oversaturating it with cutting division. The argument will follow these cuts as they turn into an innervated structure throbbing with desire. We will watch as opposition turns into obsession, the dualism of the masses following a logic of persecution, another risky theoretical construct which I will adopt from Schreber. Although they remain separate, the masses deeply interfere with one another's constitution, leaving each other differently stimulated across the dividing line. It is this irreconcilable desire that will direct the investigation of the three membranes and the symbolic structures they weave.

*

"Apart from normal human language there is also a kind of nerve-language of which, as a rule, the healthy human being is not aware" (Schreber, 1903/2000, p. 54). The *Memoirs* of Daniel Paul Schreber are a record of a language theory/experience, unconscious symbolic system whose basic unit is nerve-ray. The judge defines his predicament as linguistic right from the start, and – a good structuralist theologian that he is – proceeds to write of it in terms of the severed relation between structure and materiality of discourse. As he writes, "a human being causes his nerves to vibrate in the way which corresponds to the use of the words concerned, but the real organs of speech (lips, tongue, teeth, etc.) are either not set in motion at all or only coincidentally" (p. 54). The nerve-language needs no spelling out, no organs of speech, no actual body, although – as we shall apprise ourselves of presently – it produces an (immaterial) body of its own. The formal structures have complete autonomy, as, the judge figures, the restless conceptual fibers – the basic unit of his linguistic system – belong to none other than God:

> Naturally under normal (in consonance with the Order of the World) conditions, use of this nerve-language depends only on the will of the person whose nerves are concerned. In my case, however, since my nervous illness took the above-mentioned critical turn, *my nerves have been set in motion from without incessantly and without any respite. Divine rays above all have the power of influencing the nerves of a human being in this manner.*
>
> (pp. 54–55; emphasis added)

Schreber's delusion grows on God who is a (meta)linguistic incarnation in a state of relentless excitement. Nerve-language is its own metalanguage, Schreber's nervous illness developing into a self-referential theory. This theory is delusional, it is non-representational, it does not have language as a subject matter but constitutes it in a mechanism of relentless stimulation which we have just seen Schreber introduce.

A similarly miraculous, unstable and perverted metalanguage is the object of the study-experience of Nicolas Malebranche. In his *Dialogues on*

Metaphysics and Religion, Malebranche jumps straight to the problem of dualism as a radical severing of referential relation between thought and extension. "For the distinction of body and soul is the basis of the main tenets of philosophy, and among others of the immortality of the soul" (Malebranche, 1688/1923, p. 74). Consistent dualism, Malebranche elegantly and briefly demonstrates, means that one substance is perfectly unavailable to the other. This is all that needs to be said about the matter – this statement of its nonexistence to thinking, of the radical discontinuity of the world and experience. "No matter," Theodore tells Aristes[1] – a perfectly simple logical conclusion with shattering metaphysical consequences.

Determined to shoulder all the logical extremes of a firmly dualist position, Malebranche will not settle for dubious and evasive measures, like the Cartesian *pineal gland*, which allow us to maintain that the world somehow holds together despite the cutting division at its very core. Using such unsparing form of dualism, Malebranche thus develops a serious sickness of information. Its first logical moment is expressed in his doctrine of occasionalism which is to remedy the non-relation between substances – but it is a type of remedy which does rather aggravate the problem it is supposed to relieve; indeed it aggravates it into infinity. As there is no way for matter and mind to interact, it must be God who is responsible for holding them together. He occasions their unity by way of his direct interventions, a constant re-creation of the world incapable of existing on its own. Occasionalism is, therefore, simply, the reverse of dualism; it establishes an absolute relation which is no relation at all, as He needs to constantly intervene in order to maintain it. Thinking no more belongs to itself than extension does. They are both beside themselves, held together only by the grace of God, who constantly s(t)imulates them into (in)existence.

In a truly revelatory fashion, judge Schreber comes to identify the nerve-language with the lust of an Other, an abstract logical twitching which we will focus on throughout this chapter. Schreber's body is the vehicle of this lust; it is persecuted by the nerve-language which seeks it as a tool of constant sexual gratification. Their relationship results in a peculiar theo-linguistic formula, which is the "birth pangs of the end of the world."

> Connected with these phenomena, very early on there predominated in recurrent nightly visions the notion of an approaching end of the world, as a consequence of the indissoluble connection between God and myself. Bad news came in from all sides that even this or that star or this or that group of stars had to be "given up"; at one time it was said that even Venus had been "flooded," at another that the whole solar system would now have to be "disconnected," that the Cassiopeia (the whole group of stars) had had to be drawn together into a single sun, that perhaps only the Pleiades could still be saved, etc., etc [*sic*].
>
> (Schreber, 1903/2000, p. 75)

The intercourse – which makes Schreber's genitalia disappear along with his other organs and replaces them with an ever-changing body of conceptual brilliance produced by the nerve-language – results in the world dying. It is destruction that excites divine nerves and drives their erotic contact with the judge.

Malebranche's occasionalism sees the same destructive lust as a motor of the creative process. God has creation in hand and is responsible for its coherence – responsible beyond the limits of possible responsibility. Simply following the logical consequences of a few correlated concepts, Malebranche asserts that absolute power needs to be in constant action. It cannot rest, for it would no longer be absolute, if it were not active. And the only fit occupation for absolute power must also be absolute and that is an act of creation. And so, occasionalist God occupies himself with creation all the time, creating it anew, ex nihilo. Omnipotence needs to be petty – a rule in the spirit of nerve-rays. Rather than producing ontological stability, commonly associated with the concept, creation demands to multiply into eternity – and, in order to do so, to also cancel itself into eternity, as one creative repetition makes way for another. It thus follows from the definition of absolute power that creation is God's repetition compulsion.

Malebranche recognizes creation as a condition of existence whose absolute character drives it towards contradiction. Logically speaking, it creates (almost) nothing – an eternal plaything of the overstimulated absolute. The act is repeated, again and again, always with the same force, the same impact which immediately shatters the result. The nature of the gesture dissolves the possibility of a stable system of reference, a world as an autonomous instance, existing on its own terms. The logic of creation forbids it to develop any immanent relation. There is no continuity and no internal coherence. Occasionalism thus posits a deluded form of causality where causes are only occasions for destruction. In fact, there is only one divine cause and that is the slit separating/uniting the two substances which have no standing of their own and no agency.

"A world-economy is like an enormous envelope," writes Braudel in the third volume of *Civilisation and Capitalism* (1979/1997, p. 44). This is the third of the membranes – market as a system of prices whose tactile consistency I will try to invoke as my third ingredient. What Braudel conjures with his striking concept is a (non-)extended thing of finance, a system of prices understood in terms of their spatial distribution:

> [T]he world-economy is the greatest possible vibrating surface, one which not only accepts the conjuncture but, at a certain depth or level, manufactures it. It is the world-economy at all events which creates the uniformity of prices over a huge area, as an arterial system distributes blood throughout a living organism.
>
> (p. 83)

The envelope, Braudel reasons, consists of conjectures – trajectories of the movements of prices. In a highly unexpected argumentative turn, he defines them in speculative terms. With the envelope both accepting and manufacturing conjectures, its causality is defined as reflexive, self-stimulating. Conjectures, conceptual units of the nerve-language of the market, create a circular form of determination which Braudel recognizes as the substance of the envelope. The uniformity of prices over a huge area – the spatial turn of the phrase spells out a transformation of economic indicators into a tissue of conjectures, a space vibrating with abstract yet tangible tension. Braudel attributes to it the same spontaneity as Schreber and Malebranche do to the lust and auto-eroticism of God. Tracing the obsessive self-generation of the enormous membrane we will recognize the same destructive pettiness they both diagnose Him with.

I argue that Braudel's eerie, reflexive model evokes the global financial market; this abstract, unwieldy instance appears unexpectedly in an otherwise reasonable format of a historical narrative rich in detail. The financial envelope in its self-contained form is the result of dissociating conjectures from the historical conditionality of the social relations of production (but in truth a dissociation of these relations from themselves). It is this dissociation which surfaced during the global financial crisis triggered by the collapse of the US subprime market. The disease of this particular sector could not be contained because it was, in fact, nothing but an intensified form of the underlying disease of the entire system, or rather the entire system as an underlying disease of information.

The structure of the financial market was shaken to the core by what seemed like its erroneous construction – the malign architecture of financial instruments; wherein complex mechanisms of value-distribution turned out not to be steering away from risk and unreason, but rather accumulating them. The system occurred to revolve around repeatedly recycled and reconfigured toxic assets. Nevertheless, the uncovering of the untruth of finance did not result in any substantial correction of its logic. The multiplication of crises in the late capitalist financial economy has not diminished the key role of finance in the architecture of the contemporary market. This disease has not struck by accident. It has been no glitch in the world-system. Rather, its turbulent development may implicitly and unconsciously be recognized as its sovereign rule; it is the form of historical unconscious produced by finance, the accepting and manufacturing of conjectures, which I want to discover by referring Braudel to Schreber and Malebranche. *How* is it possible, how does the structure of nerve-market-language continue to operate? Herein, I will be asking a classic transcendental question, but with a twist, as it refers to a clearly broken, dysfunctional social structure.

I will begin by defining conjectures, linguistic units which Braudel identifies as constituting the market envelope, whereas nerve-rays are units constituting Schreber's system of language. I refer to Immanuel Wallerstein's complex definition of the term: "A major event is the result of a conjuncture (in the English sense of the word, meaning a joining point), of conjonctures (in the French sense, that is, of intermediate-length cyclical phases)" (Wallerstein, 1989/2011, pp. 93–94). For the purposes of this argument, I will concentrate on the synchronic (and spatial) dimension of conjuncture that is a joining point, a momentary effect; a splinter and reflex of the global constellation of social relations at a given point in time. Although the fragment does not name them explicitly, the term conjectures refers to prices as such joining points, disparate instances *reflecting* the complex structural organization of social causes which have brought them into being. They are, therefore, numerical perspectives on history, economic monads, perfectly contained glimpses of the totality of social relations.

It is these glimpses of history that the financial market offers in circulation. Their constitution is based in epistemological distortion tracked already by Marx whose theory of capital shows its susceptibility to the disease of information. As Beverly Best writes, "the theory of value is a theory of a specific function of representation that achieves a definitive status in the capitalist mode of production" (Best, 2010, p. 79). Marx defines this function in his theory of fetishism – it is the concealment of historical relations of production in the abstract medium of their representation, that of the market-value expressed in price. Conditions of production are not so much represented as veiled by the pricing of their products which simultaneously establishes this veiling as an objective evaluation. Capital accumulation is, therefore, defined in terms of erroneous representation where error is not accidental but constitutive of a certain historical mode of production. There is no commodity, until it is given a price. Therefore, a crucial moment of capitalist production process is entirely unproductive, a de-objectification of commodities and the labor they involve in the abstract medium of prices. Occasionalist God's creative gesture, the perverse eroticism of nerve-rays – it's all there.

Capital accumulation involves a deceptive procedure reinscribing commodities from the system of production to market circulation. Market is in fact constituted in the very gesture of reinscription, a linguistic operation performed on commodities – transformed into quantified and, therefore, exchangeable units of value embedded in the market structure. This transformation is precisely how a conjecture is constituted; a joining point forms through reflexive reversal from an effect to distorted representation of the social power relations which caused it. Defined in spatial terms as coordinates, the conjectures map history constituting the market envelope of abstraction, spatially (globally) extended structure of dissimulated evaluation. Pricing is, therefore, the distribution of conjectures, a movement attributing positions to the elements participating in the market envelope. It depends on an act of simultaneous calculation, falsification and materialization – a three-fold operation which I will continue to trace below.

Surplus (production) requires an idle component of calculation calculating nothing but itself – it is a speculative construct whose compulsion to speak mobilizes the process of accumulation. Gayatri Chakravorty Spivak is very alert to the element of self-generation encoded in capitalism and traced by Marx:

> The constitutive temporality of value – labor-time – is occluded as the material of money becomes its own measure. ... Gold is therefore nominally undecipherable, not because it alone expresses an authentic value, but because as money it expresses no value at all, but merely expresses.
>
> (Spivak, 1987, p. 32)

Spivak returns to Marx's formulas identifying the fictitious component of capital accumulation at a particular moment in history, at the height of the development of the contemporary financial market. Pure expression – Marx's definition of capital as the dream of augmenting through valorization alone gains new piquancy with economy embracing mathematics as the proper language of its processes. In the late nineteenth century figures such as Leon Walras struggle to push mathematical language to the fore of economic discourse. Some sixty years later, the paradigm, nevertheless, floods universities and influences the construction of the financial market which will explore the interpretative shift for its productive value. Economy, a science of organization of the social forces, becomes production through calculation. Pricing, which Marx identified as a crucial component of commodification, is itself commodified. Financial instruments are multilayered constellations of prices, fully exploiting the condition of "commodities," created ex nihilo, in a purely formal act of attributing market-value.

This form of capital evolves in response to the crisis of conditions of production caused repeatedly by the self-imposed tempo of re-production whose logic is succinctly described by David Harvey in *The Enigma of Capital*:

> If we conclude that it is the further expansion of production that creates the demand for yesterday's surplus product and that credit is needed to bridge the temporal gap, then it also follows that credit fuelled capital accumulation at a compound rate is also a condition of capitalism's survival. Only then can the expansion of today mop up yesterday's surplus. The reason that 3 per cent growth requires 3 per cent reinvestment then becomes clear. Capitalism, in effect, must generate and internalise its own effective demand if it is to survive under conditions where external possibilities are exhausted. If it fails to do so, as is currently the case, because of barriers to the continued expansion of production, a crisis ensues.
>
> (Harvey, 2010, pp. 112–113)

We have seen the mechanism described by Harvey in God and Schreber's couplings, which result in the end of the world, and in the occasionalist construct of deadly creation. It is reproduction unto death – with market crises functioning as symptoms of repetition compulsion which drives the process of accumulation. Harvey shows that surplus is never enough, because there is no stable standard, no given level where the conditions of reproduction are actually met. Market performance is never optimal and, thus, it cannot stabilize but requires constant re-evaluation. Growth is propelled by an immanent impossibility in which capital kills itself, and everyone else, to reproduce (itself). Market fights this contradiction and follows it; follows it, as it fights it – in a self-imposed conundrum inherent in the logic of "surplus."

The idle self-reflexivity Braudel notices in the market membrane is connected precisely to this exhausting mechanism of growth. The more the economy produces, the more drastically it lags behind. The more capital accumulates, the more it shrinks when faced with the ever more pressing demands of the future. Therefore, in a maddening, circular conclusion, it will start producing even more. Each solution leading to an increase in productivity only aggravates this problem. The principle of growth is so constructed, that to "mop up yesterday's surplus," the market needs to capitalize on value which has not yet been created. Yesterday's accumulation is today's squander, 3% growth is thus a principle of self-sacrifice applied to time itself.

As I have already mentioned, Schreber's destructive intercourse with nerve-language requires him to grow a different (im)material body which develops with a spreading of the disease of information. It is a linguistic construct apart from the physical body; the judge loses touch with the latter, as is clear from the dramatic account of physical stupor accompanying and contrasting with the turmoil of his inner experience.[2] The derailed constitution of this artificial organism follows a pattern of God's stimulations. Schreber encompasses the entirety of these transformations and perversions as God's agenda of conceptualizing the judge as a woman:

> [T]he nature of the frequently mentioned inner voices which since then have spoken to me incessantly, and also of what in my opinion is the tendency innate in the Order of the World, according to which a human being ("a seer of spirits") must under certain circumstances be "unmanned" (transformed into a woman) once he has entered into indissoluble contact with divine nerves (rays).
>
> (Schreber, 1903/2000, p. 53)

Schreber is, thus, persecuted with her own body, a purely intellectual (in)entity possessed by an Other. Its substance is pure s(t)imulation, there is no substance but openness, contact with God's language whose structures He impresses upon her. Schreber's body is a *response* to the constant taunting of logic; it is not a stable entity but a complex erotic power play between her and her Other distributed into a reflexive system, nerve-language folding upon itself through the operations performed on her body.

In Schreber's experience, a woman – beyond the sexist imagery which is sadly far from alien to his thinking – is a polymorphously abstract creature, constantly morphing in touch with nerve-language. Adam Lipszyc, in his polemic with Freud's interpretation of *Memoirs*, stresses the polymorphous sexuality of Schreber's body, the flexibility of her nervous tissue and its capacity for pleasure. He insists that it can only be understood in light of the theological register of Schreber's memoirs:

> Yielding surely to his antireligious prejudice, Freud ignores not only Schreber's stress put on centrality of religion in his world-view and mes-sage, but – more importantly – the possibility, which by the way is fully compatible with the general framework and assumptions of his own science, that theology as such has its own libidinal dynamics.
>
> (Lipszyc, 2022, p. 220)

I argue that the reading of the theological sexuality of the judge needs to involve her nerve-language theory.

> It seems to lie in the nature of the rays that they must speak as soon as they are in motion; the relevant law was expressed in the phrase "do not forget that the rays must speak," this was spoken into my nerves innu-merable times, particularly early on.
>
> (Schreber, 1903/2000, p. 126)

Symbolic system craves Schreber to become a woman whom it can fuck/speak *into* her nerves without interruption. God's revelation is pure, mindless logic, a sheer process of structuring, an endless production of patterns beyond referential purpose. The rays speak of nothing (but their compulsion). As suggested at the very beginning of this chapter, the metalinguistic component is not external, but buried within the Other's nerves, propelling this relentless flow of grammar. The sterile over-abundance is precisely a lin-guistic lust, the peculiar eroticism of deity that gets off on structures. The movement of the nerves is structured never to satiate but to keep feeding God's endless desire for the judge, which propels the mechanism of theo-linguistic persecution described in her *Memoirs*.

Just as it is with the nerves' compulsion to speak, occasionalist God's compulsion to create amounts to nothing. The endless grammatical chatter, the construction of nerve-language, is mirrored by God's frenzy which pro-duces world after world. This drive is what propels the erotic economy of the model. Gloriously blazing ontological trash – this perverse condition of creation brings us to Bataille's understanding of wealth:

> I will speak briefly about the most general conditions of life, dwelling on one crucially important fact: Solar energy is the source of life's exuberant development. The origin and essence of our wealth are given in the radiation of the sun, which dispenses energy – wealth – without any return.
>
> (Bataille, 1949/1988, p. 28)

Malebranche's and Schreber's reasoning allow us to elicit the ambiguity of Bataille's definition. The opposition between amassing wealth and its squander, which he establishes in *The Accursed Share*, is eroded by the *Memoirs* and *Dialogues* and their discussion of God's compulsions. They trace a different, more complex and sinister trajectory of surplus creation where accumulation does not oppose endless waste but proceeds as one. The Other and its compulsion to speak, to create structures without purpose, continuity or meaning – the two texts re-produce a similarly functioning figure, an unforgiving though empty sun, hyperactive nothing. Formal sterility as a source of energy and exuberance: it is wealth in this confounding sense that is a driving force of the economy of the three membranes unfolding here.

The market envelope is also a speaking one – it spews conjectures, truth-claims regarding economic conditions, which, in a self-reflexive stupor identified by Braudel, irritate the surface of the market. The dysfunctional, crisis-inducing structure of finance embodies compulsion which, in turn, results from impossibility inherent in its formula of reproduction. Writing itself into the logical and material corner following its logic of accumulation, the contemporary financial market turns the situation on its head and, in a reflexive gesture, invests in the impossibility at the heart of its condition of possibility. Thus, it takes the principle of growth to a logical conclusion, the way Malebranche does with dualism – embracing rather than alleviating its inherent contradiction and building an intricate system of delusion/financial instruments around it. Finance explores and exploits the accumulation compulsion which Harvey recognises in capitalist formula of "growth" – thus sharing an economy of desire with unlikely companions. Having next to no geographical space for further growth, it turns to its conceptual space/envelope, to the immanence of its language, producing through the impossibility built into the idle *speculative* potential inherent in the logic of "surplus," the formal insatiability of the system of pricing.

Neoclassical economy expresses the market's compulsion to speak in the efficient markets hypothesis, where "efficiency" functions as a term linking capitalist production to the representative capacity of the market understood as the language of prices. "A capital market is said to be efficient if it fully and correctly reflects all relevant information in determining security prices" (Malkiel, 1994, p. 127). It is this idealistic, reflexive definition of the market as a mechanism for *producing* truth-claims, which I will now concentrate on. The collapse of these truth-claims in 2008 and their continued presence in the economy remain our point of departure.

Surveying the disaster caused by global finance, Philip Mirowski comments sneeringly that the hypothesis takes the market to be a "transcendental superior information processor" (Mirowski, 2013, p. 61). Mirowski's distaste and disbelief are perfectly understandable; however, it is the fantastic capacity of the ridiculous pretense and blatant market untruths to exercise power over global society which his mockery needs to address. The efficient market hypothesis sees the economic system coming down with the disease of information and makes this situation *work*. The dysfunctional linguistic structure produces for the market – in a response to the impossible demands of reproduction. *Producing* truth-claims – this is the fantastic "solution" of the crisis of production and over-expansion in mid-twentieth century, a solution which fully embraced the logical contradiction and destructive impulse behind capital growth.

As Mirowski posits, financial market is a transcendental structure. Whose experience does it constitute? It is not individual, at least not directly, but rather an experience shared socially. Alain Supiot writes of "collective identities" which societies assume through their forms of organisation, when institutional order no longer functions as mere sum of parts (Supiot, 2017, pp. 14–15). The transcendental apparatus of finance produces such a form of collective identity for the late capitalist society. Defining it as a superior information processor, Mirowski shows the efficient market to be a variation on the invisible hand theme. It is precisely a figure of "collective identity," the market as a self-regulating, social order independent of whims and vices of the people. "After all, is not the 'invisible hand' of the market simply a secular version of Divine Providence?" Supiot observes (p. 9).

Retaining these theological overtones, but pushing them through occasionalism towards a more sinister and aggressive vision of divine oversight, I want to graft them onto a different matrix which Schreber brings to the argument. An invisible hand, a spontaneous, highly structured, unsupervised and uncontrollable order, spells "collective identity" as unconscious.[3] This perspective allows us to conceive of the efficient market in a defamiliarizing way. Financial packages, these extravagant products construed of calculations, are discrepant and dissociated forms of social experience. Thought of as unconscious, their filigree, self-reflexive structures create an inflating and imploding space where accumulation compulsion plays out.

Market, the great dysfunction of an information processor, creates a profoundly disruptive social logic encrypted in layered calculations. The model of an unconscious, one that undermines the rationalizing and naturalizing prejudice which inexplicably continues to protect finance capital, conceives the twisted economy behind the "invisible hand," a figure of self-regulation indiscernible from self-destruction. The dissociation of market experience is binding yet ruinous; the unconscious global market and its nerve-language of investment stimulates the development of an unsustainable, profoundly damaged social reality which we, nevertheless, agree to inhabit. Going to

Malebranche and Schreber for the methodological matrix, the argument looks at submission to this ridiculous, compromised and broken global sovereign and, rather than explaining it, attempts to put it in stark relief.

What form of experience does the global financial unconscious produce then? Mirowski notes the shift to what he defines as *processing*, thus encapsulating the turn from representative to productive function of information. This is where the efficiency of the market lies, not in the accuracy of its truth-claims. Arch-knowing information tells nothing but flow; they constitute an empty, formal medium of reproduction unto death. Production in the financial market is calculation set on a different, senseless course which overwhelms the course of history. In 2008, the claim to efficiency proved both untenable and tenacious, and for the very same reason; because the objective of erroneous market calculation is not representation but accumulation.

The judge's new body is an (erotic) accessory of this divine *jouissance*, a medium of pure linguistic construction materializing on her polymorphous symbolic skin. The speaking rays stimulate it with abstract grammatical impulses, creating a linguistic medium whose model becomes that of perverted and perverting touch:

> I have reason to assume that since then, mankind and all its activities have only been artificially maintained by means of direct divine miracles, to an extent which the restrictions under which I live do not allow me to survey fully. This is certainly the case in my own surroundings: I feel a blow on my head simultaneously with every word spoken around me, with every approaching footstep, with every railway whistle, with every shot fired by a pleasure steamer, etc.; *this causes a variable degree of pain more when God has withdrawn to a greater distance and less when He is nearby.*
>
> (Schreber, 1903/2000, p. 89; emphasis added)

The blow on the head which accompanies the rays speaking, the constant logical chatter – a pair *irritant* and *irritated* replaces *signifiant* and *signified*, changing the nature of linguistic medium into non-representational tissue, a conductor of erotic tension produced *inside* its units, nerve-rays whose spatial distribution defines the world of judge's *Memoirs*.

Experience is thus conditioned by the pattern of God's caresses. Transcendental schemata are His malicious schemes, concocted in the name of erotic obsession, and drawn directly on the multidimensional surface of judge's body (of theory). God imposes an epistemological regime which is simultaneously a changing map of erogenous zones. Pure stimulation and traveling of abstract erotic impulses replace bodily organs with configurations of linguistic nerves formed, as we have just seen Schreber argue, through constantly changing distance between her nerves and God's. An irritating and irritated mass of nerves are defined by a mutual distance.[4] Therefore, we see a simple geometrical relation being diverted in service of polymorphous linguistic production. Governing the behaviour of nerve-rays, geometry turns to surplus sense and evolves into strange, fantastic forms dubbed "divine miracles."

We find the same pattern of geometrical caresses in the text of the *Dialogues*, as it gives an account of the possibility of material experience:

> [N]ote that you can know a circle, for example, in three ways. You may conceive it, you may imagine it, you may feel or see it. When you conceive it, what happens is that intelligible extension applies itself to your mind with limits which are indeterminate as far as their length is concerned, but which are equally distant from a fixed point, and all in the same plane; and then you have a conception of a circle in general. When you imagine it, what happens is that a determinate part of this extension, the limits of which are equally distant from a point, touches your mind lightly. Finally, when you feel or see it, what happens is that a determinate part of this extension touches your soul in sensuous fashion and modifies it by a feeling of some colour.
>
> (Malebranche, 1688/1923, pp. 83–84)

A transcendental condition which Malebranche explicitly models on touch, intelligible extension is the non-representational language of Euclidean geometry which functions the same way that nerve-language does. Malebranche proposes to think of geometry as a delusional system of impressions forced upon the subject. Though purely intelligible, it is, nevertheless, not *known* but *applied* to cognition. Intelligible extension is a tactile medium which involves subject and God in acts of cognitively indecent s(t)imulation.

Just as we saw happen with nerve-language, a formal model turns into a map of erogenous zones, an Other wearing the structure of material experience as skin. Geometry constitutes divine innervation enveloping the mind. As far as cognition goes, God is an intelligible extension and, by extension, an ongoing persecution of the subject with geometrical rays:

> You do in truth see the divine Substance, for it alone is visible, it alone can illumine the mind. Yet you do not see it in itself or as it really is. You only see it in its relation to material creations, you only see it so far as they participate in it, or in so far as it is representative of them. Consequently it is not, strictly speaking, God Himself that you see, but only the matter which He can produce.
>
> (Malebranche, 1688/1923, p. 93)

Malebranche mobilizes this dumbfounding idea of geometry in order to account for the possibility of material experience in a world where thought has no access to matter. If extension is completely unavailable to thinking, then its experience should not be available either. But no matter. Malebranche never questions its possibility but turns impossibility around, redefining the non-relation between mind and matter as the condition of material experience:

> That would be true if your room had the property of being visible; but it doesn't! What I see when I look at your room – i.e. when I turn my eyes on all sides to take it in – would still be visible even if your room were destroyed and even, I may add, if it had never been built! I maintain that someone who has never left China can see everything I see when I look at your room, provided that his brain goes through the same movements that mine does when I survey the room – which is perfectly possible. People with a high fever, and people who sleep and dream – don't they see chimeras of all sorts that never were? What they see exists, at least while they see it; but what they think they see doesn't exist.
>
> (p. 82)

Proudly carrying the malicious demon's line, God introduces the experience of matter as an imposed fiction. Allowing creation no autonomy, occasionalism already made the difference between truth and deception insubstantial. This gesture is now repeated, redoubled as a transcendental principle. Experience requires divine intervention. Otherwise it won't hold; therefore, it needs to be repeatedly recreated alongside the existence of the world. Extension, the opposite of thinking, turns out to be nothing but thinking, or, strictly speaking, misinformation.

Thus, Malebranche radically distorts the Cartesian existential maxim which he opens with. He uses the logic of dualism, which is ever the point of reference, to play a very different conceptual power game. I think and, therefore, I am separated from myself by thought which surfaces right next to the mind – geometry as God's vile scheme and repeated discharge of formal constellations. To solve the problem of material experience, God creates an invagination of dualism, its logical reverse forming a separate instance between the two substances. It is their non-relation which *surfaces* as this (non-)extended thing, a fantastic conceptual growth of conflicted constitution. As vertical threads of reference are (and continue to be) severed into eternity, geometry creates a surplus, superfluous torrent of forms latching onto the senses and mind.

Schreber's body is also this unending openness to divine forms impressed directly upon his body as *miracles*; tendrils of the restless, overheated syntax of the rays:

> From the first beginnings of my contact with God up to the present day my body has continuously been the object of divine miracles. If I wanted to describe all these miracles in detail I could fill a whole book with them

alone. I may say that hardly a single limb or organ in my body escaped being temporarily damaged by miracles, nor a single muscle being pulled by miracles, either moving or paralyzing it according to the respective purpose.

(Schreber, 1903/2000, p. 141)

Schreber describes bodily alteration of linguistic nature, pulling and damage done by God's compulsion to speak. The judge experiences this keenly and with a great deal of dread, subjected to the nervously ill geometry whose hungry, destructive creativity we have on display here. Distance between rays becomes the source of voracious expression, exploding with unpredictable constructions and configurations of nerves. The application of geometry – rule against skin, nerve against concept – derails into endless proliferation of forms:

A "lung worm" was frequently produced in me by miracles; I cannot say whether it was an animal-like being or a soul-like creature; I can only say that its appearance was connected with a biting pain in the lungs similar to the pains I imagine occur in inflammation of the lungs.

(p. 142)

And just as God grooms a subject, persecuting him or her with nerve-language or Euclidean geometry, so the financial market grooms the social body persecuting it with conjectures. I will now return to the efficient market hypothesis and discuss market information in terms of this grooming. Late capitalist society is riddled by finance, a soul-like creature produced by an unconscious system of social representations, truth-claims commodified in the efficient market. It is the tireless work of this worm on the collective body which I want to touch upon towards the end.

At first, market information may seem rather modest and unobtrusive, its reach limited to stocks and securities alone. Information maps the conditions for investment in the global market. Essentially, it is the market evaluating itself, affirming its grasp on the calculation of its products. The hypothesis demonstrates its insidious character, though, when combined with another logical moment of financialization, that is the radical broadening of the reach of commodification. The productive operation performed on the immanence of the market language allows it to incorporate the extra-economical elements of the global conditions of production. This incorporation is the toxic trail left by the social worm. Truth in the efficient market is confined to the stock market; but, at the same time, the stock market radically broadens its scope and reach – no longer through geographical expansion but through exploiting its own potential for quantification, the intensive rather than extensive production based in the immanence of the language of prices. The disembodiment of production, which followed the crisis of Fordist reification, did not cause the commodification to recede but indefinitely increased its powers. It allowed the financial market to capitalize directly on social relations, political entities and institutions, which instruments like international debt turned into items of arbitrarily assigned market value.

"If a part of wealth (subject to a rough estimate) is doomed to destruction or at least to unproductive use without any possible profit, it is logical, even inescapable, to *surrender commodities without return*" (Bataille, 1949/1988, p. 25; emphasis added). Late capitalist market embraces this ruthless, simple, idle principle as its means of (perverting) production. Financial commodification operates as an act of surrender, a self-immolation of social codes. It is a history of self-sacrifice and the self-sacrifice of history (the opposite of what Fukuyama announced as its would-be end). Financial instruments transform complex relations of causes from various different registers into Schreberian/Bataillean sun, layers upon layers of prices, all beside the point. This squander of social relations results in a self-reflexive, masturbatory excess which Braudel recognizes in the global economy. Wealth is generated through structuring alone and different forms of coding social experience are to make themselves all available for *processing*. Overripe and unhealthy, the financial market keeps consuming the rot of its impossibility, reproducing the futility of reproduction. The accursed share of finance is not waste but surplus, a hyperactive nothing, pure and simple, accumulation as squander.

Value judgment, saying nothing, processes codes, commodifies different symbolic structures expressing various registers of social experience. Deleuze and Guattari define capital as an operation of *decoding*, a contradictory linguistic procedure of quantification of history – rendering it meaningless, rendering it in numbers (Deleuze and Guattari, 1972/2000, pp. 222–262). Decoding is the mechanism of financial squander and the equivalent of the violent interference of nerve-language transforming Schreber's body. Referring to Marx's theory of capital as accumulating dissemblance, the authors of *Anti-Oedipus* slightly change the accent, diagnosing not so much concealment but a loss of sense which occurs in the process of market quantification. They play with a mock-physical dimension of this loss, understood not as a state but as a transformation process, a *draining* of codes which result in sheer, difference-inducing calculations. Deleuze and Guattari (pp. 240–262) use the physical model in a fully artificial, grotesque and conceptually stylized way, as a means to express the artificial, grotesque and stylized presence of the market, a system of delusion at the center of the global social order. The argument here is also committed to these methodological choices.

The financial market capitalizes on the logical, temporal and reflexive gap, the renewed impossibility of social conditions of production to respond adequately to the demands of growth. This gap is used to make them surrender their proper, extra-economic logics which all lag behind the demands of surplus production. Different symbolic structures are punished for their inadequacy with the absurd, relentless logic of growth which they can only be inadequate to, as it is alien to their own logic. Pricing is this senseless judg-ment, worthless sentence of value which, in a perverted, reflexive develop-ment, turns inadequacy into a major s(t)imulus of growth. Worthlessness is not to be understood in terms of lack – which would mean that there exists a shared logic of value between the judged social reality and the judging market. There is no shared logic; the judgment of the market *changes* lan-guage mid-game, distributing conjectures within the global envelope. It is, therefore, nonsensical, and as such – with a switch between forms of value – it becomes productive. Financial accumulation replaces reference (and with it political recognition which capital no longer requires). The body of the totality of social relations is to become a body like Schreber's, a tissue whose perfectly responsive grammar is driven by the sense of subjection to God's demand for *jouissance*. Something which is crucial to note, although cannot be pursued here, is Schreber's ambiguity towards the language of the nerves, the dynamic of subjection and efforts to fight it.

Pricing expresses and constantly reiterates the necessary gap between the demands of the market Other and the inadequate response of the global social relations. This gap is expressed as pricing that is a compulsion to pass judgment. Produce through pricing is to produce through pure judgment, judging nothing, only stupefying and annihilating what it confronts. The efficient market theory spells out this process, introducing the idea of chance. One last thread, or cut, that I will introduce to the argument is that "all subsequent price changes represent random departures from previous prices. Thus, changes in price will be unrelated to past price changes" (Malkiel, 1994, p. 128). Random departures, one unrelated to the other; this is the broken temporal logic, radical discontinuity of senseless differentiation introduced with market value-judgment. The temporal perspective of the efficient market reflects its drive of surplus destruction. It is the perfect vehicle of vicious self-reflexivity of finance.

Let us now circle back to Wallerstein's definition and take a look at the temporal and logical discontinuity as constitutive of conjectures, or rather conjectures becoming senseless flows, effects of the efficient market's com-pulsion to speak. Joining points are formed when the trajectory of social relations is drained of its complexity and arrested in its development, by being radically undercut in its temporal unfolding. Price constitutes a per-fectly contained perspective on global history – and thus a perfect instance of judgment – but this form and its completeness results from the force of abstraction *turning* the diachronic perspective blind. Market information captures nothing. The trajectories of its grammar calculate the complex dynamic of social value into points – formal units of perverted knowledge which condenses social experience beyond recognition. Political sovereignty is dissolved in these formal bacchanalia. The construction of financial market language leaves society with no autonomy, just like occasionalist creation, with its temporal structure, has no autonomy of its own. The market consumes radical instability, with prices, reflexes of social circumstance, appearing only to disappear in the endlessly differentiating strings of calculations. There is no logical continuity and, therefore, no agency, no possibility of intervention in a cycle which is always already broken.

Logical form turns material by way of a double, non-dialectical negation. Prices are not representations, rather *they are* irrepresentations of historical events; they are events themselves. For all intents and purposes, they function as causes – their causality, a shroud swarming with conjectures:

> On some nights the souls finally dripped down onto my head, in a manner of speaking, in their hundreds, if not thousands, as "little men". I always warned them against approaching me, since I had become aware of the immensely increased power of attraction of my nerves from what had happened earlier, but the souls could not at first believe that I had such a dangerous power of attraction. Other rays which conducted themselves in the manner described above as if they were God's omnipotence itself, carried names such as "the Lord of Hosts," "the Good Shepherd," "the Almighty," etc., etc [*sic*]. Connected with these phenomena, very early on there predominated in recurrent nightly visions the notion of an approaching end of the world, as a consequence of the indissoluble connection between God and myself.
>
> (Schreber, 1903/2000, p. 75)

This is *how* the mock-physics of the formal processor of judgments operates, *how* prices debilitate codes, transforming them into quasi-stimuli which further persecute history. Once again, the logic of the efficient market is that of perverted touch. It is a body of conjectures, a structure of debilitating knowledge dripping down on the social body. Reduction breeds reduction: here, in a reproductive cycle which amounts to nothing. An anal, solar wealth is generated in the indissoluble connection between finance and the network of social codes – an economy of an approaching end of the world.

Notes

1 "In which world, Aristes, should we be passing the day? Would it not be an intelligible world? Now, note this, it is in this world that we are and that we live, though the body which we animate lives in another world and moves about in another world. It is this world which we contemplate, admire, feel. Yet the world which we pay regard to and which we concern ourselves with when we turn our heads in all directions, is nothing but matter which is invisible in itself, and which has none of those beauties which we admire, and which we feel when we are mindful of it" (Malebranche, 1688/1923, pp. 76–77).

2 In the medical opinion provided by Dr. Weber we read the following: "This physically strong man, in whom frequent jerkings of the face musculature and marked

tremor of the hands were noticeable, was at first completely inaccessible and shut off in himself, lay or stood immobile and stared with frightened eyes straight ahead of himself into space; he did not answer questions at all or only very briefly and protestingly; but clearly this rigid demeanor was far removed from indifference, rather the patient's whole state seemed tense, irritable, caused by inner uneasiness and there could be no doubt that he was continually influenced by vivid and painful hallucinations, which he elaborated in a delusional manner" (Schreber, 1903/2000, pp. 328–329).

3 Karl Polanyi, for example, writes ironically of "the alleged self-healing virtues of unconscious growth" (Polanyi, 1957, p. 35).

4 This dimension appears in de Saussure's model with the elongated tendrils which disturb the surface of the masses, indicating – a crucial thread we won't have time to pursue here – the possible heterogeneity of the masses and their internal asymmetry.

References

Bataille, G. (1988). *The Accursed Share: An Essay on General Economy*, vol. 1, *Consumption* (R. Hurley, Trans.). Zone Books. (Original work published 1949.)

Best, B. (2010). *Marx and the Dynamic of Capital Formation: An Aesthetics of the Political*. Palgrave Macmillan.

Braudel, F. (1997). *The Perspective of the World: Civilisation and Capitalism*, vol. 3 (S. Reynold, Trans.). University of California Press. (Original work published 1979.)

Cardella, V. (2017). *Language and Schizophrenia: Perspectives from Psychology and Philosophy*. Routledge.

Deleuze, G., & Guattari, F. (2000). *Anti-Oedipus: Capitalism and Schizophrenia* (R. Hurley, M. Seem & H.R. Lane, Trans.). University of Minnesota Press. (Original work published 1972.)

Spivak, G.C. (1987). Speculations on Reading Marx: After Reading Derrida. In D. Attridge, G. Bennington & R. Young (Eds.), *Post-structuralism and the Question of History*. Cambridge University Press.

Harvey, D. (2010). *The Enigma of Capital and the Crises of Capitalism*. Oxford University Press.

Lipszyc, A. (2022). On the Marrano Psychotheology of Gender: Freud, Schreber, Frank. In A. Bielik-Robson (Ed.), *The Marrano Way: Between Betrayal and Innovation*. De Gruyter.

Malebranche, N. (1923). *Dialogues on Metaphysics and Religion* (M. Ginsberg, Trans.). Allen & Unwin. (Original work published 1688.)

Malkiel, B.G. (1994). Efficient Market Hypothesis. In J. Eatwell, M. Milgate & P. Newman (Eds.), *Finance*. Macmillan.

Mirowski, P. (2013). *Never Let a Serious Crisis Go to Waste: How Neoliberalism Survived the Financial Meltdown*. Verso.

Polanyi, K. (1957). *The Great Transformation: The Political and Economic Transformations of our Time*. Beacon Press.

Schreber, D.P. (2000). Memoirs of My Nervous Illness (I. Macalpine & R.A. Hunter, Trans.). *The New York Review of Books*. (Original work published 1903.)

Supiot, A. (2017). *Governance by Numbers: The Making of a Legal Model of Allegiance* (S. Brown, Trans.). Bloomsbury.

Wallerstein, I. (2011). *The Modern World-System,* vol. 3: *The Second Era of Great Expansion of the Capitalist World-Economy, 1730s-1840s.* University of California Press. (Original work published 1989.)

Weiner, S.K. (2003). First Person Account: Living With the Delusions and Effects of Schizophrenia. *Schizophrenia Bulletin,* 29(4), 877–879.

Index

Note: *Italic* page numbers refer to *figure* and page numbers followed by 'n' reference to notes.

For Product Safety Concerns and Information please contact our EU
representative GPSR@taylorandfrancis.com
Taylor & Francis Verlag GmbH, Kaufingerstraße 24, 80331 München, Germany

9 781032 565774